How Culture Views New Media

Diverse Traditions in Modern Communication

Sam Sparrow

ISBN: 9781779665812
Imprint: First Off The Nation Dance
Copyright © 2024 Sam Sparrow.
All Rights Reserved.

Contents

Introduction to Cultural Perspectives on Digital Media   **1**
Understanding Cultural Perspectives   1

Historical Development of Digital Media and Cultural Contexts   **23**
Pre-digital Media Landscape and Cultural Traditions   23
The Role of Cultural Factors in Shaping Digital Media   35

Cultural Perspectives on Social Media   **49**
Cultural Dimensions of Social Media Use   49
Globalization and Social Media   61

Cross-Cultural Communication in the Digital Age   **75**
Language and Cultural Diversity in Digital Communication   75
Non-verbal Communication in Digital Media   84
Intercultural Communication Competence in the Digital Space   92

Cultural Perspectives on Digital Media and Identity   **101**
Individual Identity and Digital Media   101
Collective Identity and Digital Media   110

Cultural Perspectives on Digital Media and Power   **121**
Digital Media and Cultural Hegemony   121
Politics, Propaganda, and Digital Media   129

Cultural Perspectives on Digital Media and Creativity   **139**
Digital Media as Cultural Artifacts   139
Digital Media and Creative Industries   151

Cultural Perspectives on Digital Media and Education **163**
Cultural Contexts of Digital Education 163
Challenges and Opportunities of Digital Media in Education 171

Practical Strategies for Cultural Perspectives on Digital Media **181**
Promoting Cultural Awareness in Digital Media Design 181
Ethical Guidelines for Digital Media Practices 192

**Conclu-
sion: The Future of Cultural Perspectives on Digital Media** **203**
Emerging Trends in Cultural Perspectives on Digital Media 203
Recommendations for Future Research 212

Index **221**

Introduction to Cultural Perspectives on Digital Media

Understanding Cultural Perspectives

Definition and Importance of Cultural Perspectives

Cultural perspectives play a crucial role in understanding the impact and influence of digital media in our society. In this section, we will define cultural perspectives and explore their importance in the context of digital media.

Definition of Cultural Perspectives

Cultural perspectives can be understood as the lens through which individuals and communities interpret and make sense of the world around them. These perspectives are shaped by various factors, including but not limited to language, history, traditions, values, beliefs, norms, and behaviors.

In the context of digital media, cultural perspectives refer to the diverse ways in which different cultures engage with, adopt, and adapt to digital technologies. It encompasses the unique attitudes, practices, and behaviors that arise from the intersection of culture and digital media.

Importance of Cultural Perspectives

Understanding cultural perspectives is crucial for several reasons:

1. Acknowledging Diversity: Cultural perspectives highlight the rich diversity of human experiences and enable us to appreciate the multiplicity of voices and viewpoints in our global society. By recognizing cultural differences, we can move beyond a one-size-fits-all approach and design digital media that respects and reflects the uniqueness of each culture.

INTRODUCTION TO CULTURAL PERSPECTIVES ON DIGITAL MEDIA

2. Avoiding Cultural Bias: Cultural perspectives help us identify and challenge the inherent biases that may exist in digital media. Many digital technologies and platforms are designed based on cultural values and assumptions that may not be universally applicable. By considering cultural perspectives, we can strive for inclusivity and ensure that digital media caters to the needs and preferences of diverse cultural communities.

3. Enhancing Intercultural Communication: Cultural perspectives facilitate effective intercultural communication in the digital space. Each culture has its own communication norms, etiquette, and implicit rules. By understanding cultural perspectives, individuals can navigate cross-cultural interactions online with sensitivity and respect, reducing misunderstandings and fostering meaningful connections.

4. Unveiling Power Dynamics: Cultural perspectives shed light on power dynamics and cultural hegemony in the digital realm. Digital media can both empower and marginalize certain cultural groups, reinforcing existing power structures. Cultural perspectives allow us to critically examine the ways in which digital media shape cultural identity, representation, and access to resources and opportunities.

5. Promoting Ethical Considerations: Cultural perspectives bring attention to ethical considerations in digital media practices. It encourages us to question the impact of digital media on cultural heritage, intellectual property, privacy, and security. By incorporating cultural perspectives, we can develop ethical guidelines and practices that protect cultural values and promote responsible digital media use.

In summary, cultural perspectives provide valuable insights into the complex relationship between culture and digital media. By embracing and understanding these perspectives, we can foster a more inclusive, diverse, and culturally sensitive digital landscape.

Cultural Diversity and its Impact on Digital Media

Cultural diversity plays a significant role in shaping digital media. As technology continues to advance and connect people across the globe, it is crucial to understand how different cultures influence and are influenced by digital media. This section explores the various dimensions of cultural diversity and its impact on digital communication.

Cultural Diversity in the Digital Age

Cultural diversity refers to the coexistence of multiple cultures within a society or a global context. In the digital age, this diversity is not limited to physical boundaries but extends to online communities and platforms. The internet has provided a space for people from diverse cultural backgrounds to interact, share ideas, and engage in digital communication.

The impact of cultural diversity on digital media is multi-fold. First, it brings forth a wide range of perspectives, knowledge, and experiences, enriching the content available online. This diversity fosters creativity, innovation, and collaboration in creating digital media.

Second, cultural diversity in digital media allows for the representation and visibility of marginalized or underrepresented cultures. It provides an opportunity to challenge dominant narratives and stereotypes by sharing diverse cultural stories and perspectives. This inclusivity empowers individuals from different cultural backgrounds and promotes intercultural understanding.

Third, cultural diversity influences the consumption patterns of digital media. People from different cultures have unique preferences and interests when it comes to online content. Understanding these preferences helps content creators tailor their offerings, leading to more personalized and engaging digital experiences.

Lastly, cultural diversity in digital media has economic implications. It opens doors for cultural entrepreneurs and creative industries to reach global audiences, fostering cultural exchange and economic growth.

Challenges and Opportunities

While cultural diversity brings significant benefits, it also presents challenges in the digital media landscape. One of the main challenges is overcoming language barriers. Digital media platforms need to consider localization and translation to cater to diverse audiences. This requires an understanding of cultural nuances and context to ensure effective communication.

Another challenge is the potential for cultural appropriation in digital media. Cultural symbols, practices, or artifacts from marginalized cultures are sometimes commodified or taken out of context without proper acknowledgement or respect. Content creators and users need to be aware of the ethics of cultural representation and strive for cultural sensitivity and authenticity.

Opportunities arise from cultural diversity in the form of cross-cultural collaboration and learning. Online communities provide a space for individuals to share their cultural values, traditions, and knowledge. By engaging in respectful

INTRODUCTION TO CULTURAL PERSPECTIVES ON DIGITAL MEDIA

dialogue and understanding, digital media bridges cultural gaps and fosters intercultural communication.

Examples and Resources

To better understand the impact of cultural diversity on digital media, consider the case of K-pop's global popularity. The Korean music industry has been successful in promoting Korean cultural products worldwide, leveraging digital platforms and social media. This success story highlights the power of cultural diversity and its ability to transcend borders in the digital age.

For further exploration, the following resources provide valuable insights:

- "Cultural Diversity and the Digital Divide" by D. P. S. Bhawuk

- "Digital Diversity: The Impact of New Media on Cultural Diversity" by Rebecca Blood

- "Intercultural Communication in the Global Age" by Fred E. Jandt

Exercises

1. Reflect on your own digital media consumption habits. How does your cultural background influence the type of content you engage with? Provide examples.

2. Choose a popular digital media platform and analyze how it embraces cultural diversity. Consider its content, user base, and features. Discuss the impact of this diversity on the platform's success.

3. Research a case study of cultural appropriation in digital media. Describe the specific instances and discuss the ethical implications. Suggest strategies to promote cultural sensitivity and avoid cultural appropriation.

Tricks and Caveats

When exploring cultural diversity and its impact on digital media, it is essential to approach the topic with respect and open-mindedness. Recognize that cultural diversity is not a monolithic concept; it encompasses a wide range of experiences and identities. Avoid generalizations or stereotyping when discussing specific cultures or communities.

It is also crucial to consider the power dynamics that exist within digital media. Acknowledge the potential for cultural hegemony, where dominant cultural perspectives may overshadow or marginalize others. Strive for inclusive representation and give voice to underrepresented cultures and communities.

Summary

Cultural diversity has a profound impact on digital media, shaping its content, consumption patterns, and economic implications. Embracing cultural diversity in the digital age promotes intercultural understanding, challenges stereotypes, and fosters creativity. However, challenges such as language barriers and cultural appropriation must be addressed. By recognizing the power of cultural diversity and being culturally sensitive, digital media can truly become a platform for global engagement and connection.

INTRODUCTION TO CULTURAL PERSPECTIVES ON DIGITAL MEDIA

Cultural Bias in Digital Media

Cultural bias refers to the tendency to favor certain cultural perspectives while marginalizing or ignoring others. In the context of digital media, cultural bias can have a significant impact on the content that is created, disseminated, and consumed. It can influence the way information is presented, the representation of different cultures, and the overall narratives that dominate the digital space.

1. The Influence of Cultural Bias in Digital Media Content Creation:

Cultural bias can shape the content that is produced and shared on digital platforms. Content creators may unconsciously incorporate their own cultural beliefs, values, and assumptions into their work, which can result in the marginalization or misrepresentation of certain cultures. For example, biased portrayals of certain racial or ethnic groups can perpetuate stereotypes and reinforce prejudices.

To illustrate this point, let's consider a scenario where a group of content creators from a particular cultural background produces a video about a traditional festival. If their perception of the festival is influenced by their own cultural biases, they may inadvertently present a skewed or incomplete representation of the event. This can lead to the misinterpretation or misrepresentation of the festival by the audience, who may not have any cultural context or understanding of the event.

2. Cultural Bias and the Amplification of Certain Voices:

Cultural bias can also influence which voices and perspectives are amplified or silenced in the digital space. Dominant cultural groups or regions tend to have more influence and visibility, while marginalized cultures or communities may struggle to have their voices heard. This can perpetuate power imbalances and further marginalize certain cultures or communities.

For example, social media algorithms often prioritize content that aligns with the dominant culture or mainstream narratives. This can result in the underrepresentation of diverse voices and perspectives. As a result, certain cultures may find it more challenging to gain visibility and recognition in the digital media landscape.

3. The Impact of Cultural Bias on Digital Media Consumption:

Consumers of digital media are also susceptible to cultural bias. The content they consume and engage with is often shaped by algorithms and recommendations that are influenced by their past behavior and preferences. This can create filter bubbles and echo chambers, reinforcing existing biases and limiting exposure to diverse perspectives.

To address cultural bias in digital media consumption, individuals can take proactive steps to seek out diverse voices and perspectives. This can include

UNDERSTANDING CULTURAL PERSPECTIVES 7

following people from different cultural backgrounds on social media, actively engaging with content that challenges one's own biases, and being critical of the information presented.

4. Strategies to Mitigate Cultural Bias in Digital Media:

To reduce cultural bias in digital media, content creators and platforms can adopt several strategies:

- Promoting diversity and inclusivity: Platforms can actively promote content from diverse cultural backgrounds and underrepresented communities. This can be done by featuring a diverse range of creators, implementing inclusive algorithms, and providing resources for content creators from marginalized communities.

- Cultural sensitivity training: Content creators can undergo training to improve their awareness of cultural biases and develop the skills to create more inclusive and culturally sensitive content. This can help them avoid perpetuating stereotypes and misrepresentations.

- Auditing content: Platforms can conduct regular audits to identify and address any biases present in their algorithms and content recommendations. This can help ensure that diverse voices and perspectives are given fair visibility.

- User feedback and moderation: Users should be encouraged to report any instances of cultural bias or misrepresentation they come across. Platforms should have effective moderation systems in place to address such complaints and take appropriate action.

Overall, addressing cultural bias in digital media is crucial for promoting diversity, inclusivity, and cross-cultural understanding. By recognizing and mitigating cultural biases, digital media can become a powerful tool for fostering cultural exchange, challenging prejudices, and promoting a more equitable and inclusive society.

Cultural Competence in Digital Communication

In the context of digital communication, cultural competence refers to the ability to interact effectively and respectfully with individuals from different cultural backgrounds. It is essential for ensuring a successful and inclusive digital environment that respects diversity and promotes meaningful connections. This section will explore the importance of cultural competence in digital communication, the challenges it presents, and strategies for developing and enhancing cultural competence in the digital space.

INTRODUCTION TO CULTURAL PERSPECTIVES ON DIGITAL MEDIA

Understanding Cultural Competence

Cultural competence in digital communication involves understanding, appreciating, and adapting to cultural differences. It goes beyond mere tolerance and aims to foster positive and meaningful interactions that acknowledge and respect diversity. Developing cultural competence requires individuals to acquire knowledge about different cultures, develop self-awareness, and possess effective communication skills.

Importance of Cultural Competence

Cultural competence is crucial in digital communication for several reasons. Firstly, the digital world has shrunk the distance between individuals from diverse cultural backgrounds, increasing the frequency of cross-cultural interactions. Without cultural competence, misunderstandings and misinterpretations are more likely to occur, leading to communication breakdowns and conflicts.

Secondly, cultural competence promotes inclusivity and equality in digital spaces. It ensures that individuals from all cultures have an equal opportunity to participate and contribute, regardless of their cultural background. By valuing and respecting cultural differences, digital communication platforms can become more welcoming and inclusive for everyone.

Furthermore, cultural competence is essential for building trust and strengthening relationships in the digital world. When individuals demonstrate cultural competence, they are better equipped to navigate cultural nuances, avoid stereotypes, and communicate in a way that is respectful and meaningful.

Challenges in Developing Cultural Competence

Developing cultural competence in digital communication can be challenging due to various factors. Some of the key challenges include:

1. **Stereotyping and Cultural Bias:** Individuals may unconsciously hold stereotypes and biases towards different cultures, which can hinder their ability to communicate effectively. Overcoming these biases requires self-reflection and a willingness to challenge and unlearn cultural stereotypes.

2. **Limited Cultural Knowledge:** Cultural competence requires individuals to have a deep understanding of different cultural practices, norms, values, and communication styles. Acquiring this knowledge can be time-consuming and requires continuous learning and curiosity about different cultures.

UNDERSTANDING CULTURAL PERSPECTIVES

3. **Language Barriers:** Language plays a vital role in cultural communication, and language barriers can hinder effective cross-cultural interactions. Overcoming language barriers may involve using translation tools, learning basic phrases, or seeking assistance from interpreters.

4. **Miscommunication and Misinterpretation:** Cultural differences can lead to miscommunication and misinterpretation of messages. Cultural competence involves developing effective communication skills, such as active listening, empathy, and the ability to ask clarifying questions.

Strategies for Developing Cultural Competence

Developing and enhancing cultural competence in digital communication requires a combination of self-reflection, knowledge acquisition, and active practice. Here are some strategies to consider:

1. **Self-reflection:** Start by reflecting on your own cultural values, biases, and assumptions. This self-awareness is essential for recognizing and challenging your own cultural lens.

2. **Cultural Education:** Take the initiative to learn about different cultures, their customs, traditions, and communication styles. Read books, watch documentaries, or engage in online courses that explore cultural diversity.

3. **Interact with Individuals from Different Cultures:** Actively seek out opportunities to interact with individuals from different cultural backgrounds. Engage in online forums, social media groups, or virtual communities that embrace cultural diversity.

4. **Practice Active Listening:** Cultivate active listening skills by being fully present in conversations, suspending judgment, and paraphrasing to ensure understanding. This helps to foster effective communication and prevent misunderstandings.

5. **Ask Questions and Seek Clarification:** If you encounter cultural practices or behaviors that you don't understand, politely ask questions for clarification. Avoid assumptions, as they may lead to misunderstandings.

6. **Embrace Flexibility and Adaptability:** Cultivate a mindset of flexibility and adaptability when engaging with individuals from different cultures. Be open to new perspectives and willing to modify your communication style to accommodate cultural differences.

7. **Respect and Value Cultural Differences:** Show respect for cultural differences by avoiding stereotypes, treating everyone with dignity, and acknowledging the richness of diverse cultural backgrounds.

By consciously applying these strategies, individuals can develop and enhance their cultural competence, leading to more effective and inclusive digital communication.

Case Study: Enhancing Cultural Competence in Online Education

One area where cultural competence is particularly relevant is online education. As online courses and e-learning platforms become increasingly popular, it is essential to ensure that cultural differences are acknowledged and accommodated in the digital learning environment.

In a case study conducted at a virtual university, researchers explored the impact of cultural competence training on the interactions between students from diverse cultural backgrounds. The training included modules on cultural diversity, communication styles, and strategies for developing cultural competence in online education.

The study found that after the cultural competence training, students reported increased awareness and understanding of cultural differences. They were more likely to engage in respectful and inclusive discussions, and misunderstandings stemming from cultural differences were minimized. The training also led to higher levels of satisfaction and engagement among students from diverse backgrounds, contributing to a more positive learning experience.

This case study highlights the importance of integrating cultural competence training into online education settings. By providing students and educators with the tools and knowledge to navigate cultural differences, digital learning platforms can create an environment that promotes inclusivity and enhances the overall educational experience.

Conclusion: Fostering Cultural Competence in Digital Communication

Cultural competence is essential for navigating the complexities of digital communication in a globalized world. By valuing and respecting cultural differences, individuals can enhance their ability to communicate effectively and build meaningful relationships in the digital space.

This section has explored the importance of cultural competence, the challenges it presents, and strategies for developing and enhancing cultural competence in the digital context. Building cultural competence requires self-reflection, cultural education, active listening, and a willingness to embrace flexibility and adaptability.

In the ever-evolving digital landscape, being culturally competent allows us to bridge cultural divides, foster inclusivity, and promote positive interactions. By continuously striving to develop cultural competence, we can create a digital world that harnesses the power of diversity and facilitates meaningful connections.

Ethical Considerations in Cultural Perspectives on Digital Media

Ethics plays a crucial role in the study of cultural perspectives on digital media. As digital technologies continue to shape our communication landscape, it is essential to consider the ethical implications that arise from the intersection of culture and digital media. In this section, we will explore the ethical considerations that researchers, practitioners, and users should take into account when examining cultural perspectives on digital media.

Ethical Frameworks for Cultural Perspectives on Digital Media

To navigate ethical challenges in cultural perspectives on digital media, scholars and practitioners can rely on established ethical frameworks. These frameworks provide a systematic approach to analyze and evaluate ethical issues. Two key ethical frameworks relevant to this field are:

1. **Utilitarianism:** This ethical framework emphasizes maximizing overall social welfare and utility. When applying utilitarianism to cultural perspectives on digital media, we consider the potential positive impact of digital media on cultural preservation, representation, and empowerment. For example, digital media platforms can amplify marginalized voices and foster cultural exchange, leading to a more inclusive and diverse digital landscape.

2. **Principle-based ethics:** This framework relies on a set of moral principles to guide ethical decision-making. In the context of cultural perspectives on digital media, important principles include cultural sensitivity, respect for diversity, and protection of cultural heritage. These principles guide researchers and practitioners to consider the potential harm caused by cultural misappropriation, stereotypes, or exclusionary practices.

By utilizing these ethical frameworks, researchers and practitioners can identify potential ethical concerns and develop strategies to address them.

INTRODUCTION TO CULTURAL PERSPECTIVES ON DIGITAL MEDIA

Ethical Challenges

The cultural diversity inherent in digital media presents several ethical challenges that need to be addressed. Some of the key challenges include:

1. **Cultural misappropriation:** Digital media platforms can facilitate the appropriation of cultural artifacts, practices, and identities without proper acknowledgment or respect. This can lead to the distortion, commodification, and devaluation of cultures. Addressing cultural misappropriation requires ethical guidelines for content creators, platform operators, and users to ensure that cultural expressions are treated with sensitivity and respect.

2. **Digital divide and cultural marginalization:** Access to digital media is not uniform across different cultures and regions. The digital divide can exacerbate existing cultural inequalities, excluding certain communities from participating and benefiting from digital platforms. Ethical considerations involve addressing structural barriers, promoting digital inclusion, and ensuring equal access to cultural representation and expression online.

3. **Representation and power imbalances:** Digital media platforms have the potential to perpetuate power imbalances by privileging certain cultural perspectives while marginalizing others. Ethical considerations should include ensuring diverse and authentic cultural representation, addressing algorithmic biases, and empowering underrepresented communities to shape digital media narratives.

4. **Privacy and security in cultural contexts:** Cultures often have different norms and expectations around privacy and security. Ethical considerations involve understanding and respecting these cultural differences while ensuring the protection of individuals' privacy and security in digital media practices.

Mitigating Ethical Concerns

To address these ethical challenges, it is important to develop practical strategies and guidelines. Here are a few examples:

1. **Cultural awareness and sensitivity training:** Researchers, content creators, and platform operators should receive training on cultural awareness and sensitivity. This training can help them understand and navigate the

complexities of cultural diversity, avoid cultural misappropriation, and promote inclusivity.

2. **Collaboration with communities:** Engaging and collaborating with communities can ensure that digital media projects respect and reflect their cultural values. By involving community members in design, decision-making, and content creation processes, ethical concerns can be effectively addressed.

3. **Ethical guidelines and codes of conduct:** Developing and implementing ethical guidelines and codes of conduct specific to cultural perspectives on digital media can provide a roadmap for researchers, practitioners, and users. These guidelines should emphasize respect for cultural diversity, authenticity in cultural representation, and responsible content creation.

4. **User empowerment and consent:** Digital media platforms should empower users to control and manage their cultural identity and expressions. This includes clear consent mechanisms, allowing users to determine how their cultural content is shared and accessed.

5. **Auditing and accountability:** Regular audits of digital media platforms can help identify and address ethical concerns. Transparency in decision-making processes and accountability mechanisms are essential to ensure that cultural perspectives are respected and ethical standards are upheld.

Case Study: Cultural Representation in Virtual Reality

Virtual reality (VR) technology presents unique ethical considerations when it comes to cultural perspectives. A case in point is the representation of cultural heritage sites in VR experiences. While VR can provide immersive and educational experiences for users, it also raises questions about authenticity, ownership, and respectful representation.

To address these ethical concerns, VR developers can collaborate with local communities and cultural experts to ensure accurate representations of heritage sites. They can also implement consent mechanisms that allow communities to have control over how their cultural heritage is represented in VR experiences. Additionally, clear guidelines on avoiding stereotypes, cultural misappropriation, and commodification can help create a more ethical approach to cultural representation in VR.

Conclusion

Ethical considerations are vital in cultural perspectives on digital media as they shape the impact and implications of digital technologies on diverse cultures. By applying ethical frameworks, recognizing the challenges, and implementing practical strategies, we can foster a more inclusive, respectful, and culturally sensitive digital media landscape. It is crucial for researchers, practitioners, and users alike to be aware of and actively address the ethical dimensions of cultural perspectives on digital media.

Research Approaches to Studying Cultural Perspectives on Digital Media

Studying cultural perspectives on digital media requires a multidisciplinary approach that combines insights from sociology, anthropology, communication studies, media studies, and other related fields. This section will explore various research approaches that can be used to investigate the complex intersection of culture and digital media.

Qualitative Research Methods

Qualitative research methods are essential for understanding the nuanced and context-dependent nature of cultural perspectives on digital media. These methods allow researchers to delve deep into the cultural meanings, practices, and experiences associated with digital media use.

Ethnography Ethnography involves immersing oneself in a particular social group or community to gain an in-depth understanding of their culture and digital media practices. Ethnographic research in the digital media context may involve participant observation, interviews, and the collection of artifacts such as online posts, images, and videos. By spending time with participants, researchers can uncover the cultural dynamics shaping digital media use.

For example, a researcher conducting an ethnographic study on social media use among a specific cultural group might join online communities, observe interactions, and conduct interviews to gain insights into how members navigate social media platforms and express their cultural identities.

In-depth Interviews In-depth interviews provide a valuable means of exploring individual experiences and perspectives regarding digital media and culture. This

UNDERSTANDING CULTURAL PERSPECTIVES 15

approach allows researchers to capture the richness and diversity of individuals' beliefs, values, and practices related to digital media use. Researchers can conduct open-ended interviews, asking probing questions to elicit detailed accounts of participants' experiences.

For instance, a researcher might conduct in-depth interviews with members of a community to understand their motivations for sharing cultural content online and how they perceive the impact of digital media on cultural identity.

Focus Groups Focus groups involve bringing together a small group of participants to engage in facilitated discussions on specific topics related to digital media and culture. This approach allows researchers to explore shared experiences, norms, and beliefs within a cultural group.

For instance, a focus group discussion could explore how different cultural communities perceive and engage with digital media platforms differently, uncovering the underlying cultural values and practices influencing their usage patterns.

Quantitative Research Methods

Quantitative research methods complement qualitative approaches by providing statistical insights into broader patterns and trends within cultural perspectives on digital media. While quantitative research may sacrifice some depth, it allows for the generalization of findings to larger populations.

Surveys Surveys involve administering standardized questionnaires to a large number of participants to gather data on their attitudes, behaviors, and perceptions related to digital media use. By using statistical techniques, researchers can identify correlations and associations between variables.

For example, a researcher might conduct a survey to investigate the relationship between cultural values and social media use across different cultural groups, providing quantitative evidence of the impact of cultural factors on digital media practices.

Content Analysis Content analysis involves systematically analyzing digital media content, such as social media posts, user-generated content, or online news articles, to uncover prevalent themes, discourses, and representations. Researchers can examine patterns and trends in the content to gain insights into cultural perspectives.

INTRODUCTION TO CULTURAL PERSPECTIVES ON DIGITAL MEDIA

For instance, a content analysis of online discourse around a particular cultural event or movement can reveal how digital media platforms are used to negotiate cultural identities and social dynamics.

Mixed Methods Approaches

Combining qualitative and quantitative research methods through mixed-methods approaches offers a more comprehensive understanding of cultural perspectives on digital media. Integrating different data collection and analysis techniques enables researchers to triangulate findings and explore the complexities of the research topic.

For instance, a researcher might conduct initial qualitative interviews to explore cultural values and practices related to digital media, followed by a quantitative survey to assess the prevalence of those perspectives within a larger population. The integration of both approaches provides a more holistic understanding of the research question.

Intercultural Research Collaborations

Given the global nature of digital media, intercultural research collaborations can provide unique insights into cultural perspectives. By engaging scholars from different cultural backgrounds, researchers can incorporate diverse viewpoints and challenge potential biases in their research.

For example, a collaborative research project between researchers from Western and non-Western cultures can lead to a richer understanding of how culture shapes digital media practices and challenge ethnocentric assumptions.

Challenges and Limitations

Studying cultural perspectives on digital media comes with its unique challenges and limitations. Researchers must navigate sensitive ethical considerations, such as obtaining informed consent and mitigating potential harm to participants. Additionally, ensuring the representation of diverse cultural perspectives within research samples is crucial for avoiding generalizations or stereotypes.

Moreover, cultural dynamics are dynamic and ever-evolving, which poses a challenge for researchers to capture the rapidly changing landscape of digital media and culture. Longitudinal studies and ongoing engagement with cultural communities can help address this limitation.

Conclusion

Studying cultural perspectives on digital media requires a range of research approaches that combine qualitative, quantitative, and mixed-methods techniques. Ethnography, in-depth interviews, focus groups, surveys, and content analysis offer different lenses for understanding the complex interplay between culture and digital media. Intercultural research collaborations can further enrich the understanding of cultural perspectives. Researchers must anticipate and address challenges such as ethical considerations and the ever-changing nature of digital media and culture. By employing diverse research approaches, scholars can uncover the intricate ways in which culture shapes digital media practices and vice versa, ultimately contributing to a more nuanced understanding of this rapidly evolving field.

Theoretical Frameworks for Analyzing Cultural Perspectives on Digital Media

Understanding cultural perspectives on digital media requires the application of theoretical frameworks that help to analyze and interpret the complex interplay between culture and technology. These frameworks provide a lens through which we can examine how cultural factors shape and are shaped by digital media platforms and practices. In this section, we will explore some key theoretical frameworks that contribute to a deeper understanding of cultural perspectives on digital media.

Cultural Studies

Cultural studies is an interdisciplinary field that emerged in the 1960s and 1970s, drawing on insights from sociology, anthropology, literary criticism, and media studies. It aims to analyze the relationship between culture, power, and identity within societal contexts. Cultural studies offers a valuable framework for understanding cultural perspectives on digital media by examining how digital technologies are embedded within broader social, political, and economic structures.

One key concept in cultural studies is the idea of cultural representation. It examines how digital media platforms represent diverse cultural groups and identities, and how these representations shape perceptions and power dynamics. For example, the underrepresentation or misrepresentation of certain cultural groups can perpetuate stereotypes and inequalities.

Cultural studies also emphasizes the role of resistance and agency. It examines how individuals and communities use digital media to challenge dominant cultural norms and practices. This framework helps to illuminate the ways in which digital media can be a site of cultural empowerment and social change.

Media Ecology

Media ecology is a theoretical framework that views media as environments that shape human perception, communication, and social interactions. It emphasizes the interplay between media technologies, cultural practices, and human behavior. In the context of cultural perspectives on digital media, media ecology helps to analyze how digital technologies mediate cultural experiences and shape cultural norms.

One key concept in media ecology is the idea of technological determinism. This perspective argues that technological developments have a deterministic influence on social and cultural change. In the case of digital media, technological determinism suggests that the affordances and constraints of digital technologies shape cultural practices and norms. For example, the widespread use of social media platforms has led to the emergence of new forms of communication and social interaction.

Media ecology also emphasizes the idea of media symbiosis, which refers to the mutually reinforcing relationship between media and culture. This perspective examines how digital media and culture coevolve and shape each other. For instance, the rise of user-generated content on digital platforms has blurred the boundaries between media producers and consumers, allowing for new forms of cultural expression and participation.

Postcolonial Theory

Postcolonial theory examines the cultural, political, and economic legacies of colonialism and imperialism. It provides a critical framework for analyzing the power dynamics and cultural hierarchies embedded in digital media. Postcolonial theorists argue that digital media can reproduce existing power structures, perpetuate cultural imperialism, or provide platforms for subaltern voices to challenge dominant narratives.

One key concept in postcolonial theory is the idea of cultural resistance. This perspective emphasizes the ways in which marginalized communities use digital media to contest dominant cultural representations and reclaim their agency. For example, social media platforms have been used by indigenous communities to assert their cultural identity and challenge stereotypes.

UNDERSTANDING CULTURAL PERSPECTIVES

Postcolonial theory also highlights the importance of decolonizing digital spaces. It calls for a critical examination of the colonial legacies and power imbalances that shape digital media platforms. This framework prompts us to consider how digital media can be more inclusive, equitable, and respectful of diverse cultural perspectives.

Actor-Network Theory

Actor-network theory (ANT) is a sociological framework that seeks to understand how social actors, both human and non-human, interact and shape each other within networks. In the context of cultural perspectives on digital media, ANT provides a useful lens for analyzing the complex web of relationships between users, digital technologies, and cultural practices.

ANT emphasizes the agency of non-human actors, such as algorithms, data structures, and interfaces, in shaping cultural perspectives on digital media. It explores how these technologies mediate and shape our interactions, preferences, and access to information. For example, algorithms used in social media platforms can prioritize certain types of content, leading to the formation of filter bubbles and echo chambers.

ANT also highlights the role of controversies and translations in shaping cultural perspectives on digital media. It examines the tensions and negotiations that occur when different actors and interests come together within a network. This perspective helps to uncover the power dynamics and conflicts that influence the design, use, and impact of digital media platforms.

In conclusion, these theoretical frameworks provide valuable tools for understanding and analyzing cultural perspectives on digital media. Cultural studies, media ecology, postcolonial theory, and actor-network theory offer different perspectives on how culture and technology intersect, and how digital media shape and are shaped by cultural practices and power dynamics. By applying these frameworks, we can gain deeper insights into the complex relationship between culture and digital media in our increasingly interconnected world.

Overview of the Book

In this book, "Cultural Perspectives on Digital Media: How Diverse Traditions, Revolutionary Ideas, and Practical Strategies Shape Modern Communication," we explore the complex relationship between culture and digital media. We delve into the various cultural perspectives that influence the design, use, and impact of digital media in our interconnected world.

INTRODUCTION TO CULTURAL PERSPECTIVES ON DIGITAL MEDIA

The study of cultural perspectives is crucial in understanding the ways in which different cultures shape, interpret, and engage with digital media. By examining the diversity of cultural traditions, revolutionary ideas, and practical strategies, we aim to shed light on the complex interplay between digital media and cultural contexts. This book seeks to provide readers with a comprehensive understanding of cultural perspectives as they apply to digital media.

Throughout the book, we cover a wide range of topics, offering both theoretical frameworks and practical strategies for analyzing and navigating the cultural dimensions of digital media. We begin in Chapter 1 with an introduction to the concept of cultural perspectives and their importance in shaping digital communication. We explore definitions and the impact of cultural diversity and bias in digital media. Additionally, we delve into ethical considerations and research approaches for studying cultural perspectives on digital media.

Chapter 2 takes a historical approach, tracing the development of digital media in different cultural contexts. We explore how oral, written, print, and broadcast traditions have influenced the evolution of digital media. Furthermore, we examine the role of cultural factors in shaping digital media, including adaptation, appropriation, consumption patterns, and platform evolution.

Moving on to Chapter 3, we specifically focus on social media and its cultural dimensions. We explore how cultural values, identity, norms, and privacy concerns shape social media use. Furthermore, we analyze the impact of globalization and how it affects transcultural communication and cultural hybridity on social media platforms. Lastly, we delve into the relationship between social media activism and cultural empowerment.

Chapter 4 concentrates on the challenges and opportunities of cross-cultural communication in the digital age. We examine the role of language barriers, multilingualism, and adaptation strategies in digital communication. Additionally, we explore the impact of non-verbal communication, such as visual communication, emojis, and gestures, on cultural interpretation. Finally, we discuss strategies for developing intercultural communication competence in the digital space.

In Chapter 5, we shift the focus to digital media and identity. We explore how digital media influences individual identity construction, self-expression, and cultural identity formation in virtual communities. Furthermore, we delve into the relationships between digital media and collective identity, including national and ethnic identities, as well as identity politics on digital platforms.

Chapter 6 dives into the intersection of digital media and power. We analyze the concept of cultural hegemony and the influence of global media corporations. Furthermore, we explore the digital divide and its implications for cultural

UNDERSTANDING CULTURAL PERSPECTIVES

marginalization. Additionally, we discuss representation and power dynamics in digital media. We examine the role of digital media in political mobilization, the spread of fake news, and the emergence of online public spheres and digital democracy.

In Chapter 7, we explore the relationship between digital media and creativity. We examine digital media as cultural artifacts and their role in preserving cultural heritage, facilitating cultural expressions, and enabling cultural production and consumption. Furthermore, we discuss the intersection of digital media and creative industries, including cultural entrepreneurship, cultural policy, and intellectual property considerations.

Chapter 8 focuses on the cultural perspectives of digital media in education. We address the impact of cultural contexts on digital education, including the digital divide and educational inequality. Additionally, we explore cultural factors in digital literacy and the importance of culturally-responsive pedagogy in digital learning. We also examine the challenges and opportunities that digital media brings to the field of education.

In Chapter 9, we present practical strategies for incorporating cultural perspectives into digital media design. We discuss user interface design, localization, and inclusive design as ways to promote cultural awareness in digital products. Additionally, we explore ethical guidelines for digital media practices, including cultural appropriation, responsible content creation, and privacy and security considerations.

Finally, in Chapter 10, we discuss the future of cultural perspectives on digital media. We explore emerging trends, such as artificial intelligence, virtual reality, and big data, and their impact on cultural communication. Furthermore, we provide recommendations for future research, including bridging gaps in cultural perspectives and addressing ethical challenges. We also emphasize the importance of interdisciplinary approaches to understanding cultural perspectives on digital media.

This book is intended for students, scholars, and professionals interested in digital media, cultural studies, communication, and related fields. We aim to provide a comprehensive and insightful exploration of the intricate relationship between culture and digital media, highlighting the diverse traditions, revolutionary ideas, and practical strategies that shape modern communication. Throughout the book, readers will find thought-provoking examples, engaging exercises, and valuable resources to deepen their understanding of the subject matter.

Historical Development of Digital Media and Cultural Contexts

Pre-digital Media Landscape and Cultural Traditions

Oral Tradition and Cultural Communication

In this section, we will explore the significance of oral tradition in cultural communication. Oral tradition refers to the transmission of cultural knowledge, beliefs, and practices through spoken words from one generation to another. It plays a vital role in preserving and disseminating cultural heritage, shaping identities, and fostering social cohesion within communities. Understanding the dynamics of oral tradition can provide valuable insights into the cultural perspectives on digital media.

The Importance of Oral Tradition

Oral tradition has been a fundamental mode of communication for human societies throughout history. Before the advent of written language, oral tradition was the primary means of sharing information, preserving cultural values, and expressing collective memory. It encompassed various forms of verbal expression such as storytelling, songs, chants, proverbs, and rituals.

One of the main reasons oral tradition has been vital to cultural communication is its ability to convey nuanced meanings, emotions, and cultural context that may be lost in written texts. The spoken word allows for improvisation, intonation, and gestures that enhance the richness of communication. Additionally, oral tradition fosters a sense of community and shared identity, as individuals gather to listen, participate, and interact with the storyteller or performer.

Characteristics of Oral Tradition

Oral tradition exhibits distinctive characteristics that differentiate it from other forms of communication. These characteristics have shaped cultural perspectives and influenced the development of digital media:

1. **Oral Performances:** Oral tradition often involves live performances where the knowledge, stories, and cultural expressions are shared in a communal setting. The audience actively engages with the speaker or performer, creating an immersive and participatory experience.

2. **Dynamic and Flexible:** Oral tradition allows for dynamic and flexible narratives that evolve with time and context. Each performance may differ slightly as the speaker adapts the content to the audience, incorporating current events or personal storytelling. This flexibility reflects the fluid nature of cultural communication.

3. **Preservation of Collective Memory:** Oral tradition serves as a repository of collective memory, preserving historical events, cultural practices, and ancestral wisdom. It ensures the continuity and transmission of cultural heritage from one generation to another.

4. **Orality and Emotion:** Oral tradition relies heavily on oral language, gestures, intonation, and other non-verbal cues to convey emotion and meaning. These components enhance the emotional resonance of the narratives, fostering an empathetic connection between the performer and the audience.

5. **Contextual Embeddedness:** Oral tradition is deeply embedded in its cultural context. The narratives and performances are influenced by local customs, geographical landscapes, social structures, and historical events, reflecting the diversity and uniqueness of each culture.

6. **Oral Tradition as a Living Tradition:** Unlike written texts, oral tradition is a living tradition that evolves and adapts to changing circumstances. It accommodates new cultural influences, incorporates contemporary experiences, and responds to societal transformations.

Digital Media and Oral Tradition

The emergence of digital media has both challenged and complemented the practices of oral tradition. On one hand, digital media provides new platforms for oral performances to reach broader audiences and be preserved for future generations. Oral narratives and cultural expressions can be recorded, shared, and accessed globally, transcending physical and temporal boundaries.

However, the digitization of oral tradition also raises ethical and cultural concerns. Digital media may not fully capture the performative nature and embodied experience of oral tradition. The cultural context, non-verbal cues, and interactive elements that are crucial to the communication process may be lost or distorted in digital formats. Additionally, issues of ownership, intellectual property, and cultural appropriation arise when oral traditions are digitized without consent or proper attribution.

Examples and Resources

To delve deeper into the significance of oral tradition and cultural communication, here are some examples and resources to explore:

+ **Example:** The preservation of indigenous oral traditions through digital storytelling initiatives in collaboration with indigenous communities.

+ **Resource:** "Orality and Literacy: The Technologizing of the Word" by Walter J. Ong. This book provides a comprehensive exploration of oral tradition and its relationship with literacy and communication technologies.

+ **Resource:** "Indigenous Knowledge and the Integration of Digital Technologies" edited by Jeremy Hunsinger and Anna Malina. This collection of essays explores the intersection of indigenous knowledge systems and digital technologies, including the challenges and opportunities for oral tradition.

+ **Resource:** The UNESCO Oral and Intangible Heritage of Humanity program, which safeguards and raises awareness about oral traditions worldwide. Their website contains valuable information and resources related to oral tradition.

Understanding the role of oral tradition in cultural communication is essential for grasping the diverse perspectives that shape modern digital media. By appreciating the distinct characteristics and value of oral tradition, we can navigate the ethical challenges and leverage digital media to promote cultural diversity and inclusivity.

Exercise: Reflect on your own cultural heritage and identify an oral tradition that holds significance. Consider how this oral tradition has been passed down through generations and how it contributes to the cultural fabric of your community. Discuss your findings with a partner and reflect on the potential impact of digital media on the preservation and dissemination of this oral tradition.

Remember, oral tradition is not just a relic of the past but an ongoing practice that continues to shape our cultural landscapes.

Written Tradition and Its Evolution

The written tradition is an important aspect of human culture and communication. It has evolved over time and has had a significant impact on the development of digital media. In this section, we will explore the evolution of the written tradition and its influence on the digital media landscape.

Origins of Writing

Writing is believed to have originated around 5,000 years ago in ancient Mesopotamia. The earliest form of writing was cuneiform, a system of symbols made by pressing a wedge-shaped stylus into clay tablets. These clay tablets preserved important historical, administrative, and religious records.

Writing also independently developed in other regions, such as ancient Egypt, where hieroglyphs were used to record events and communicate information. The invention of writing revolutionized human communication by enabling the preservation and dissemination of knowledge across time and space.

Impact of Writing on Culture

The evolution of writing had a profound impact on different aspects of culture. Here are a few key areas where the written tradition influenced cultural development:

Knowledge Preservation and Transmission The written tradition allowed for the preservation of knowledge and ideas. Prior to writing, knowledge was primarily passed down orally, which was susceptible to loss or distortion over time. With writing, knowledge could be recorded and transmitted accurately, ensuring its longevity. This led to the accumulation of knowledge and the growth of civilizations.

Standardization of Language Writing played a crucial role in standardizing languages. As writing systems developed, they provided a visual representation of spoken words, establishing rules and conventions for the written form of language. This standardization allowed for effective communication across regions and facilitated the development of literature, legal systems, and religious texts.

Formation of Literary Traditions The written tradition laid the foundation for the development of literary traditions. Ancient epics, myths, legends, and religious texts were written down, enabling their preservation and widespread dissemination. These literary works became an integral part of cultural identity and shaped the collective imagination of communities. They also provided inspiration for future generations of writers and artists.

Transition to Digital Media

The advent of digital media has revolutionized the way we produce, distribute, and consume written content. The transition from traditional written forms to digital media has brought about significant changes in the way we interact with information. Here are a few key aspects of this transition:

Digitization of Texts With the development of optical character recognition (OCR) technology, printed texts can now be digitized and stored in electronic formats. This has led to the creation of vast digital libraries, making a vast amount of knowledge accessible to a global audience. Digitization has also facilitated the preservation of fragile and rare texts, ensuring their availability for future generations.

Electronic Publishing and E-books The rise of the internet and digital publishing platforms has enabled the creation and distribution of electronic books (e-books). E-books are portable, searchable, and easily accessible on a variety of devices. They have transformed the publishing industry, allowing authors to reach global audiences without the need for traditional publishing channels. E-books have also made reading more interactive by incorporating multimedia elements and hyperlinks.

Impact on Reading Practices Digital media has influenced reading practices and the way we engage with written content. With the proliferation of smartphones, tablets, and e-readers, reading has become more mobile and convenient. The ability to adjust font sizes and customize reading experiences has made reading more accessible to individuals with visual impairments. However, digital distractions and information overload have also posed challenges to sustained and deep reading.

Emergence of Social Reading and Writing Digital media platforms have facilitated social reading and writing experiences. Online book clubs, forums, and social media platforms have provided avenues for readers to connect, discuss, and share their reading experiences. Similarly, writing platforms and blogging tools have empowered individuals to express their thoughts, opinions, and stories, reaching a broader audience instantly. This has democratized the writing process and fostered online communities of writers and readers.

Challenges and Opportunities

The evolution of the written tradition in the digital age has brought both challenges and opportunities. Here are a few important factors to consider:

Digital Divide While digital media has increased access to written content, there remains a digital divide that limits access to technology and connectivity. Socioeconomic factors, infrastructure limitations, and educational disparities contribute to unequal access and usage of digital media. Bridging the digital divide is essential to ensure equal opportunities for individuals to engage with written content in the digital age.

Evaluating Online Sources The abundance of digital information requires individuals to develop critical evaluation skills. Online sources may vary in terms of accuracy, reliability, and credibility. Understanding how to discern trustworthy sources from misleading or false information is crucial in the digital era. Digital literacy education plays a vital role in equipping individuals with the skills to navigate and evaluate online sources effectively.

Preserving Cultural Diversity Digital media has the potential to amplify diverse voices and promote cultural diversity. However, there is a risk of dominant cultural narratives overpowering marginalized voices in the digital landscape. Ensuring the preservation and representation of diverse cultural perspectives requires conscious efforts in content creation, dissemination, and platform design.

PRE-DIGITAL MEDIA LANDSCAPE AND CULTURAL TRADITIONS 29

New Modes of Expression Digital media has expanded the possibilities for creative expression. From interactive storytelling to multimedia presentations, new modes of expression have emerged. Individuals can combine text, images, videos, and sound to create rich and immersive narratives. The digital space offers opportunities for experimentation, collaboration, and the exploration of unconventional forms of writing and storytelling.

In conclusion, the written tradition has evolved from ancient forms of writing to the digital media landscape we see today. The transition to digital media has had profound implications for knowledge preservation, language standardization, literary traditions, and reading practices. While digital media presents challenges such as the digital divide and the need for critical evaluation of online sources, it also offers exciting opportunities for cultural diversity, new modes of expression, and global access to written content. As digital media continues to evolve, it is essential to consider the cultural perspectives and implications of these transformations.

Print Media and Cultural Impact

Print media has played a significant role in shaping cultural norms, values, and perceptions. From the advent of the printing press to the rise of newspapers, magazines, and books, print media has been a powerful medium for disseminating information, ideas, and ideologies. In this section, we will explore the cultural impact of print media and how it has influenced societies throughout history.

The Evolution of Print Media

The invention of the printing press by Johannes Gutenberg in the 15th century revolutionized the way information was produced and distributed. With the ability to mass-produce books, pamphlets, and other printed materials, literacy rates began to rise, and the spread of knowledge became more widespread. This led to the democratization of information and the empowerment of individuals to engage in intellectual discourse and critical thinking.

The development of newspapers in the 17th century further expanded the reach of print media. Newspapers became a primary source of news and information, allowing people to stay informed about local and global events. They also played a vital role in shaping public opinion and political discourse. In many cases, newspapers became the mouthpiece for political movements and ideologies, influencing the way societies thought about various issues.

The rise of magazines in the 19th century added another dimension to print media. Magazines focused on specific topics, such as fashion, literature, or politics, and catered to niche audiences. They provided a platform for in-depth analysis, commentary, and cultural exploration. Magazines became vehicles for promoting cultural trends, ideologies, and societal values.

Cultural Influence of Print Media

Print media has had a profound impact on cultural development, as it played a significant role in disseminating cultural ideas, values, and traditions. Here are some key ways in which print media shaped culture:

Preservation of Cultural Heritage Print media has been instrumental in preserving and transmitting cultural heritage. Books, newspapers, and magazines have documented historical events, literature, and cultural practices, ensuring that they are passed down through generations. Through printed materials, cultural traditions, language, and historical narratives have been preserved and continue to inform contemporary cultural identities.

Formation of Cultural Identities Print media has played a crucial role in the formation of cultural identities. By providing stories, literature, and narratives that reflect specific cultural experiences, printed materials have helped communities understand and express their unique cultural identities. Books, magazines, and newspapers have empowered marginalized groups by providing a platform for their voices and perspectives to be heard and acknowledged.

Promotion of Cultural Values and Ideologies Print media has often been used as a tool for promoting specific cultural values and ideologies. Newspapers and magazines have propagated political ideologies, religious beliefs, and societal norms, influencing public opinion and behavior. Print media has the power to shape attitudes, opinions, and behaviors by presenting information and perspectives that align with certain cultural values or agendas.

Cultural Resistance and Alternative Narratives Print media has also been a medium for cultural resistance and the dissemination of alternative narratives. Underground newspapers, zines, and self-published books have challenged dominant cultural norms and ideologies, providing platforms for marginalized voices and perspectives. These alternative forms of print media have fostered cultural diversity, creativity, and social change.

Contemporary Challenges and Opportunities

While print media continues to be influential, it faces numerous challenges in the digital age. The widespread availability of online news sources, blogs, and social media has shifted the way people consume information. The decline in print media readership has led to financial constraints and reduced resources for traditional print publications.

However, print media still holds unique advantages and opportunities. The physicality of printed materials provides a tactile and immersive reading experience that digital media cannot replicate. Print publications can also cater to specific audiences and provide focused, in-depth analysis and commentary.

To remain relevant, print media has had to adapt and innovate. Many newspapers and magazines have embraced digital platforms and incorporated multimedia elements into their print publications. They have also focused on creating diverse and inclusive content that reflects the cultural experiences and perspectives of their readers.

Case Study: The Impact of Print Media on Cultural Movements

An excellent example of print media's cultural impact is the role it played in various social and political movements throughout history. Print media has been instrumental in mobilizing communities, disseminating ideologies, and shaping cultural movements.

One prominent example is the role of newspapers and pamphlets during the American Revolution. Revolutionary leaders used print media as a platform to rally support for independence, disseminate revolutionary ideas, and challenge British authority. Newspapers like "Common Sense" by Thomas Paine played a crucial role in shaping public sentiment and galvanizing the colonists towards revolution.

Similarly, during the civil rights movement in the United States, print media played a vital role in spreading awareness, organizing protests, and challenging systemic racism. Magazines like "Jet" and newspapers like "The Chicago Defender" provided platforms for African American activists and journalists to share their stories, challenge discriminatory policies, and ignite social change.

These examples highlight the power of print media in shaping cultural narratives, promoting social justice, and creating a sense of collective identity among communities.

Conclusion

Print media has been a powerful force in shaping cultural perspectives and influencing societies throughout history. From the invention of the printing press to the rise of newspapers, magazines, and books, print media has played a crucial role in preserving cultural heritage, shaping cultural identities, promoting ideologies, and fostering cultural resistance.

While print media faces challenges in the digital age, it continues to hold unique opportunities for in-depth analysis, focused content, and the preservation of physical cultural artifacts. Understanding the cultural impact of print media provides insights into our historical and cultural development and serves as a foundation for exploring the broader cultural perspectives on digital media.

Broadcast Media and Cultural Contexts

Broadcast media has played a significant role in shaping cultural contexts throughout history. From radio to television, these mass communication platforms have influenced cultural practices, norms, and values. In this section, we will explore the relationship between broadcast media and cultural contexts, examining the impact and influence of radio and television on society.

The Emergence of Broadcast Media

The development of broadcast media marked a significant shift in how information and entertainment were distributed. With the invention of the radio in the early 20th century, for the first time, people could hear news, music, and other forms of audio content from the comfort of their homes. Radio became an essential part of people's lives, connecting them to distant voices, cultures, and ideas.

The introduction of television in the mid-20th century revolutionized the way people consumed media. Television brought moving images and sounds directly into people's homes, providing a visual and auditory experience like no other. The advent of television introduced new possibilities and challenges for cultural representation and communication.

Cultural Diversity in Broadcast Media

One of the significant impacts of broadcast media is its ability to disseminate cultural content on a mass scale. Radio and television have brought cultural diversity to people's homes, exposing them to different traditions, languages, and perspectives. This exposure has increased awareness and understanding of diverse cultures and fostered multiculturalism in many societies.

Broadcast media has also served as a platform for underrepresented cultures to assert their identities and share their narratives. Minorities, indigenous communities, and marginalized groups have used radio and television as a means of cultural expression and empowerment. They have been able to counter mainstream narratives and challenge stereotypes by creating their own media spaces.

Cultural Influence on Broadcast Media

While broadcast media has enabled the dissemination of diverse cultural content, it is important to recognize that cultural influences also shape the production and consumption of broadcast media. Cultural values, beliefs, and norms are embedded in the programs, advertisements, and narratives presented through radio and television.

For example, in some cultures, modesty and conservativeness are highly valued. As a result, television shows and advertisements in these cultures may reflect these values, presenting characters and content that align with societal expectations. On the other hand, in more liberal cultures, broadcast media may showcase a wider range of perspectives and content that pushes boundaries.

Cultural Representations in Broadcast Media

Cultural representations in broadcast media have a significant impact on how individuals perceive themselves and others. The media plays a crucial role in shaping cultural identities and influencing societal norms. Consequently, it is essential to critically analyze the representations and portrayals of different cultures in broadcast media.

Misrepresentation or exoticization of cultures can perpetuate stereotypes and contribute to cultural misunderstandings. For instance, certain cultures may be depicted as backward or primitive, reinforcing negative stereotypes and biases. On the other hand, some cultural groups may be idealized or fetishized, leading to cultural appropriation or commodification.

Challenges of Cultural Representation

The challenge of cultural representation in broadcast media lies in striking a balance between accurately representing different cultures and catering to audience expectations. Content creators and media professionals need to be sensitive to cultural nuances and avoid simplification or generalization of complex cultural identities.

Additionally, cultural representation in broadcast media should be inclusive and equitable. It should ensure that historically marginalized and underrepresented cultures have a voice and presence in media narratives. Efforts must be made to provide opportunities for diverse cultural groups to participate in the creation and production of media content.

The Power of Broadcast Media

Broadcast media holds immense power in shaping cultural contexts due to its wide reach and influence. It has the ability to reinforce existing cultural norms, challenge outdated beliefs, and introduce new ideas. The content presented through broadcast media can shape public opinion, impact social movements, and influence cultural changes.

However, with great power comes responsibility. Media organizations should be aware of the potential impacts of their content and act ethically. They should strive to create a media landscape that respects cultural diversity, promotes inclusivity, and fosters meaningful dialogue.

Case Study: Cultural Impact of Soap Operas

Soap operas are a prime example of the cultural influence of broadcast media. These serialized dramas have captivated audiences worldwide and have often been instrumental in shaping cultural attitudes and behaviors. In many cultures, soap operas have played a significant role in initiating discussions on social issues, challenging traditional values, and advocating for gender equality.

For instance, in Latin American countries, telenovelas have successfully highlighted social issues such as domestic violence, class disparities, and political corruption. These programs have sparked national conversations and contributed to social change. Similarly, soap operas in India have addressed topics like arranged marriages, dowry, and women's rights, raising awareness and influencing societal norms.

Soap operas' immense popularity and longevity provide a unique opportunity for social messaging and cultural representation. They have the ability to reach millions of viewers on a daily basis, making them a powerful tool for cultural education and social commentary.

Conclusion

Broadcast media has had a profound impact on cultural contexts. It has brought cultural diversity and representation to millions of people, while also being shaped by cultural influences. Cultural representations in broadcast media have the power to shape identities, influence societal norms, and facilitate social change. It is essential for media organizations to utilize this power responsibly, promoting inclusivity, diversity, and ethical practices. By recognizing the influence of broadcast media on culture, we can foster a more inclusive and culturally sensitive media landscape.

The Role of Cultural Factors in Shaping Digital Media

Cultural Adaptation and Localization of Digital Media

In the digital age, cultural adaptation and localization of digital media play a crucial role in ensuring effective communication and engagement with diverse audiences across different cultural contexts. Cultural adaptation refers to the process of modifying digital media content to align with the cultural values, norms, and preferences of a specific target audience. Localization, on the other hand, involves translating and adapting digital media content to suit the language and cultural context of a particular region or country.

2.2.1.1 Cultural adaptation strategies

Cultural adaptation strategies vary depending on the medium, platform, and intended audience. Here are some key strategies:

1. Content customization: Adapting digital media content to resonate with the cultural references, symbols, and storytelling styles of the target audience. For example, a video game set in Japan may customize its characters, scenery, and narrative to reflect Japanese cultural elements such as traditional festivals, cuisine, and historical landmarks.

2. User interface design: Modifying the user interface (UI) of digital media platforms to accommodate the cultural preferences of different regions. This includes features such as date formats, fonts, color schemes, and layout designs that align with the cultural aesthetics and usability preferences of the target audience. For instance, a social media platform may offer different UI options for users in Middle Eastern countries to ensure compatibility with right-to-left reading orientation.

3. Cultural sensitivity in marketing: Tailoring promotional campaigns and branding strategies to avoid cultural insensitivity or misinterpretation. This

involves conducting thorough research into cultural taboos, religious sensitivities, and local customs. For instance, a global e-commerce company may need to adapt its marketing messages to respect cultural norms related to modesty, gender roles, or religious holidays in different regions.

4. Localized user-generated content (UGC): Encouraging users to generate and share content that is relevant and culturally appropriate for their respective communities. This approach facilitates the co-creation of content that reflects the diverse cultural perspectives within a digital media platform.

2.2.1.2 Challenges and considerations

Cultural adaptation and localization of digital media are not without challenges. Here are some considerations to address:

1. Cultural research: Conducting comprehensive cultural research and understanding the target audience's values, beliefs, and cultural practices is essential. This involves employing qualitative research methods such as interviews, focus groups, and ethnographic studies to gain insights into the cultural nuances that should be considered during adaptation and localization.

2. Avoiding stereotypes: Care must be taken to avoid reinforcing cultural stereotypes or perpetuating biases through adapted or localized content. It is crucial to strike a balance between cultural authenticity and avoiding harmful representations that may perpetuate cultural misunderstandings or reinforce existing power dynamics.

3. Linguistic and contextual appropriateness: The localization of digital media should go beyond mere translation. To ensure linguistic and contextual appropriateness, professional translators and cultural experts should be involved in the process. This includes adapting idiomatic expressions, cultural references, and humor that may not have direct translations.

4. Technical challenges: Adapting digital media across different devices, platforms, and operating systems can present technical challenges. Compatibility issues, font support, encoding formats, and multimedia integration are just a few examples of the technical considerations that need to be addressed during the localization process.

2.2.1.3 Case study: McDonald's cultural adaptation in different countries

One notable example of cultural adaptation and localization in digital media is McDonald's, a global fast-food chain. McDonald's has successfully adapted its marketing and digital strategies to appeal to diverse cultural markets across the globe.

For instance, in India, McDonald's introduced vegetarian menu options to accommodate cultural preferences and religious dietary restrictions. The menu includes items such as the McAloo Tikki burger, which features a potato and vegetable patty, and the McVeggie burger, which incorporates a vegetable-based patty.

In China, McDonald's embraced digital technology to localize its digital media offerings. They launched a mobile app that integrates with popular Chinese social media platforms such as WeChat and offers features like personalized promotions, virtual red envelopes during Chinese New Year, and interactive games that incorporate Chinese cultural elements.

These examples demonstrate how cultural adaptation and localization can contribute to the success of digital media strategies in diverse cultural contexts. By respecting cultural values, preferences, and sensitivities, digital media can bridge cultural gaps and foster meaningful engagement with audiences globally.

2.2.1.4 Resources and further reading

- Belk, R. W., & McCracken, G. (Eds.). (2020). Handbook of Research on Digital Consumption: Frontiers and Future Directions. Edward Elgar Publishing.

- Ess, C. (Ed.). (2014). Cultural Attitudes Towards Technology and Communication 2012 Proceedings of the Eighth International Conference on Cultural Attitudes Towards Technology and Communication (CATaC'12). School of Communication, University of Oslo.

- Lai, F., & Resmini, A. (2015). Cultural adaptation and localisation of digital media. In Human-Computer Interaction and Innovation in Handheld, Mobile and Wearable Technologies (pp. 141-156). Springer.

- Mori, J., & Yamashita, S. (2019). Localization strategies of multinational corporations on social media: A case study of McDonald's in Japan and China. Journal of World Business, 54(6), 101002.

- Zhoa, Y., & Rau, P. L. (2014). The culture-performance nexus in e-business: revealing the impact of national culture on e-commerce across the globe. Electronic Commerce Research and Applications, 13(3), 189-204.

2.2.1.5 Exercises

1. Choose a popular digital media platform and research how it has adapted its features and content for different cultural markets. Analyze the strategies employed and discuss the impact on user engagement and adoption in those markets.

2. Imagine you are tasked with localizing a popular mobile game for a new market. Identify the cultural factors that need to be considered and propose adaptation strategies to ensure a successful launch in the target market.

3. Conduct a small-scale research study to explore the impact of cultural adaptation in digital media. Choose a specific digital medium or platform and collect user feedback to evaluate the effectiveness of cultural adaptation strategies implemented. Analyze the findings and propose recommendations for further improvement.

Note: XeLaTeX code portion ends here.

Cultural Appropriation and Digital Media

Cultural appropriation refers to the adoption, borrowing, or imitation of elements from another culture, often without understanding or respecting their historical, social, and cultural significance. In the context of digital media, cultural appropriation has become a significant issue due to the ease and speed with which content can be shared and disseminated.

Understanding Cultural Appropriation

Cultural appropriation in digital media occurs when individuals or groups from a dominant culture adopt elements from marginalized cultures, often without acknowledging or understanding their origins. This can include clothing, hairstyles, music, art, language, and symbols. While cultural exchange and appreciation are valuable, cultural appropriation becomes problematic when it leads to the commodification and exploitation of cultural expressions, reinforcing power imbalances and perpetuating stereotypes.

Digital media platforms, such as social media, have amplified the spread of cultural appropriation by providing a global reach and instant accessibility. Content creators, influencers, and even brands often appropriate elements from different cultures to attract attention, gain followers, or increase profits. This can result in the erasure and misrepresentation of cultural traditions, stripping them of their original meaning and context.

Implications of Cultural Appropriation in Digital Media

The implications of cultural appropriation in digital media are far-reaching. They can contribute to the marginalization and commodification of marginalized cultures by reinforcing stereotypes, commodifying cultural practices, and perpetuating cultural hierarchy. Cultural appropriation can also lead to the erasure of cultural identity, as elements are divorced from their original context and repackaged for mass consumption.

Furthermore, cultural appropriation in digital media can have economic consequences. When dominant cultures appropriate cultural elements, they often profit from them, while the communities from which those elements originate may not receive recognition or compensation. This can perpetuate economic inequality and further marginalize already disadvantaged communities.

THE ROLE OF CULTURAL FACTORS IN SHAPING DIGITAL MEDIA 39

Examples of Cultural Appropriation in Digital Media

There have been numerous instances of cultural appropriation in digital media that have sparked controversies and raised awareness about the issue. For example, the use of Native American headdresses as fashion accessories or costumes in music festivals and on social media platforms has been criticized for disrespecting indigenous cultures and reducing sacred symbols to fashion trends.

Similarly, the adoption of African-American Vernacular English (AAVE) phrases and slang by non-Black social media influencers without crediting or acknowledging their origins has been condemned for profiting off Black culture while disregarding the systemic oppression faced by the Black community.

Addressing Cultural Appropriation in Digital Media

Addressing cultural appropriation in digital media requires a multi-faceted approach that involves individuals, content creators, platform owners, and society as a whole. Here are a few strategies that can help mitigate the issue:

1. **Educate and raise awareness:** It is essential to educate individuals about the concept of cultural appropriation and its implications. This can be done through educational campaigns, workshops, and the inclusion of cultural sensitivity training in digital media-related courses and programs.

2. **Promote cultural exchange rather than appropriation:** Encouraging respectful and reciprocal cultural exchange can help foster understanding and appreciation between cultures. This involves engaging in meaningful dialogue, seeking permission, and giving proper credit to the originators of cultural practices and expressions when incorporating them into digital media content.

3. **Diversify representation:** Platform owners and content creators should strive for diversity and inclusivity in digital media. This involves featuring voices and perspectives from marginalized communities, avoiding stereotypes, and providing opportunities for individuals from these communities to share their own narratives.

4. **Accountability and transparency:** Content creators and influencers should take responsibility for their actions and be transparent about their sources of inspiration. This includes acknowledging the cultural origins of their content, engaging in open discussions when called out for cultural appropriation, and making amends when necessary.

5. **Collaboration and partnership:** Foster collaboration between content creators from different cultures. This can help ensure that cultural expressions are represented accurately and authentically.

By implementing these strategies, we can begin to address the issue of cultural appropriation in digital media and work towards a more inclusive and respectful online environment.

Ethical Considerations

Ethical considerations play a crucial role in combating cultural appropriation in digital media. Content creators and platform owners have a responsibility to act ethically, respecting the cultural rights and intellectual property of marginalized communities. Ethical guidelines can help navigate the complexities of cultural exchange and ensure that content is created and shared in a manner that is respectful and inclusive.

Some ethical considerations include:

+ **Research and understanding:** Before creating or sharing content, it is crucial to research and understand the cultural significance, history, and context of the elements being used. This helps to avoid misrepresentation, distortion, or trivialization.

+ **Informed consent:** When featuring individuals from different cultures in digital media content, it is important to obtain their informed consent and ensure that they understand how their image or representation will be used. This is particularly relevant when using traditional cultural practices or symbols.

+ **Credit and attribution:** Giving credit and attribution to the originators of cultural expressions is essential. This helps recognize and honor their contributions and prevents erasure or misrepresentation.

+ **Collaborative partnerships:** When incorporating elements from different cultures, consider collaborating with individuals from those cultures. This ensures that their voices and perspectives are included in the creative process and helps foster mutual respect and understanding.

+ **Continuous learning and adaptability:** Recognize that cultural dynamics and perspectives are constantly evolving. Stay open to feedback, learn from mistakes, and adapt your approach accordingly.

By adhering to ethical guidelines in digital media practices, we can promote a more inclusive and culturally sensitive online environment.

Conclusion

Cultural appropriation in digital media is a complex and consequential issue that requires attention and action. By understanding the concept, recognizing its implications, and implementing strategies to address it, we can create a digital landscape that is respectful, inclusive, and appreciative of diverse cultures. It is crucial that individuals, content creators, platform owners, and society as a whole work together to promote cultural exchange rather than appropriation and ensure that digital media reflects the rich and vibrant diversity of our global community.

Cultural Influences on Digital Media Consumption Patterns

The consumption of digital media is heavily influenced by cultural factors. People from different cultures have varying preferences, behaviors, and attitudes towards digital media, which in turn shape their consumption patterns. Understanding these cultural influences is essential for marketers, content creators, and digital media professionals to effectively reach and engage diverse audiences. In this section, we will explore some key cultural factors that impact digital media consumption patterns and discuss their implications in a rapidly changing technological landscape.

Cultural Values and Digital Media Consumption

Cultural values play a significant role in shaping the way individuals consume digital media. Different cultures prioritize various values that influence their preferences, expectations, and behaviors. For example, individualistic cultures, such as those in Western countries, emphasize personal expression, freedom, and autonomy. As a result, individuals from these cultures may gravitate towards digital media platforms that allow them to customize their online identities and share their thoughts and experiences freely.

On the other hand, collectivist cultures, prevalent in Asian countries, emphasize group harmony, conformity, and interconnectedness. In such cultures, individuals may value social bonds and community-oriented platforms for digital media consumption. These platforms often prioritize group interactions and shared experiences, encouraging users to engage in activities such as online gaming, social networking, or content sharing.

The implications of cultural values on digital media consumption are evident in the success of different platforms. For example, Facebook, with its focus on self-expression and individual connections, is dominant in Western cultures. In contrast, platforms like WeChat, which provides a more integrated and community-oriented experience, are widely popular in China.

Cultural Identity and Digital Media Consumption

Cultural identity plays a crucial role in influencing digital media consumption patterns. People's cultural identity, which includes factors such as nationality, ethnicity, language, and religion, shapes their preferences, interests, and content consumption choices.

Individuals often seek digital media content that aligns with their cultural identity, allowing them to connect with their roots, express themselves, and find a sense of belonging. For instance, members of the Indian diaspora may actively consume Bollywood movies or music videos on YouTube to maintain a connection with their cultural heritage, even if they reside in a different country.

Cultural identity also influences the adoption of specific digital media platforms. For example, in regions where English is not the primary language, individuals may favor platforms that provide content in their native language. This preference can be seen in the popularity of regional social media platforms in countries like China (Weibo) or Russia (VKontakte), where local language content dominates.

Cultural Norms and Digital Media Consumption

Cultural norms, defined as socially accepted behaviors and expectations within a culture, significantly impact digital media consumption patterns. Norms related to family, gender, social hierarchy, and etiquette shape people's perceptions and behaviors regarding digital media usage.

For example, in some cultures, it is customary to seek the opinions of family and close friends before making any significant decisions. This applies to digital media consumption as well, where recommendations from trusted individuals hold considerable influence. In such cultures, the word-of-mouth promotion of digital media content through personal networks can significantly impact consumption patterns.

Gender norms and expectations also play a role in digital media consumption. For instance, in certain cultures, men may be more inclined towards consuming sports-related content, while women may show greater interest in fashion or beauty-related content. These gender-driven preferences can shape the design and marketing strategies of digital media platforms, ensuring that they cater to the specific interests and expectations of their target audiences.

Cultural Differences in Digital Media Usage Patterns

Cultural differences also manifest in the usage patterns of digital media. For instance, some cultures may have a higher preference for consuming long-form content, such as articles or podcasts, due to a preference for detailed information and in-depth analysis. Other cultures may prefer shorter, concise content that can be easily consumed on the go.

Cultural differences in time orientation also impact digital media usage. Some cultures prioritize immediate gratification and instant access to information, favoring platforms like Twitter or Instagram, known for their real-time updates. In contrast, cultures that value patience and reflection may gravitate towards platforms that allow for long-form content creation and engagement, such as blogs or forums.

Moreover, cultural attitudes towards technology and its role in everyday life can influence digital media consumption patterns. For example, in countries where traditional media outlets are perceived as more trustworthy, people may be less inclined to rely on digital media for news or information. Similarly, cultural norms around privacy and data security can impact individuals' willingness to engage with digital media platforms that collect personal information or have perceived vulnerabilities.

Case Study: Cultural Influences on Gaming Consumption

Gaming is a popular form of digital media consumption that provides insights into the influence of culture on consumption patterns. Different cultures have unique attitudes towards gaming, which shape the types of games consumed, the platforms used, and the social interactions surrounding gaming.

In Japan, for instance, gaming is deeply embedded in the culture and is associated with communal experiences. Gaming arcades, where people gather to play multiplayer games, have been an integral part of Japanese society for decades. Japanese gamers' preference for console gaming and multiplayer experiences reflects their cultural value of social cohesion and shared experiences.

In South Korea, esports (competitive video gaming) is highly popular and has become a significant part of the country's culture. The success of esports in South Korea can be attributed to cultural factors like collectivism, competitive spirit, and the Korean Wave (popular culture phenomenon), which has elevated the status of gaming and esports.

In contrast, gaming consumption patterns in Western countries, like the United States, have been shaped by a different set of cultural influences. Here, gaming is often viewed as an individual leisure activity rather than a social experience. The rise of online multiplayer games and streaming platforms has allowed gamers from different cultural backgrounds to interact and form communities, transcending traditional geographic boundaries.

Implications and Future Considerations

Understanding cultural influences on digital media consumption patterns is essential for businesses, marketers, and content creators to effectively reach and engage diverse audiences. Here are a few key implications to consider:

- Localization: Adapting digital media content to cater to cultural preferences and norms can enhance engagement and resonance with the target audience. This includes translating content into local languages, incorporating cultural references, and considering cultural sensitivities in content creation.

- Cultural Sensitivity: Taking into account cultural values and norms when designing digital media platforms or campaigns can help avoid potential misunderstandings or cultural insensitivity that may alienate or offend users.

- Personalization: Offering personalized digital media experiences based on cultural preferences can enhance user satisfaction and engagement. This includes providing content recommendations tailored to the user's cultural interests and enabling customization of user interfaces to align with cultural preferences.

- Cross-cultural Collaboration: Embracing cross-cultural collaboration in digital media production and consumption can lead to the creation of diverse, inclusive content that resonates with global audiences. Encouraging the sharing of perspectives and experiences from different cultural backgrounds can enrich the digital media landscape.

As technology continues to advance and the world becomes more interconnected, understanding the role of cultural influences on digital media consumption patterns will become increasingly crucial. By recognizing and valuing cultural diversity, digital media professionals can create more inclusive and engaging experiences for audiences worldwide.

Conclusion

In this section, we explored the cultural influences on digital media consumption patterns. We discussed how cultural values, cultural identity, cultural norms, and cultural differences shape the way individuals consume digital media. Understanding these influences is vital to effectively reach and engage diverse audiences in a rapidly evolving technological landscape.

We examined the implications of cultural influences on digital media consumption, highlighting the importance of localization, cultural sensitivity, personalization, and cross-cultural collaboration. By considering and embracing cultural diversity, digital media professionals can create more inclusive and engaging experiences for audiences worldwide.

In the next section, we will delve into the cultural perspectives on social media, exploring how social media platforms are influenced by diverse cultural dimensions and their impact on communication and behavior.

Cultural Factors in the Evolution of Digital Media Platforms

The evolution of digital media platforms has been greatly influenced by various cultural factors. These factors, such as language, cultural values, and technological advancements, have shaped the development and adoption of digital media platforms around the world. In this section, we will explore how these cultural factors have played a crucial role in the evolution of digital media platforms.

Language and Cultural Diversity

Language diversity is a significant cultural factor that impacts the evolution of digital media platforms. As the internet becomes more accessible globally, the need for multilingual content and interfaces becomes crucial. Different cultures have diverse language preferences, and catering to these preferences is essential for the success of digital media platforms.

For instance, major social media platforms like Facebook and Twitter have incorporated language localization features, allowing users to interact with the platforms in their preferred language. This not only improves user experience but also enables individuals from diverse cultural backgrounds to engage with digital media platforms more effectively.

Cultural Values and User Preferences

Culture shapes people's values and preferences, which, in turn, influence the content and features offered by digital media platforms. Cultural values, such as individualism vs. collectivism, hierarchical vs. egalitarian societies, and high-context vs. low-context communication styles, impact the design and functionality of these platforms.

For example, in collectivist cultures where community and harmony are important, digital media platforms may emphasize group-based communication and collaboration. In contrast, platforms designed for individualistic cultures may prioritize personalization and self-expression.

Understanding cultural values is crucial for digital media platform developers as it helps them tailor their platforms to meet the preferences and expectations of specific cultural groups. By incorporating cultural values into the design and functionality of the platforms, developers can create a more inclusive and engaging user experience.

Technological Infrastructure and Cultural Contexts

Technological infrastructure and cultural contexts also play a significant role in the evolution of digital media platforms. The availability and accessibility of internet connectivity, devices, and other technological resources differ across cultures and regions.

For instance, in some developing countries, limited access to high-speed internet can hinder the adoption and usage of certain digital media platforms. Similarly, economic factors and cultural attitudes towards technology can also influence the growth and acceptance of digital media platforms in specific contexts.

To address these challenges, digital media platform developers must consider the cultural and technological context in which their platforms are being used. They need to ensure that their platforms are optimized for different devices, internet connectivity situations, and cultural norms to provide an equitable and enjoyable user experience for all users.

Cultural Content and Representation

The content available on digital media platforms is heavily influenced by cultural factors. Different cultures have unique traditions, customs, and interests that shape the type of content produced and consumed on these platforms.

For instance, video-sharing platforms like YouTube have seen the emergence of content creators from diverse cultural backgrounds, who create content that reflects

THE ROLE OF CULTURAL FACTORS IN SHAPING DIGITAL MEDIA 47

their cultural values, traditions, and interests. This cultural diversity in content not only enriches the digital media landscape but also provides users with a wide range of perspectives and experiences.

It is essential for digital media platforms to promote cultural diversity and representation by providing tools and resources to support content creators from different cultural backgrounds. This enables users to access a diverse range of content that goes beyond mainstream cultural narratives.

Technological Innovation and Cultural Adaptation

Technological innovations often disrupt and transform digital media platforms, and cultural adaptation plays a crucial role in this process. Digital media platforms must continuously evolve to meet the changing needs and expectations of users from different cultural backgrounds.

For instance, the rise of mobile technology has led to the development of mobile-based social media platforms that cater to the preferences of users who primarily access the internet through their smartphones. This shift has not only influenced the way people consume and share digital content but has also created new opportunities for cultural exchange and global connectivity.

Digital media platform developers need to be aware of cultural nuances and adapt their platforms to suit the changing technological landscape while respecting diverse cultural perspectives. By embracing cultural adaptation, platforms can continue to evolve and remain relevant to a global audience.

Conclusion

Cultural factors have a profound impact on the evolution of digital media platforms. Language diversity, cultural values, technological infrastructure, cultural content, and technological innovations all contribute to shaping the development and adoption of these platforms. By understanding and integrating these cultural factors, digital media platform developers can create more engaging, inclusive, and culturally relevant platforms for users around the world.

As we move forward into the future, it is crucial for researchers, developers, and users to continue exploring the relationship between culture and digital media. By bridging gaps in cultural perspectives, addressing ethical challenges, and adopting interdisciplinary approaches, we can gain deeper insights and make informed decisions about the future of digital media platforms in a culturally diverse world.

Cultural Perspectives on Social Media

Cultural Dimensions of Social Media Use

Cultural Values and Social Media Behavior

Cultural values play a crucial role in shaping individuals' behavior, including their use of social media platforms. These values, deeply rooted in various cultural traditions and societal norms, influence how people perceive and navigate the digital world. Understanding cultural values is essential for analyzing and explaining the diverse behaviors observed on social media.

Definition and Importance of Cultural Values

Cultural values refer to the beliefs, attitudes, and principles that guide individuals and communities within a particular culture. These values are shared among members of the culture and shape their behaviors and perspectives. They are transmitted through socialization processes, such as family, education, and media.

The importance of cultural values lies in their ability to guide individuals' decision-making and actions. They provide a framework for interpreting and evaluating social behaviors, including those on social media. By examining cultural values, we can gain insights into the underlying motivations and intentions behind people's social media behaviors.

Impact of Cultural Values on Social Media Behavior

Cultural values have a significant impact on how individuals engage with social media platforms. Different cultural values influence the frequency and nature of social media use, the content individuals share, and the interactions they have with others. Let's explore some of the ways cultural values shape social media behavior:

- **Collectivism vs. Individualism:** Cultures that prioritize collectivism tend to emphasize group harmony, cooperation, and interdependence. In such cultures, social media use is often aimed at maintaining social connections, sharing community-oriented content, and seeking consensus. On the other hand, individualistic cultures value personal achievement, self-expression, and independence. In these cultures, social media behaviors may reflect self-promotion, personal branding, and individualistic aspirations.

- **Hierarchy vs. Equality:** Cultural values regarding power distance and social equality influence social media behavior. In high-power distance cultures, where hierarchical relationships are emphasized, individuals may be more cautious about expressing their opinions or challenging authority figures on social media platforms. In contrast, cultures that emphasize equality and egalitarianism may foster more open and democratic discussions on social media.

- **Long-term Orientation vs. Short-term Orientation:** Cultures with a long-term orientation prioritize virtues such as perseverance, thrift, and societal stability. In these cultures, social media behaviors may reflect a long-term perspective, such as sharing content related to cultural heritage, tradition, and sustainable development. On the other hand, cultures with a short-term orientation may exhibit a focus on immediate gratification, novelty, and trends in their social media usage.

- **Uncertainty Avoidance:** Cultural values related to uncertainty avoidance influence individuals' comfort levels with ambiguity and risk-taking. In cultures with high uncertainty avoidance, individuals may be more cautious about sharing personal information and engaging in controversial discussions on social media. Cultures with low uncertainty avoidance, on the other hand, may exhibit more openness to diverse viewpoints and experimentation on social media platforms.

These examples highlight the diverse ways in which cultural values shape social media behavior. It is important to note that cultural values are not fixed or deterministic but rather provide a broad framework for understanding different patterns of behavior.

Cultural Values and Social Media Strategies

Recognizing the influence of cultural values on social media behavior is essential for designing effective social media strategies. Here are some considerations to keep in mind:

- **Localization and Cultural Sensitivity:** Social media platforms should be adapted and localized to reflect the cultural values and norms of specific target audiences. This includes language translation, cultural references, and visual elements that resonate with the local culture.

- **Emphasis on Community and Collaboration:** Understanding the collective nature of some cultures can inform the development of social media features that prioritize community-building and collaboration. This can include features that facilitate group discussions, collective decision-making, and community-based initiatives.

- **Respect for Diversity:** Social media platforms should promote inclusivity and respect for diverse cultural values. This includes addressing issues such as hate speech, discrimination, and stereotypes that go against cultural sensitivity.

- **User Empowerment:** Recognizing the importance of individualism in certain cultures, social media platforms should provide users with tools and options for self-expression and customization. This can include personalized privacy settings, profile customization, and content curation features.

By aligning social media strategies with cultural values, organizations and individuals can enhance their engagement, reach, and effectiveness on social media platforms.

Case Study: Cultural Values and Social Media Behavior in China

As an example of the influence of cultural values on social media behavior, let's look at China, where cultural values shape the landscape of social media platforms. Chinese society places a strong emphasis on collectivism, hierarchy, and long-term orientation. These values are reflected in the following social media trends:

- **Group-oriented Social Media:** Chinese social media platforms, such as WeChat and Weibo, emphasize group interactions, where users join various communities based on shared interests or affiliations. This group-oriented approach aligns with the collectivist values prevalent in Chinese culture.

- **Respect for Authority:** Chinese social media users tend to show deference to authority figures and government regulations. Criticizing government policies or expressing controversial opinions is less common due to the hierarchical cultural values, emphasizing respect for authority.

- **Emphasis on Tradition and Heritage:** Chinese social media users often share content related to traditional customs, cultural heritage, and family values. The long-term orientation of Chinese culture translates into a focus on preserving and celebrating cultural traditions through social media.

- **Strong Digital Communities:** Online communities in China play a crucial role in social media behavior. These communities promote collaboration, shared learning, and the exchange of practical knowledge, reflecting the collectivist values embedded in Chinese culture.

Understanding the cultural values at play provides insights into the preferences and behaviors of social media users in China. Social media strategies targeting this audience need to consider these cultural values to effectively engage with Chinese users.

Conclusion

Cultural values significantly influence individuals' social media behavior, shaping how they engage, share, and interact on these platforms. Recognizing and understanding these cultural values is essential for designing effective social media strategies and fostering meaningful connections in diverse cultural settings. By incorporating cultural values into social media platforms, organizations, and individuals can create a more inclusive and engaging digital space. Further research and exploration of cultural values in social media behavior will continue to uncover nuanced insights for the future of digital communication.

Cultural Identity and Social Media Representation

Cultural identity plays a crucial role in shaping how individuals represent themselves on social media platforms. In this section, we will explore the relationship between cultural identity and social media representation, examining how individuals express their cultural values, beliefs, and practices through their online personas.

Cultural Identity and its Significance

Cultural identity refers to the sense of belonging and identification with a particular cultural group. It encompasses aspects such as nationality, ethnicity, language, religion, and traditions. Cultural identity is a fundamental part of an individual's self-concept, shaping their values, beliefs, behaviors, and interactions.

In the digital age, social media platforms provide individuals with opportunities to express their cultural identities publicly. Representation on social media allows individuals to share their cultural background, experiences, and perspectives with others, forming connections and understanding across cultures.

Self-Presentation and Cultural Identity

On social media, individuals engage in self-presentation, shaping their online persona to communicate specific aspects of their identity. Cultural identity is often a significant component of self-presentation, as individuals use social media to showcase their cultural heritage and values.

1. **Online Cultural Signifiers:** Online cultural signifiers are symbols, language, or imagery that individuals use to indicate their cultural identity. For example, someone may use a flag emoji or traditional clothing in their profile picture to signify their national or ethnic background. These signifiers create a visual representation of cultural identity and help establish connections with others sharing similar cultural backgrounds.

2. **Content Sharing:** Social media users share content that reflects their cultural identity, such as cultural events, traditions, or celebrations. For instance, individuals may post pictures or videos of themselves participating in cultural festivals or engage in discussions about cultural customs. Through sharing cultural content, individuals not only express their identity but also educate and raise awareness about their culture among their online connections.

3. **Language Use:** Language plays a crucial role in expressing cultural identity on social media. Users may choose to communicate in their native language, or use specific terms, phrases, or slang associated with their cultural background. By using language specific to their culture, individuals enhance their sense of belonging and connection within their cultural community.

Cultural Identity and Social Media Influence

Social media has the power to influence both individual and collective cultural identity in several ways. Here are a few examples:

1. **Cultural Homogenization**: Social media platforms can promote cultural homogenization by spreading dominant cultural values, trends, and norms. As individuals from diverse cultural backgrounds engage with these platforms, they may feel compelled to conform to the prevailing cultural standards, leading to a loss of unique cultural identities.

2. **Cultural Preservation**: Conversely, social media allows marginalized or minority cultural groups to preserve and promote their cultural identity. Through online communities, individuals can share their cultural heritage, language, and traditions with a wider audience, fostering a sense of pride and encouraging the preservation of cultural customs.

3. **Cultural Hybridity**: Social media facilitates cultural hybridity by enabling cross-cultural interactions and exchanges. As individuals from different cultural backgrounds engage in online discussions, collaborations, and shared experiences, new cultural practices and ideas emerge. These hybrid cultural expressions challenge traditional notions of identity and encourage the celebration of diversity.

Challenges and Considerations

While social media offers a platform for cultural representation, it also presents challenges and considerations:

1. **Stereotyping and Misrepresentation**: Stereotyping and misrepresentation can occur when individuals assume or project stereotypes onto others based on their cultural identity. It is crucial to promote positive and accurate representations of cultures, emphasizing their diversity, complexity, and individuality.

2. **Cultural Appropriation**: Cultural appropriation, the adoption or use of cultural elements without understanding or respect, is a concern on social media. It is essential for individuals to engage with cultural practices respectfully, acknowledging and learning about their meaning and significance.

3. **Digital Divide**: The digital divide, the gap in access to technology and the internet, can affect individuals' ability to represent their cultural identity online. Lack of access hinders marginalized communities from expressing their cultural perspectives and participating fully in online discussions.

Resources and Further Reading

1. Cultural Identity and Social Media (Smithsonian Folklife): https://s.si.edu/3ld4e1y 2. Cultural Diversity in the Digital World (UNESCO): https://bit.ly/3Cg63pD 3. Cultural Appropriation: Definition, Examples, and Implications (Everyday Feminism):

https://bit.ly/3XJp7RY 4. The Influence of Social Media on Cultural Identity Formation (Academia.edu): https://bit.ly/3FdG5Ro

Exercises

1. Reflect on your own social media presence. How do you express your cultural identity on social media? Are there specific signifiers, content, or language that represent your cultural background? 2. Research and analyze instances of cultural appropriation on social media. Discuss the impact of these instances on the affected cultures and propose strategies to address cultural appropriation in digital spaces. 3. Conduct a case study on a social media campaign that successfully promotes and celebrates cultural diversity. Analyze its effectiveness and identify key elements that contribute to its positive impact.

Remember, representing cultural identity on social media is a personal and nuanced process. Respect, empathy, and understanding should guide our interactions to foster an inclusive and culturally diverse digital environment.

Cultural Norms and Social Media Etiquette

In the age of digital media, social media platforms have become an integral part of our lives, allowing us to connect and communicate with people from all over the world. However, it is important to recognize that different cultural norms and values shape the way we use and interact on social media. In this section, we will explore the cultural perspectives on social media etiquette and the norms that guide our online behavior.

Understanding Cultural Norms

Cultural norms are the unwritten rules and expectations that govern behavior within a particular society or group. These norms vary across cultures and influence how individuals communicate and interact with others. When it comes to social media, cultural norms play a significant role in shaping our online behavior.

Respect for Authority and Hierarchical Structures

In many cultures, there is a strong emphasis on respect for authority and hierarchical structures. This can be reflected in social media etiquette, where individuals tend to show deference to those in positions of power or authority. For example, in some cultures, it is common to address your elders or superiors with honorifics or formal language, even in online interactions. Understanding and respecting these cultural norms is crucial when engaging with individuals from different backgrounds on social media.

Individualistic vs. Collectivist Cultures

Cultural norms also reflect the balance between individualism and collectivism within societies. In individualistic cultures, such as the United States and Western European countries, there is a greater emphasis on personal achievements and individual rights. In contrast, collectivist cultures, such as many Asian and African countries, prioritize group harmony and social cohesion.

These cultural differences can influence social media etiquette. In individualistic cultures, self-promotion and expressing personal opinions are often encouraged. However, in collectivist cultures, there may be a greater emphasis on maintaining harmony and consensus, which can result in more cautious and reserved online behavior.

Communication Styles and Directness

Differences in communication styles also shape social media etiquette. Some cultures value direct and assertive communication, while others may prefer indirect and nuanced expression. For example, in Western cultures, straightforward and concise communication is often valued. On social media, this may translate to using clear language, avoiding ambiguity, and getting straight to the point.

In contrast, cultures that value indirect communication, such as many Asian cultures, may prefer to communicate implicitly or through subtle cues. On social media, this can be observed in the use of emojis, sarcasm, or metaphors to convey meaning. Understanding and adapting to these cultural communication styles can help foster effective and respectful online interactions.

Privacy and Sharing Personal Information

Privacy norms also vary across cultures, and this has important implications for social media etiquette. In some cultures, such as in parts of Europe, privacy is highly valued, and individuals are cautious about sharing personal information online. On the other hand, in countries like the United States, there may be a culture of oversharing and a greater willingness to disclose personal details.

These cultural differences can lead to misunderstandings and conflicts on social media. It is important to be mindful of cultural expectations regarding privacy and to respect others' boundaries when engaging in online discussions.

Online Conflict and Resolution

Conflict is inevitable in online interactions, but cultural norms influence how conflict is addressed and resolved. In some cultures, open disagreement or confrontation may be seen as confrontational and disrespectful. In others, direct and frank exchanges of differing opinions may be expected.

Understanding cultural norms around conflict and resolution can help navigate disagreements on social media. Practicing active listening, showing empathy, and finding common ground are important skills that can contribute to more constructive and productive online discussions.

Case Study: Cultural Norms on Social Media Platforms

Let's take a look at a case study that illustrates the impact of cultural norms on social media etiquette:

Case Study: Facebook in India

Facebook is a widely used social media platform in India, with a growing number of users from diverse cultural backgrounds. In this context, it is crucial to understand the cultural norms that shape online interactions.

In Indian culture, respect for elders and authority figures is highly valued. This is often reflected in the way individuals address and communicate with others on social media. Users may use honorifics or formal language to show respect, especially when interacting with older family members, teachers, or public figures.

Additionally, collectivism is an important cultural value in India. This can be seen in the way individuals prioritize the harmony of the group and the respect for authority. Discussions on social media often take into account the perspectives and opinions of the larger community and emphasize the importance of maintaining positive relationships.

Privacy is also a key consideration in India. Users are generally more cautious about sharing personal information online and may limit their privacy settings to control who has access to their content. Respect for privacy norms is essential to maintain trust and foster meaningful connections on social media platforms.

Understanding these cultural norms helps users navigate social media etiquette in India. By recognizing and respecting the values of respect, collectivism, and privacy, individuals can engage in online interactions that are sensitive to the cultural context and foster positive relationships.

Best Practices for Cross-cultural Social Media Etiquette

To navigate social media in a culturally sensitive way, here are a few best practices to keep in mind:

1. Educate yourself: Take the time to learn about different cultural norms and practices. Familiarize yourself with the values and customs of the cultures you interact with on social media.

2. Show respect: Always approach online interactions with respect and sensitivity. Be aware of your language, tone, and the cultural implications behind your words.

3. Empathize and listen: Practice active listening and empathy when engaging with individuals from different cultural backgrounds. Seek to understand their perspectives and values before responding.

4. Adapt your communication style: Be mindful of different communication styles and adjust your approach accordingly. If you are unsure, ask for clarification to avoid misunderstandings.

5. Maintain privacy and boundaries: Respect others' privacy preferences and be cautious about sharing personal information online. Consider the cultural norms around privacy in your interactions.

6. Resolve conflicts with cultural sensitivity: In the event of disagreements or conflicts, approach resolution with cultural sensitivity. Seek common ground and emphasize understanding rather than direct confrontation.

By following these best practices, you can navigate social media with cultural awareness and contribute to a more inclusive and respectful digital environment.

Conclusion

Cultural norms and social media etiquette are intricately linked, shaping our online behavior and interactions. Understanding and respecting these cultural perspectives is crucial for effective communication and fostering positive relationships on social media platforms. By being mindful of cultural differences, adapting our communication styles, and practicing empathy, we can create a more inclusive and meaningful digital space for people from diverse backgrounds.

In the next section, we will explore the globalization of social media and its impact on cultural norms and communication patterns.

Cultural Differences in Privacy and Security Concerns on Social Media

In this section, we will explore the cultural differences in privacy and security concerns on social media. As digital communication continues to shape our lives, it is essential to understand the diverse cultural perspectives that influence individuals and communities' attitudes towards privacy and security on social media platforms.

Cultural Values and Privacy

Privacy is a fundamental aspect of human existence, but its interpretation and importance vary across cultures. Some cultures prioritize individual privacy, emphasizing personal space and the right to control one's information. Other cultures place more significance on communal or collective privacy, focusing on the preservation of family or group secrets.

For example, in Western cultures such as the United States, privacy is often seen as an individual right, and people are cautious about sharing personal information online. On the other hand, in more collectivist cultures like Japan, there is a greater emphasis on maintaining group harmony, and individuals might be more willing to share personal information with others.

These cultural values significantly influence how individuals approach privacy on social media platforms. Understanding these differences is crucial for designing culturally sensitive privacy settings that align with users' expectations and comfort levels.

Cultural Norms and Information Sharing

Cultural norms also play a significant role in shaping individuals' attitudes towards information sharing on social media. Different cultures have varying levels of comfort in sharing personal details, photos, and experiences online. Factors such as religious beliefs, societal norms, and traditional customs influence these perceptions.

For instance, in some cultures with a strong emphasis on modesty and privacy, individuals may be more hesitant to share personal information or photographs publicly. In contrast, cultures that value open communication and self-expression might be more inclined to share personal moments on social media platforms.

These cultural norms create distinct expectations of privacy and influence individuals' decisions about what they choose to share or keep private on social media.

Perceived Risks and Security Concerns

Perceived risks and concerns regarding security on social media also vary across cultures. Different cultures might have varying levels of trust in social media platforms, government surveillance, or online scams. These variations influence individuals' attitudes towards sharing personal information and engaging in online activities.

For example, in countries with a history of government censorship or suppression, individuals may be wary of sharing political opinions or sensitive information on social media. In contrast, cultures with higher trust in online platforms might be more open to sharing personal information but remain concerned about data breaches or identity theft.

Understanding these cultural differences in perceived risks and security concerns is crucial for developing effective security measures and privacy policies that address the specific needs and fears of various cultural groups.

Strategies for Addressing Cultural Differences

To address cultural differences in privacy and security concerns on social media, platform developers and policymakers need to take into account the following strategies:

1. User Education: Providing comprehensive education and awareness campaigns that highlight cultural differences in privacy and security concerns can help users make informed decisions about their online activities.

2. Customizable Privacy Settings: Allowing users to customize their privacy settings according to their cultural preferences can provide a sense of control and align with their cultural norms.

3. Transparency and Consent: Ensuring transparency in data collection and obtaining informed consent from users regarding data usage can help build trust and address cultural concerns about privacy.

4. Collaboration with Cultural Experts: Collaborating with cultural experts and ethnographers can provide valuable insights into understanding cultural differences and incorporating them into platform design and policies.

5. Localized Policies and Features: Developing localized policies and features that consider cultural nuances and legal frameworks can enhance privacy and security experiences for users from different cultural backgrounds.

By actively addressing cultural differences in privacy and security concerns, social media platforms can foster a more inclusive and culturally sensitive digital environment.

Conclusion

In this section, we explored the cultural differences in privacy and security concerns on social media. We discussed how cultural values, norms, perceived risks, and security concerns shape individuals' attitudes towards privacy and information sharing online. To address these cultural differences, strategies such as user education, customizable privacy settings, transparency and consent, collaboration with cultural experts, and localized policies and features can play a crucial role. By recognizing and accommodating these cultural differences, social media platforms can create a more inclusive and culturally sensitive digital space.

Globalization and Social Media

Transcultural Communication through Social Media

In today's globalized world, social media has become an essential tool for communication, allowing individuals from different cultures to connect and interact with each other. Transcultural communication refers to the exchange of ideas, values, and information across cultural boundaries, and social media platforms play a pivotal role in facilitating this communication. This section explores the various dimensions of transcultural communication through social media, including its benefits, challenges, and impact on cultural diversity.

Benefits of Transcultural Communication through Social Media

Transcultural communication through social media offers several advantages, fostering interaction and understanding among individuals from diverse cultural backgrounds. Firstly, it allows for the dissemination of cultural knowledge and the exploration of different perspectives. By connecting with individuals from different cultures, users can gain insights into distinct customs, traditions, and worldviews. This exposure enhances their cultural intelligence and promotes empathy and tolerance.

Secondly, social media platforms provide opportunities for intercultural dialogue and collaboration. Through the exchange of ideas and experiences, individuals can engage in meaningful discussions and collaborate on projects transcending cultural boundaries. This virtual space enables the blending of unique cultural perspectives, leading to the creation of innovative solutions and the cultivation of inclusive communities.

Finally, transcultural communication through social media strengthens personal connections and promotes friendships across cultures. It allows individuals to build relationships, share experiences, and celebrate cultural diversity. Language barriers, which can hinder face-to-face communication, are overcome through translation tools and multilingual content, enabling seamless interaction and mutual understanding.

Challenges of Transcultural Communication through Social Media

While transcultural communication through social media offers numerous benefits, it also presents challenges that need to be addressed. One of the primary challenges is the potential for misinterpretation and cultural misunderstandings. Differences in language, gestures, symbols, and cultural norms can lead to miscommunication and unintentional offense.

Moreover, the digital divide and access to social media platforms vary across different cultures and regions. Some communities may not have equal access to the internet or the necessary technological infrastructure to engage in transcultural communication. This disparity can perpetuate existing inequalities and hinder the potential for cross-cultural exchange.

Another challenge is the risk of cultural appropriation and the commodification of culture on social media. Cultural elements, such as music, fashion, and rituals, can be appropriated without proper respect or understanding, leading to the erasure of cultural significance and reinforcing stereotypes. It is essential for individuals and communities to be aware of the ethical considerations associated with cultural representation and consumption on social media.

Impact of Transcultural Communication on Cultural Diversity

Transcultural communication through social media has both positive and negative impacts on cultural diversity. On the one hand, it provides a platform for marginalized communities to represent and express their cultural identities. Social media enables cultural activists and individuals to challenge dominant narratives and promote cultural diversity. It empowers communities to preserve and revitalize their cultural heritage in the face of globalization.

On the other hand, there is a risk of cultural homogenization and the loss of distinct cultural traditions. The dominance of certain social media platforms and the widespread adoption of global trends can overshadow local cultural practices. This can result in cultural assimilation and the erosion of cultural diversity. It is

GLOBALIZATION AND SOCIAL MEDIA

crucial to strike a balance between the promotion of transcultural communication and the preservation of cultural integrity.

Case Study: Cultural Exchange through Virtual Communities

To understand the practical implications of transcultural communication on social media, let's take a look at a case study involving a virtual community called "Culture Connect." This online platform brings together individuals from different cultures to share their cultural practices, traditions, and experiences.

Through Culture Connect, users can join discussion forums, participate in virtual events, and collaborate on cultural projects. For example, users can join a group dedicated to celebrating traditional music and engage in cross-cultural music collaborations. They can also share recipes, learn about traditional cooking techniques, and organize virtual cooking classes to explore diverse cuisines.

This virtual community acts as a bridge between cultures, allowing users to appreciate and respect the richness of cultural diversity. It encourages active participation, stimulates cultural learning, and promotes the cultivation of global citizens who are knowledgeable about different cultures.

Key Takeaways

Transcultural communication through social media opens up opportunities for individuals from diverse cultural backgrounds to connect, collaborate, and celebrate cultural diversity. It promotes empathy, enhances cultural intelligence, and expands intercultural dialogue. However, challenges such as miscommunication, the digital divide, and cultural appropriation need to be addressed to ensure responsible and inclusive use of social media for transcultural communication.

To foster effective transcultural communication on social media, individuals should strive to develop intercultural sensitivity, educate themselves about other cultures, and engage in respectful and meaningful interactions. By embracing the benefits and overcoming the challenges, transcultural communication through social media can contribute to a more inclusive and harmonious global society.

Exercises

1. Reflect on your experience with transcultural communication through social media. Discuss the benefits and challenges you have encountered. How have these experiences shaped your perspective on cultural diversity?

2. Conduct research on a case study of successful transcultural communication through social media. Analyze how this initiative promotes understanding, collaboration, and cultural exchange. Present your findings in a report format, highlighting the key strategies and outcomes.

3. Identify a social media campaign or post that exemplifies cultural appropriation. Critically analyze the elements of cultural appropriation present in the content and discuss its impact on cultural diversity. Propose alternative approaches that could have respected and celebrated the culture in question.

4. Imagine you are designing a social media platform dedicated to transcultural communication. Outline the key features, functionalities, and strategies you would incorporate to ensure a responsible and inclusive space for cultural exchange. Justify your choices based on the challenges and benefits outlined in this section.

5. Organize a virtual cultural event on social media that promotes transcultural communication. Develop a plan for the event, including the activities, target audience, and strategies for facilitating cross-cultural interaction. Evaluate the success of the event based on participant feedback and the achievement of specific learning objectives.

Further Reading

- Alfred, T. (2015). Culture at the cutting edge: Tracking transnational film culture. Routledge. - Danesi, M. (2019). Cultural Studies: Theory and Practice. Routledge. - Wang, Y., & Fesenmaier, D. R. (2017). Transforming destination marketing through user-generated content. Journal of Travel Research, 56(3), 318-330.

Social Media and Cultural Homogenization

Social media has become an integral part of our daily lives, impacting various aspects of society, including culture. One of the effects that social media has on culture is the potential for cultural homogenization. Cultural homogenization refers to the process by which diverse cultural traditions, practices, and beliefs are reduced or even eliminated, leading to a more uniform global culture. In this section, we will explore the role of social media in cultural homogenization, its underlying mechanisms, and its implications for society.

Cultural Homogenization: An Overview

Cultural homogenization is not a new phenomenon but has been accelerated by the rise of social media platforms. These platforms enable individuals from different parts of the world to connect and interact with each other, transcending geographical and cultural boundaries. As a result, cultural exchange and fusion take place, leading to the spread of dominant cultural values and practices.

Several factors contribute to cultural homogenization through social media. First, the dominance of major social media platforms, such as Facebook, Instagram, Twitter, and YouTube, creates a globalized space where people from diverse backgrounds converge. These platforms have immense influence and reach, making them powerful agents of cultural diffusion. The content shared on these platforms, from popular music to fashion trends, can quickly become viral and influence the behavior and preferences of users worldwide.

Second, the algorithms and recommendation systems employed by social media platforms play a significant role in cultural homogenization. These algorithms are designed to show users content that aligns with their interests and preferences. While this personalized experience can enhance user satisfaction, it also creates filter bubbles, where people are exposed only to content that reinforces their existing beliefs and values. As a result, users become less exposed to diverse cultural perspectives, leading to a narrowing of cultural experiences.

Mechanisms of Cultural Homogenization

Social media contributes to cultural homogenization through various mechanisms. One such mechanism is the spread of globalized consumer culture. Brands and influencers on social media promote specific products, lifestyles, and aesthetics, which often adhere to Western ideals of beauty, success, and happiness. As a result, individuals across different cultures may adopt similar consumer behaviors and aspirations, leading to a convergence of preferences and tastes.

Another mechanism is the standardization of communication norms. Social media platforms have their own conventions, etiquettes, and symbols, which influence the way people interact and communicate online. For example, the use of emojis and hashtags has become widespread across different cultures, creating a common language of expression. While this can facilitate cross-cultural communication, it may also lead to the loss of unique cultural forms of communication.

Additionally, social media platforms provide spaces for cultural content production and consumption. This enables the dominant cultural industries, such as Hollywood and the music industry, to reach a global audience easily. As a result, cultural products that are commercially successful in one region can quickly spread and dominate the global market, overshadowing local cultural productions. This unequal distribution of cultural influence and power can further contribute to cultural homogenization.

Implications and Critiques

The cultural homogenization facilitated by social media has both positive and negative implications. On one hand, it promotes cultural exchange and intercultural understanding. People can learn about different traditions, languages, and perspectives through social media interactions. This exposure can foster empathy and appreciation for diversity, breaking down cultural barriers.

On the other hand, cultural homogenization can lead to the erosion of cultural diversity and the dominance of mainstream cultures. This can be particularly detrimental to marginalized communities and minority cultures, as their voices and traditions may be marginalized or even erased. The standardization of communication norms can also lead to the loss of linguistic diversity and the homogenization of languages.

Critics argue that the cultural homogenization facilitated by social media is a form of cultural imperialism, where dominant cultures exert their influence and control over others. They contend that this can lead to the loss of cultural autonomy and the commodification of culture for profit. Furthermore, cultural homogenization may contribute to a loss of cultural heritage and identity, as traditional practices and values are overshadowed by globalized trends.

Navigating Cultural Homogenization

While cultural homogenization through social media may seem inevitable, there are strategies to navigate its impact and preserve cultural diversity.

One approach is to raise awareness about the potential consequences of cultural homogenization. Educating individuals about the importance of cultural diversity and the need to value local traditions and practices can cultivate a sense of cultural appreciation and sensitivity. Encouraging users to seek out and engage with diverse cultural content can also counteract the narrow exposure created by social media algorithms.

Promoting cultural self-expression and representation is equally crucial. Encouraging individuals to share their unique cultural experiences, stories, and perspectives on social media platforms can counter the dominance of mainstream

GLOBALIZATION AND SOCIAL MEDIA

cultures. This can foster a more inclusive and diverse online environment that celebrates the richness of different cultures.

Another important strategy is the development and promotion of alternative social media platforms that prioritize cultural diversity and representation. These platforms can provide spaces for underrepresented cultures to share their stories and traditions, enabling a more balanced representation in the digital sphere.

In conclusion, social media plays a significant role in cultural homogenization. While it has the potential to foster cultural understanding and exchange, it can also contribute to the dominance of mainstream cultures and the erosion of cultural diversity. Navigating the impact of cultural homogenization requires raising awareness, promoting cultural self-expression, and supporting platforms that prioritize diversity and representation. By recognizing the value of diverse cultural perspectives, we can strive for a more inclusive and equitable digital landscape.

Social Media and Cultural Hybridity

Social media platforms have transformed the way people from different cultures interact and communicate with each other. In this section, we will explore the concept of cultural hybridity in the context of social media and how it shapes our understanding of society, identity, and globalization.

Understanding Cultural Hybridity

Cultural hybridity refers to the blending and mixing of different cultural elements, practices, and perspectives. In the digital age, social media platforms have become spaces where individuals from diverse cultural backgrounds interact and share ideas, leading to the emergence of new cultural forms and expressions. This cultural hybridity challenges traditional notions of identity and allows for the creation of alternative cultural narratives.

Social media platforms enable users to connect with people from different cultures, enabling the exchange of ideas, values, and practices. Users have the opportunity to learn about, engage with, and incorporate elements of other cultures into their own, leading to the creation of distinctive cultural identities that incorporate multiple influences.

Examples of Cultural Hybridity on Social Media

One example of cultural hybridity on social media is the rise of "K-pop" (Korean pop) music and its global impact. K-pop has garnered a massive international following, and social media platforms have played a crucial role in its success. Fans from different cultures and backgrounds share their love for K-pop artists through fan-created content, such as dance covers and fan art. This blending of Korean music and global fan participation has resulted in a unique cultural phenomenon that transcends national boundaries.

Another example of cultural hybridity is the diverse online communities that have emerged around the world. Platforms like Reddit and Twitter allow for the formation of niche interest groups, where individuals with similar interests from different cultural backgrounds can come together and exchange ideas. These online communities often develop their own distinct culture, blending elements from various cultural traditions.

Effects of Cultural Hybridity on Social Media

Cultural hybridity on social media has several significant effects on individuals and societies worldwide:

1. **Increased cultural exchange and understanding:** Social media platforms provide opportunities for individuals to engage with different cultures, broadening their understanding and appreciation of diverse perspectives. Exposure to different cultural practices fosters tolerance and empathy, promoting a more inclusive and interconnected global society.

2. **Reinforcement of cultural stereotypes:** The blending of different cultures on social media can sometimes reinforce existing stereotypes and biases. Cultural elements may be cherry-picked or misrepresented, leading to the perpetuation of harmful stereotypes. It is essential to promote critical thinking and cultural sensitivity to avoid such pitfalls.

3. **Emergence of new forms of expression:** Cultural hybridity on social media encourages the emergence of new artistic and creative expressions. Individuals draw inspiration from various cultural influences, leading to the development of innovative approaches and the reimagining of traditional art forms.

4. **Challenges to cultural preservation:** The rapid exchange and blending of cultural elements on social media can pose challenges to the preservation of traditional cultural practices. Aspects of culture may become diluted or altered in the process of hybridity. Efforts must be made to safeguard and protect cultural heritage in the digital age.

5. **Facilitation of cultural activism:** Social media provides a platform for individuals and communities to mobilize and advocate for cultural causes.

GLOBALIZATION AND SOCIAL MEDIA

Cultural activists can use social media to raise awareness about cultural issues, seek solidarity across borders, and promote cultural preservation and empowerment.

Addressing Challenges and Maximizing Opportunities

To make the most of cultural hybridity on social media, it is crucial to address the challenges it presents and maximize its opportunities. Here are some strategies:

1. **Cultural sensitivity and education:** Promote cultural sensitivity and education to foster understanding and respect for diverse cultural practices. Educational initiatives can help individuals critically evaluate and appreciate cultural hybridity without falling into cultural appropriation or misrepresentation.

2. **Encouraging dialogue and collaboration:** Social media platforms should facilitate cross-cultural dialogue and collaboration. Encouraging users to engage in conversations and collaborate with individuals from different cultural backgrounds promotes mutual understanding and the exchange of ideas.

3. **Supporting cultural preservation:** Social media can be utilized to document and preserve traditional cultural practices. Digital archives and cultural repositories can help safeguard and raise awareness about endangered traditions, ensuring their continuity in the face of cultural hybridity.

4. **Promoting diverse representation:** Social media platforms should prioritize diverse representation to counterbalance the perpetuation of stereotypes. Providing visibility to marginalized cultural groups and amplifying their voices helps challenge dominant narratives and fosters a more inclusive online environment.

5. **Responsible content creation:** Users should be encouraged to create content that respects cultural traditions and avoids appropriating or misrepresenting them. Awareness campaigns and guidelines can help users navigate the potential pitfalls of cultural hybridity and engage in responsible content creation.

Conclusion

Cultural hybridity on social media brings both opportunities and challenges. It has the potential to connect individuals from different cultures, foster understanding, inspire creativity, and empower cultural movements. However, it requires vigilance to ensure cultural sensitivity, respect, and responsible engagement. By embracing the possibilities of cultural hybridity and addressing its complexities, we can cultivate a more diverse and inclusive digital space that celebrates and preserves cultural diversity in the era of social media.

Further Reading

1. Appadurai, Arjun. "Disjuncture and Difference in the Global Cultural Economy." *Theory, Culture & Society* 7, no. 2-3 (1990): 295-310.

2. Castells, Manuel. *The Rise of the Network Society*. John Wiley & Sons, 2010.

3. Morley, David, and Kevin Robins. *Spaces of Identity: Global Media, Electronic Landscapes and Cultural Boundaries*. Routledge, 2018.

4. Couldry, Nick, and Andreas Hepp. "The Mediated Construction of Reality." *Annual Review of Sociology* 43 (2017): 93-116.

5. Hjorth, Larissa, and Olga Goriunova. *Gaming Cultures and Place in Asia-Pacific*. Routledge, 2019.

Social Media Activism and Cultural Empowerment

Social media has become a powerful platform for activism, providing individuals and communities with an opportunity to raise awareness about social and cultural issues, mobilize support, and drive meaningful change. This section explores the relationship between social media activism and cultural empowerment, highlighting the ways in which digital media has empowered marginalized groups to challenge the status quo, amplify their voices, and shape cultural narratives.

Understanding Social Media Activism

Social media activism refers to the use of online platforms, such as Facebook, Twitter, and Instagram, to advocate for social, political, and cultural change. It involves the use of hashtags, viral campaigns, and digital tools to draw attention to various issues, spark conversations, and mobilize communities. Social media activism has gained prominence in recent years due to its ability to reach a large and diverse audience, promote grassroots movements, and facilitate collective action.

GLOBALIZATION AND SOCIAL MEDIA

The Role of Cultural Empowerment in Social Media Activism

Cultural empowerment, within the context of social media activism, refers to the ability of individuals and communities to assert their cultural identities, challenge dominant narratives, and reclaim their voices in the digital space. Through social media, marginalized groups can share their stories, express their concerns, and articulate their demands, ultimately promoting cultural diversity and inclusivity.

Social media activism has played a crucial role in empowering various cultural communities. For instance, the #BlackLivesMatter movement emerged as a powerful force on social media, providing a platform for African Americans to speak out against systemic racism and police brutality. The movement not only raised awareness about these issues but also brought about policy changes, grassroots organizing, and community empowerment. Similarly, the #MeToo movement, sparked on social media, empowered survivors of sexual assault to share their experiences and shed light on the pervasive nature of gender-based violence.

Challenges and Limitations of Social Media Activism

While social media activism has proven to be a powerful tool for cultural empowerment, it also faces certain challenges and limitations. One of the key challenges is the risk of slacktivism, where individuals engage in token gestures of support without taking meaningful action. Additionally, social media activism can sometimes lead to online harassment, doxxing, and threats, particularly when individuals challenge deeply entrenched power structures.

Another limitation is the digital divide, as marginalized communities may lack access to technology and internet connectivity, limiting their participation in online activism. Moreover, social media platforms are governed by algorithms and policies that may prioritize certain voices and perspectives, amplifying existing power imbalances.

Strategies for Effective Social Media Activism

Effective social media activism requires careful planning, strategic thinking, and an understanding of the digital landscape. Here are some strategies for maximizing the impact of cultural empowerment through social media activism:

1. **Storytelling:** Sharing personal stories and lived experiences can be a powerful way to humanize social issues and create empathy among online audiences. By highlighting the cultural dimensions of their struggles, individuals and communities can engage and mobilize support.

2. **Coalition Building:** Facilitating collaborations and alliances across different cultural communities can enhance the collective power of social media activism. By finding common ground and working together, activists can amplify their messages and advocate for broader social change.

3. **Digital Tools and Tactics:** Leveraging the full range of digital tools and tactics, such as infographics, videos, live streams, and petitions, can help capture attention, engage audiences, and drive action. Additionally, using hashtags effectively can increase the visibility and reach of social media campaigns.

4. **Engaging with Opposing Views:** Engaging with individuals who hold opposing views can be challenging but can also open up opportunities for dialogue, understanding, and transformation. Constructive conversations can help break down cultural barriers and foster empathy and understanding.

5. **Offline Activism:** While social media is a powerful platform, combining online activism with offline actions can have a greater impact. Organizing protests, community events, and engaging in policy advocacy can complement social media initiatives and create lasting change.

Case Study: #NoDAPL Movement

The #NoDAPL (No Dakota Access Pipeline) movement serves as an illustrative case study of how social media activism can empower marginalized communities and challenge cultural and environmental injustices. The movement, led by the Standing Rock Sioux Tribe and their allies, utilized social media platforms to mobilize support and raise awareness about the potential impacts of the pipeline on indigenous lands and water sources.

Through the use of videos, images, and personal testimonies shared on social media platforms, the movement gained international attention and garnered support from diverse groups worldwide. Activists effectively utilized hashtags such as #NoDAPL and #WaterIsLife to create a cohesive and inclusive narrative around the issue. This collective mobilization ultimately led to a temporary halt in the construction of the pipeline, highlighting the power of social media activism in challenging large-scale infrastructure projects.

Conclusion

Social media activism has revolutionized the way individuals and communities engage with social, cultural, and political issues. By embracing digital media, marginalized groups have gained the power to challenge dominant narratives, amplify their voices, and drive cultural change. While it faces challenges and limitations, proper planning, strategic thinking, and an understanding of the digital landscape can help maximize the impact of social media activism. As we look to the future, social media activism will continue to play a vital role in cultural empowerment, creating opportunities for dialogue, inclusivity, and meaningful social transformation.

Cross-Cultural Communication in the Digital Age

Language and Cultural Diversity in Digital Communication

Language Barriers and their Impact on Digital Communication

Language is a fundamental aspect of human communication. It allows us to express our thoughts, share information, and connect with others. In the digital age, language continues to play a crucial role in facilitating communication through various digital platforms and technologies. However, language barriers can significantly impact digital communication, posing challenges for individuals and communities in accessing and engaging with digital media. In this section, we will explore the concept of language barriers in digital communication and examine their impacts on different aspects of our interconnected digital lives.

Understanding Language Barriers in Digital Communication

Language barriers refer to the difficulties or hindrances that arise when individuals with different linguistic backgrounds try to communicate effectively. In the context of digital communication, language barriers can manifest in various forms, such as differences in languages spoken, written scripts, dialects, accents, and levels of language proficiency. These barriers can create obstacles in understanding and expressing ideas, leading to communication breakdowns and misunderstandings.

Digital communication platforms, including social media, online forums, messaging apps, and email, have greatly expanded the reach and accessibility of communication. However, they do not automatically bridge the gaps caused by language barriers. While technological advancements have made it easier to

CROSS-CULTURAL COMMUNICATION IN THE DIGITAL AGE

translate, transcribe, or interpret different languages, language barriers can still pose significant challenges in digital communication due to issues related to accuracy, cultural nuances, and context.

Impacts of Language Barriers on Digital Communication

Language barriers can have a profound impact on various aspects of digital communication. Let us explore some key areas where these barriers can pose challenges:

Limited Access to Information   Language barriers can restrict individuals' access to information available on the internet and other digital platforms. Websites, online articles, and other digital resources may be primarily available in dominant languages, making it difficult for non-native speakers to access and benefit from the information. This limitation can hinder educational opportunities, limit the acquisition of new knowledge, and perpetuate inequalities in digital access.

Ineffective Communication   When individuals with different linguistic backgrounds try to communicate through digital platforms, language barriers can impede effective communication. Misinterpretations, misunderstandings, and miscommunications may occur due to language differences, leading to frustration, confusion, and possible conflicts. This can limit collaboration, hinder social interaction, and impact personal and professional relationships.

Exclusion and Marginalization   Language barriers in digital communication can result in exclusion and marginalization of individuals and communities who are not fluent in the dominant languages used online. This exclusion may limit opportunities for participation in online communities, career advancement, cultural expression, and social integration. Language-related biases and discrimination may arise, reinforcing existing power imbalances and inequalities in digital spaces.

Cybersecurity Concerns   Language barriers can also contribute to cybersecurity concerns in digital communication. For instance, individuals who are not proficient in the language used in emails or online messages may have difficulty understanding and identifying phishing attempts, scams, or other malicious activities. This vulnerability can increase the risk of falling victim to cybercrimes and compromising personal or sensitive information.

LANGUAGE AND CULTURAL DIVERSITY IN DIGITAL COMMUNICATION

Addressing Language Barriers in Digital Communication

To minimize the negative impacts of language barriers on digital communication, several strategies can be implemented:

Translation and Localization Efforts should be made to provide accurate translation and localization services for digital content, ensuring that information and resources are accessible to individuals who speak different languages. This includes employing automated translation tools, hiring professional translators, and considering cultural adaptation in the design and content of digital platforms.

Language Learning and Digital Literacy Programs Promoting language learning opportunities and digital literacy programs can empower individuals to overcome language barriers in digital communication. By enhancing language proficiency skills and digital literacy, individuals can navigate digital platforms more effectively, express themselves clearly, and engage in meaningful online interactions.

Collaborative Online Communities Creating inclusive and collaborative online communities can foster a supportive environment for individuals with different linguistic backgrounds. These communities can encourage multilingualism, cultural exchange, and the sharing of diverse perspectives. Platforms that facilitate language exchange programs, language-specific interest groups, or translation support can be valuable in bridging language gaps.

Technological Advancements for Language Support Continued advancements in technology can play a significant role in addressing language barriers in digital communication. Improved machine translation tools, language processing algorithms, and voice recognition systems can help overcome communication challenges. However, it is essential to acknowledge the limitations of technology and ensure a balanced approach that integrates human involvement and cultural sensitivity.

Real-World Examples and Exercises

To better understand the impact of language barriers in digital communication, let us consider a few real-world examples:

Example 1: Online Customer Support Imagine a non-English speaker encountering a technical issue with a product they purchased. They reach out to the company's online customer support, but the only available support is provided in English. The language barrier creates frustration and hampers effective communication, leading to an unsatisfactory customer experience. How can companies overcome such language barriers to provide better support to diverse customers?

Example 2: Language Diversity on Social Media Social media platforms like Twitter and Facebook have a global user base, making them incredibly diverse in terms of languages and cultures. However, language barriers can limit effective communication and understanding among users. How can social media platforms address these barriers to foster meaningful connections and interactions, especially in contexts where machine translation is not sufficient?

Exercise Think about a situation where language barriers impacted your own digital communication experiences. Reflect on the challenges you faced and consider potential strategies or solutions that could have improved the communication. Share your thoughts and experiences with your peers or on an online forum to foster learning and engagement.

Conclusion

Language barriers can significantly impact digital communication, limiting access to information, hindering effective communication, perpetuating exclusion and marginalization, and posing cybersecurity concerns. Overcoming these barriers requires a multifaceted approach that combines technological advancements, language learning programs, inclusive online communities, and support for translation and localization. By addressing language barriers, we can strive for more inclusive and equitable digital communication spaces, enabling individuals and communities to connect, collaborate, and thrive.

Multilingualism and the Internet

In today's interconnected world, the Internet plays a crucial role in facilitating communication and information exchange. With billions of users accessing online platforms, the Internet has become a space where people from diverse linguistic backgrounds come together. This section explores the relationship between

LANGUAGE AND CULTURAL DIVERSITY IN DIGITAL COMMUNICATION

multilingualism and the Internet, examining the challenges and opportunities that arise when multiple languages intersect in the digital realm.

The Linguistic Landscape of the Internet

The Internet is a multilingual space, encompassing a vast array of languages and scripts. The linguistic landscape of the Internet reflects the diverse linguistic heritage of its users. While English remains the dominant language used in digital content, the increasing significance of non-English languages cannot be overlooked. The rise of social media platforms, blogs, and discussion forums has provided an avenue for individuals to express themselves in their native languages, ultimately contributing to the linguistic diversity online.

Challenges of Multilingualism on the Internet

Despite the potential benefits of multilingualism on the Internet, numerous challenges need to be addressed to ensure effective communication and inclusivity. One significant challenge is the digital divide, which refers to the unequal access to digital technologies, including the Internet. This divide disproportionately affects individuals from marginalized linguistic communities, hindering their participation in online spaces.

Moreover, the use of different scripts and character encoding presents technical hurdles. Historically, many computer systems primarily focused on English and Latin alphabets, leading to issues with displaying and rendering non-Latin scripts like Chinese or Arabic accurately. Efforts to develop standardized encoding systems, such as Unicode, have aimed to address these challenges, allowing for the representation of various scripts on the Internet.

Another challenge lies in the machine translation of online content. While machine translation tools have improved significantly in recent years, they often struggle to accurately translate contextual nuances and cultural nuances in diverse languages. This can result in misinterpretation or miscommunication, affecting the quality of online interactions.

Opportunities for Multilingualism on the Internet

Despite the challenges, multilingualism on the Internet presents numerous opportunities for communication, collaboration, and cultural exchange. By embracing multilingualism, online platforms can foster inclusivity and create spaces where individuals can express themselves in their preferred language.

One significant advantage of multilingualism on the Internet is the preservation of linguistic diversity. Digital platforms enable the documentation and dissemination of endangered languages, promoting language revitalization efforts. Online language communities and resources provide a means for language learners to connect, practice, and immerse themselves in different linguistic contexts.

Additionally, multilingualism online facilitates cross-cultural understanding and global collaboration. It exposes individuals to diverse perspectives and allows for the sharing of knowledge and ideas across linguistic boundaries. This creates opportunities for multicultural dialogue and cooperation, promoting intercultural communication and empathy.

Addressing Multilingualism on the Internet

To effectively address multilingualism on the Internet, various stakeholders need to collaborate and implement practical strategies. Here are a few approaches that can be taken:

1. Localization: Online platforms should prioritize localization efforts, ensuring that their interfaces, content, and user experiences are adapted to cater to various language communities. This includes not only translation but also cultural adaptation to accommodate different linguistic norms and practices.

2. Language technology development: Further research and development in language technologies, such as machine translation and natural language processing, can help overcome barriers faced in multilingual online communication. Improving the accuracy and efficacy of these tools will enhance cross-linguistic understanding and facilitate seamless linguistic interactions.

3. Digital literacy programs: Educating individuals on the benefits and opportunities presented by multilingualism on the Internet can promote inclusivity and bridge the digital divide. Digital literacy programs should focus on improving language skills and raising awareness about linguistic diversity online.

4. Community-driven initiatives: Encouraging grassroots initiatives and community-driven platforms that cater to specific linguistic communities can foster a sense of belonging and empowerment. These initiatives provide spaces for language preservation, cultural expression, and community building.

By adopting these strategies, we can build a more inclusive and linguistically diverse digital ecosystem where all individuals can fully participate and benefit from the opportunities that the Internet offers.

Conclusion

Multilingualism and the Internet are intricately connected, presenting both challenges and opportunities for online communication. To harness the benefits of linguistic diversity, it is essential to address the technical, social, and cultural barriers that hinder effective multilingual communication. By implementing inclusive practices, promoting language technologies, and fostering community-driven initiatives, we can create a digital landscape that celebrates and embraces the richness of languages and cultures worldwide.

Language Adaptation Strategies in Digital Media

Language plays a crucial role in digital communication, as it is the primary medium through which information is exchanged. However, language barriers can hinder effective communication and limit access to digital media for non-native speakers. In this section, we will explore various language adaptation strategies in digital media that aim to bridge these gaps and enhance cross-cultural communication.

The Importance of Language Adaptation

In an increasingly globalized and interconnected world, digital media platforms have become important tools for communication and collaboration across cultures. However, language differences can create communication obstacles, affecting inclusivity and participation. Language adaptation strategies involve making adjustments to digital media content, user interfaces, and communication platforms to accommodate diverse linguistic backgrounds.

Effective language adaptation strategies in digital media can benefit individuals, organizations, and societies. They enable the inclusion of multicultural voices, enhance user experience, and promote intercultural understanding. Moreover, businesses and content creators can expand their reach and appeal to broader audiences by adopting appropriate language adaptation practices.

Machine Translation

One of the key language adaptation strategies in digital media is machine translation. Machine translation refers to the automated translation of text or speech from one language to another using computational methods. It utilizes algorithms and statistical models to analyze and generate translations.

Machine translation has evolved significantly in recent years, thanks to advancements in artificial intelligence and natural language processing. Platforms such as Google Translate and Microsoft Translator have greatly improved translation accuracy and usability. These tools have become indispensable in bridging language barriers in digital media.

However, it is important to note that machine translation is not perfect and can still produce inaccurate or awkward translations, especially for languages with complex structures or cultural nuances. Therefore, human involvement in the translation process, either through post-editing or quality assurance, is often necessary to ensure translation quality.

Transcreation

Transcreation is a language adaptation strategy that goes beyond translation. It involves the creative adaptation of content to convey its intended meaning and emotional impact in the target language and culture. Transcreation is particularly relevant for marketing, advertising, and creative industries, where cultural nuances and context are vital.

Transcreation requires a deep understanding of both the source and target cultures. It involves not only linguistic adaptation but also cultural adaptation, taking into account idioms, metaphors, humor, and cultural references. By adapting content to resonate with the target audience on an emotional level, transcreation can significantly enhance the effectiveness of digital media campaigns.

For example, a slogan or tagline that works well in one language may not have the same impact in another language due to cultural differences. Transcreation allows marketers to adapt the message to ensure it captures the essence and spirit of the original content while resonating with the target audience.

Localization

Localization is another crucial language adaptation strategy, particularly for software, websites, and applications. It involves customizing digital media content to meet the linguistic, cultural, and functional requirements of a specific locale or target audience.

Localization goes beyond translation and transcreation by considering cultural norms, preferences, and local regulations. It involves adapting user interfaces, date formats, currency symbols, measurement units, and other elements to align with the target culture. Additionally, it may involve replacing images, icons, and colors to ensure they are culturally appropriate and meaningful to the target audience.

By implementing localization strategies, digital media developers can provide a more user-friendly and culturally relevant experience for their target users.

LANGUAGE AND CULTURAL DIVERSITY IN DIGITAL COMMUNICATION

Localization not only facilitates access to digital media but also ensures that users can navigate and interact with content seamlessly.

Community-driven Translation

Community-driven translation, also known as crowd-sourced translation, involves harnessing the power of a community to translate and adapt digital media content. This approach allows users to collaboratively contribute to the translation process, providing a more diverse range of perspectives and expertise.

Platforms such as Transifex and Crowdin facilitate community-driven translation by providing tools for collaboration and project management. Users can contribute translations, suggest improvements, and vote on the best translations. This shared effort can result in more accurate and contextually appropriate translations.

Crowd-sourced translation can be particularly effective for niche languages, dialects, or less-resourced languages that may not have extensive available resources for translation. By tapping into the collective knowledge and linguistic skills of the community, digital media platforms can provide more comprehensive language support and promote linguistic diversity.

Challenges in Language Adaptation

While language adaptation strategies in digital media offer significant benefits, they also come with challenges. Some of these challenges include:

- **Translation accuracy:** Machine translation, while continually improving, can still produce inaccurate translations. Human involvement is often necessary to ensure translation quality.

- **Cultural nuances:** Adapting content to different cultural contexts requires a deep understanding of cultural nuances, idioms, and references, which can be challenging, especially for less-resourced languages.

- **Maintaining brand voice:** Transcreation, while important for marketing and creative content, may involve changing the original message, leading to potential challenges in maintaining brand voice and consistency.

- **User-generated content:** Language adaptation strategies often face challenges when dealing with user-generated content, such as social media posts or comments, where translations may not be available or accurate.

To address these challenges, organizations and content creators should implement comprehensive language adaptation strategies that blend automation with human involvement. This ensures accurate translations, appropriate cultural adaptations, and the preservation of brand voice.

Conclusion

Language adaptation strategies in digital media play a crucial role in bridging language barriers and promoting cross-cultural communication. Machine translation, transcreation, localization, and community-driven translation are among the key strategies employed to enhance language accessibility and inclusivity in digital media.

While these strategies offer significant benefits, challenges such as translation accuracy and cultural adaptation must be carefully addressed. By adopting comprehensive language adaptation strategies and leveraging the collective intelligence of both technology and human expertise, digital media can become more accessible, culturally inclusive, and effective in facilitating global communication.

Now that we have explored language adaptation strategies in digital media, let us delve into another important aspect of cross-cultural communication in the digital age - non-verbal communication.

Non-verbal Communication in Digital Media

Visual Communication and Cultural Differences

Visual communication plays a significant role in shaping the way we perceive and interpret information. It involves the use of visual elements such as images, icons, colors, typography, and layout to convey messages and meanings. However, cultural differences can significantly impact how visuals are understood and interpreted by individuals from different cultural backgrounds. In this section, we will explore the influence of cultural differences on visual communication and discuss strategies to navigate these differences effectively.

The Impact of Cultural Differences on Visual Communication

Visual communication is deeply rooted in cultural contexts, and different cultures have distinct aesthetic preferences, symbolism, and interpretations of visual elements. These cultural differences can pose challenges when communicating visually across cultures. Here are some key factors to consider:

1. **Symbolism and Meanings:** Visual symbols often carry specific meanings in different cultures. For example, the color red may symbolize luck and celebration in Chinese culture but can signify danger or warning in Western cultures. Similarly, gestures and body language can vary in their interpretation across cultures. To ensure effective communication, it is crucial to understand the cultural connotations and associations of visual symbols.

2. **Design Principles:** Design principles differ across cultures. For instance, Western cultures tend to prioritize simplicity, minimalism, and symmetry in visual design, while Eastern cultures may embrace complexity, intricacy, and asymmetry. These differences can affect the visual composition, layout, and aesthetics of communication materials. It is essential to adapt design principles to align with the cultural sensibilities of the target audience.

3. **Typography and Text:** Fonts, typography, and the use of text can vary significantly across cultures. Different scripts, writing systems, and languages have distinctive typographic conventions and aesthetics. Consideration should be given to the choice of fonts, readability, and the presentation of text in different languages to ensure effective communication.

4. **Visual metaphors and analogies:** Visual metaphors and analogies are powerful communication tools but can be culture-specific. Certain metaphors may be easily understood in one culture but not in another. For example, the use of animal symbolism may differ across cultures. In Western cultures, a lion is often associated with strength and leadership, while in African cultures, it may symbolize royalty and power. It is important to ensure that visual metaphors are universally understood or adapt them to fit the cultural context.

Strategies for Effective Visual Communication across Cultures

To bridge cultural differences and ensure effective visual communication, consider the following strategies:

1. **Cultural Research:** Conduct in-depth cultural research on the target audience to understand their visual preferences, symbolism, and cultural nuances. This can involve studying cultural norms, visual traditions, and appreciating the historical and social context. Understanding the target culture will help in making informed decisions during the visual communication process.

2. **Collaboration and Feedback:** Involve individuals from the target culture in the design process. Seek their feedback and input to ensure cultural sensitivity and

appropriateness. Collaborative approaches can lead to more inclusive and effective visual communication outcomes.

3. **Adaptation and Localization:** Adapt visual designs to accommodate cultural differences. This may involve adjusting color palettes, typography, and visual metaphors to align with the target culture's preferences and conventions. Localization of visuals can enhance cultural relevance and resonance.

4. **User Testing:** Conduct user testing with representatives from the target culture to gauge the effectiveness of visual communication materials. Gathering feedback and insights from the end-users can help identify potential cultural barriers and refine the visual design accordingly.

5. **Contextualize and Explain:** Provide contextual information and explanations alongside visuals, particularly when dealing with symbols and metaphors that may be unfamiliar to the target culture. This helps avoid misinterpretations and ensures clarity of communication.

6. **Sensitivity to Diversity:** Recognize that cultures are heterogeneous and adapt visual communication materials to be inclusive of diverse cultural perspectives within the target audience. Consider nuances within cultural groups and avoid generalizations that may oversimplify or stereotype cultures.

Understanding and navigating cultural differences in visual communication is essential for effective cross-cultural communication. By considering cultural preferences and adapting design approaches, visual communication can transcend cultural boundaries and connect with diverse audiences in meaningful ways.

Example: Visual Communication in International Advertising Campaigns

A real-world example that highlights the impact of cultural differences on visual communication is international advertising campaigns. Companies often face challenges in crafting visuals that resonate with diverse global audiences while maintaining brand consistency. Let's consider an example of a multinational technology company launching a new product globally.

The company's marketing team needs to create visual advertisements that appeal to consumers in various cultural contexts. They realize that using the same visual elements and design approach may not be effective across different markets due to cultural variations. To address this, the team conducts extensive cultural research and collaborates with local marketing experts in target countries.

Based on their research, they discover that the use of specific colors and symbols can significantly influence consumer perception and purchase behavior in each market. With this knowledge, they adapt the visual elements of their advertisements to align with the cultural preferences of each target audience.

For instance, in the ads targeting Asian markets, they use red and gold, which are considered auspicious and symbolic of prosperity in many Asian cultures. In contrast, the ads targeting Western markets utilize a more minimalist and sleek design aesthetic, aligning with the design preferences of those cultures.

Additionally, the team conducts user testing and seeks feedback from focus groups in each target market to ensure the effectiveness of their visual communication. They contextualize the visuals by incorporating culturally relevant imagery, gestures, and symbols that resonate with the target audience.

By implementing these strategies, the advertising campaign successfully navigates cultural differences in visual communication, effectively engaging consumers across various cultural backgrounds. The company's product gains popularity globally, and the campaign serves as an example of how cultural sensitivity and adaptation can enhance visual communication in diverse markets.

In conclusion, cultural differences significantly impact visual communication, and understanding these differences is crucial for effective cross-cultural communication. By considering cultural preferences, conducting research, collaborating with cultural experts, adapting designs, and user-testing visuals, we can bridge cultural gaps and create impactful visual communication that resonates with diverse audiences.

Emojis and Cultural Interpretation

Emojis have become an integral part of digital communication in recent years. These small pictorial icons allow individuals to express emotions, convey messages, and add a touch of personalization to their digital interactions. However, the interpretation of emojis can vary across cultures, highlighting the influence of cultural norms, values, and symbols on their meaning. In this section, we will explore the cultural perspectives on emojis and the challenges in their interpretation.

Understanding Emojis

Emojis originated in Japan in the late 1990s and have since gained global popularity. They are now used across various digital platforms, including social media, messaging apps, and email. Emojis cover a wide range of emotions, objects, activities, and symbols, allowing users to enhance their textual messages with visual elements.

Cultural Variations in Emoji Interpretation

While emojis are designed to be universally understood, their interpretation can vary significantly across cultures. Different cultures have distinct ways of expressing emotions, and these cultural variations can influence how emojis are perceived and understood.

For example, the thumbs-up emoji is generally associated with approval and positivity in Western cultures. However, in some Middle Eastern and West African countries, the same gesture may be considered offensive or rude. This cultural variation stems from different cultural norms and gestures associated with the thumbs-up gesture in these regions.

Similarly, the smiley face emoji is commonly used to convey happiness. However, in some Asian cultures, where saving face and maintaining social harmony are highly valued, individuals may use this emoji to mask their true emotions or politely acknowledge a message without fully agreeing with it. This cultural nuance highlights the importance of considering cultural context in emoji interpretation.

Challenges in Emoji Translation

As emojis have gained global popularity, there have been efforts to translate them across languages and cultures. However, translating emojis can be challenging due to their cultural specificity and lack of direct equivalents in different languages.

Translating emojis involves capturing their intended meaning and cultural connotations accurately. This task requires a deep understanding of both the source and target cultures, including their linguistic expressions, historical references, and social norms.

For example, the emoji of folded hands is commonly used to represent prayer or gratitude in many cultures. However, translating this emoji to languages with different religious or cultural practices may require adapting the symbol to align with local customs.

Addressing Cultural Variations in Emojis

To address the cultural variations in emoji interpretation, it is essential to develop culturally inclusive emoji sets. Unicode Consortium, the organization responsible for standardizing emojis, has recognized the need for diversity and cultural representation in emoji design.

In recent years, Unicode has introduced emojis representing a broader range of cultural practices, identities, and symbols. These additions aim to ensure that emojis are inclusive and resonate with diverse cultural backgrounds.

To enhance cross-cultural understanding, it is important for individuals using emojis to be aware of the potential cultural variations in interpretation. Being sensitive to cultural differences and open to discussions about emoji meanings can help mitigate miscommunications and misunderstandings.

Example: Emoji Misinterpretation

Let's consider a real-world example of emoji misinterpretation in a multicultural context. A company with global operations sends an email to its multicultural team, announcing a pay raise for all employees. The email includes a champagne bottle emoji to symbolize celebration.

While the intention of using the champagne bottle emoji is to convey excitement and joy, it may be misinterpreted by team members from cultures where alcohol consumption is restricted or considered inappropriate. In such cases, the emoji can unintentionally create confusion or discomfort among team members.

To avoid such misinterpretations, one possible solution is to use a more culturally neutral symbol, such as confetti or balloons, that can convey the same celebratory message without the potential cultural implications.

Further Reading and Resources

- The Emoji Handbook by David Sansone provides an in-depth exploration of the cultural significance of emojis and their impact on digital communication. - The Unicode Consortium's website (unicode.org/emoji) offers information on the latest emoji additions, including those representing diverse cultural backgrounds. - "Emojis and Cross-cultural Communication: An Exploratory Analysis" by Nishanth Sastry and Isabel H. Twesigomwe discusses the challenges and opportunities of emojis in cross-cultural communication.

Key Takeaways

- Emojis are widely used in digital communication to express emotions and enhance messages. - The interpretation of emojis can vary across cultures, highlighting the influence of cultural norms and values. - Translating emojis can be challenging due to their cultural specificity and lack of direct equivalents in different languages. - Culturally inclusive emoji sets aim to address the diversity of cultural practices and identities. - Being aware of cultural variations in emoji interpretation and using culturally neutral symbols can help avoid miscommunications.

Gestures and Body Language in Digital Communication

In the realm of digital communication, where interactions are often mediated by screens and keyboards, the significance of non-verbal communication, particularly gestures and body language, may seem diminished. However, even in the digital space, these non-verbal cues play a vital role in conveying meaning, expressing emotions, and establishing connections between individuals from diverse cultural backgrounds.

The Importance of Gestures and Body Language

Gestures and body language are powerful tools for communication. They can enhance the understanding of spoken or written messages, add nuances to the meaning conveyed, and provide crucial contextual information. In face-to-face interactions, people rely heavily on visual cues, such as facial expressions, hand movements, and body posture, to interpret the intentions and emotions of others. In digital communication, where visual cues are limited, the absence of gestures and body language can result in misunderstandings or misinterpretations.

By incorporating gestures and body language into digital communication, individuals can bridge the gap between the virtual and physical worlds, bringing a sense of human connection to their interactions. These non-verbal cues can facilitate empathy, establish rapport, and foster a greater sense of understanding between individuals from different cultural backgrounds.

Cultural Variations in Gestures and Body Language

Gestures and body language are deeply rooted in cultural traditions and vary widely across different societies. What may be considered a polite and respectful gesture in one culture could be interpreted as rude or offensive in another. Therefore, it is crucial to recognize and understand the cultural variations in gestures and body language to avoid misunderstandings or unintended offenses in digital communication.

For example, a thumbs-up gesture is commonly used to convey approval or agreement in many Western cultures. However, in some Middle Eastern and West African cultures, the thumbs-up gesture is considered offensive. Similarly, the use of eye contact varies across cultures, with some cultures perceiving direct eye contact as a sign of respect and attentiveness, while others may view it as a challenge or invasion of privacy.

To navigate these cultural variations, individuals engaging in digital communication need to be mindful of the cultural norms and expectations of the intended audience. This awareness can help avoid misinterpretation and build stronger connections in cross-cultural interactions.

Digital Platforms and Non-verbal Communication

While digital platforms may limit the direct expression of gestures and body language, they offer alternative means for individuals to convey non-verbal cues digitally. Emojis, stickers, and GIFs have become popular tools for expressing emotions and adding contextual information to digital messages. These visual elements serve as substitutes for facial expressions, hand gestures, and body movements, allowing individuals to infuse their digital communication with non-verbal cues.

However, it is important to note that the interpretation of these digital non-verbal cues can vary across cultures. For example, an emoji that represents happiness in one culture may be perceived differently in another culture. Therefore, it is essential to consider cultural nuances when using digital non-verbal cues to ensure effective communication and avoid any unintended cultural misunderstandings.

Exploring Cultural Gestures in Digital Communication: The Smileys Project

To further explore the role of gestures and body language in digital communication, let's introduce the Smileys Project. This project aims to capture and analyze cultural variations in the interpretation of smileys, one of the most commonly used digital non-verbal cues.

The Smileys Project invites participants from different cultural backgrounds to rate and describe their interpretations of various smiley faces. Through an online survey, participants are presented with a series of smileys and asked to indicate their emotional response and perception of each smiley. The data collected from this project provide insights into the cultural differences in the interpretation of digital non-verbal cues and can help inform cross-cultural communication strategies in the digital space.

Conclusion

In the digital age, gestures and body language still hold significant importance in communication, even though they may be expressed differently through digital means. Understanding the cultural variations in gestures and body language is crucial to ensuring effective and inclusive cross-cultural digital communication. By incorporating non-verbal cues and digital alternatives, individuals can enhance the richness of their interactions, bridge cultural divides, and foster more meaningful connections in the digital realm.

Intercultural Communication Competence in the Digital Space

Developing Intercultural Sensitivity in Digital Communication

In today's interconnected world, digital communication has become an integral part of our daily lives. We interact with people from diverse cultural backgrounds through various digital platforms such as social media, email, and online forums. However, communicating effectively across cultures in the digital space can be challenging due to differences in language, cultural norms, and communication styles. Developing intercultural sensitivity is crucial for successful and meaningful digital communication.

Understanding Intercultural Sensitivity

Intercultural sensitivity refers to the ability to recognize, understand, and appreciate cultural differences in communication. It involves being open-minded, empathetic, and curious about other cultures, beliefs, and values. Developing intercultural sensitivity is essential not only for avoiding misunderstandings but also for building positive relationships in the digital world.

Challenges in Intercultural Digital Communication

When communicating with individuals from different cultural backgrounds, we may encounter several challenges that can impede effective communication. These challenges include:

- **Language barriers:** Language differences can lead to misunderstandings and misinterpretations. It is important to be mindful of language proficiency levels and use clear and simple language in digital communication.

INTERCULTURAL COMMUNICATION COMPETENCE IN THE DIGITAL SPACE

- **Cultural norms and etiquette:** Cultural norms and etiquette vary across cultures, including expectations of politeness, formality, and directness. Understanding and respecting cultural norms can help avoid offense and misunderstandings.

- **Non-verbal cues:** Non-verbal cues, such as body language and facial expressions, play a significant role in face-to-face communication. However, in digital communication, these cues may be absent or easily misinterpreted. It is important to be aware of this limitation and clarify any potential misunderstandings.

- **Stereotypes and biases:** Stereotypes and biases can hinder intercultural understanding and communication. It is crucial to challenge and overcome preconceived notions, actively seek to understand different perspectives, and avoid making assumptions based on cultural stereotypes.

Strategies for Developing Intercultural Sensitivity

To develop intercultural sensitivity in digital communication, consider the following strategies:

- **Educate yourself about different cultures:** Take the initiative to learn about different cultures, their customs, traditions, and communication styles. Engage in cultural immersion experiences, read books, and participate in online courses focusing on cultural awareness.

- **Practice active listening:** Be attentive and demonstrate a genuine interest in understanding others' perspectives. Active listening involves paraphrasing and clarifying what others are saying to ensure accurate comprehension.

- **Ask questions and seek clarification:** If you are unsure about something, ask open-ended questions to seek clarification. Avoid making assumptions based on your own cultural perspective.

- **Adapt your communication style:** Recognize that different cultures may have different communication styles. Be flexible and adapt your communication style to accommodate cultural differences. For example, some cultures value indirect communication, while others prefer directness.

- **Recognize and challenge your biases:** Be aware of your own cultural biases and stereotypes. Challenge these biases by seeking diverse perspectives and actively challenging stereotypes.

Example Scenario

Consider the following scenario that highlights the importance of intercultural sensitivity in digital communication:

Emma, a student from the United States, is collaborating on a group project with Koji, a student from Japan. They are communicating through email and Google Docs. Emma, accustomed to direct and assertive communication, finds Koji's emails excessively polite and indirect. She interprets this as a lack of confidence or competence. However, after learning about Japanese communication styles, Emma realizes that Koji's emails are a reflection of cultural norms and respect.

In response, Emma adapts her communication style by being more patient and providing clearer instructions to Koji. She also makes an effort to show appreciation for his contributions. Through this understanding and adaptation, Emma and Koji build a stronger working relationship and successfully complete the project.

Additional Resources

Developing intercultural sensitivity in digital communication requires ongoing learning and self-reflection. Here are some additional resources that can help you expand your knowledge:

- *Intercultural Communication in the Global Workplace* by Iris Varner and Linda Beamer: This book provides insights into intercultural communication and strategies for effective global communication.

- *The Culture Map: Breaking Through the Invisible Boundaries of Global Business* by Erin Meyer: This book explores cultural differences in communication and provides practical advice for navigating diverse cultural contexts.

- *Intercultural Competence: Interpersonal Communication Across Cultures* by Myron W. Lustig and Jolene Koester: This textbook offers a comprehensive overview of intercultural competence and communication skills.

- Online courses: Platforms like Coursera and edX offer various courses on intercultural communication and cultural sensitivity.

Conclusion

Developing intercultural sensitivity is essential for effective digital communication. By understanding and appreciating cultural differences, actively listening, asking

INTERCULTURAL COMMUNICATION COMPETENCE IN THE DIGITAL SPACE

questions, and being mindful of cultural biases, we can navigate the complexities of intercultural communication in the digital age. Cultivating intercultural sensitivity not only enhances our communication skills but also promotes inclusivity, respect, and meaningful connections in the diverse online world.

Remember, the key to successful digital communication across cultures lies in being open-minded, curious, and adaptable. Embrace the opportunity to learn from others and foster intercultural understanding in the digital space.

Overcoming Communication Challenges in Multicultural Online Communities

In the digital age, online communities have become increasingly multicultural, allowing individuals from various cultural backgrounds to interact and collaborate. However, communication in multicultural online communities can be challenging due to language barriers, cultural differences, and misunderstandings. In this section, we will explore strategies to overcome these communication challenges and promote effective intercultural communication.

Understanding Communication Challenges

Communication challenges arise when individuals from different cultures attempt to interact and exchange information in online communities. These challenges can be attributed to several factors:

- **Language Barriers:** Language differences make it difficult for individuals to understand each other. Misinterpretation of words, idiomatic expressions, and cultural nuances can lead to misunderstandings and miscommunication.

- **Cultural Differences:** Cultural variations in communication styles, non-verbal cues, and social norms can create barriers to effective communication. These differences may affect the interpretation of messages, humor, and tone.

- **Technological Constraints:** Limited access to technology, internet connectivity, and digital literacy can create disparities in communication capabilities, hindering meaningful interaction in online communities.

Strategies for Effective Intercultural Communication

To overcome communication challenges in multicultural online communities, it is important to adopt strategies that promote understanding, respect, and inclusivity. Here are some practical approaches:

- **Language Adaptation:** Encourage participants to use plain and concise language, avoiding jargon, idioms, and cultural-specific references. Providing translation tools or offering multilingual support can also help bridge language gaps.

- **Cultural Sensitivity:** Develop cultural awareness and sensitivity among community members, fostering an environment that values different perspectives. Encourage participants to ask for clarification and assume positive intent in communication.

- **Active Listening:** Emphasize active listening skills, encouraging individuals to pay attention, clarify information, and paraphrase to ensure accurate comprehension. Cultivate an environment where individuals are open to seeking clarification and clarification is provided respectfully.

- **Facilitating Intercultural Exchange:** Promote intercultural exchange by facilitating dialogue and encouraging individuals to share their cultural backgrounds, traditions, and experiences. This can foster understanding, build empathy, and break down stereotypes.

- **Educational Resources:** Provide resources, such as cultural guides, language tutorials, and etiquette tips, to help individuals navigate cultural differences and enhance their communication skills. These resources can serve as references and tools for self-directed learning.

- **Moderation and Conflict Resolution:** Appoint moderators or community managers who are trained in intercultural communication and conflict resolution. They can help address misunderstandings, mediate conflicts, and promote respectful communication practices.

Real-World Example: Overcoming Language and Cultural Barriers in Online Gaming

Online gaming communities often consist of players from diverse cultural backgrounds. Language and cultural barriers can pose significant challenges to

INTERCULTURAL COMMUNICATION COMPETENCE IN THE DIGITAL SPACE

effective communication and collaboration in these environments. To address these challenges, game developers can implement the following strategies:

- **Built-in Translation:** Incorporate built-in translation features that automatically translate text chat into the preferred language of each player. This helps overcome language barriers and enables seamless communication between players.

- **Cultural Sensitivity Training:** Provide cultural sensitivity training to in-game moderators to ensure they can address issues related to cultural differences and promote respectful communication among players.

- **In-game Communication Tools:** Develop communication tools, such as gestures, emojis, and symbols, that transcend language barriers and allow players to express themselves and communicate non-verbally.

- **Community Guidelines:** Establish community guidelines that outline expected behavior and encourage players to respect cultural differences. Implement reporting and enforcement mechanisms to address cases of harassment or cultural insensitivity.

By implementing these strategies, online gaming communities can create inclusive spaces where players from different cultural backgrounds can communicate effectively and enjoy meaningful gaming experiences.

Exercises

To further enhance your understanding of overcoming communication challenges in multicultural online communities, consider the following exercises:

1. Think about a time when you encountered a communication challenge in a multicultural online community. How did you navigate through it? What strategies did you employ to overcome the challenge?

2. Conduct a case study on an online community that successfully promotes effective intercultural communication. Analyze the strategies they have implemented and evaluate their effectiveness.

3. Imagine you are a community manager of a multicultural online platform. Develop a set of guidelines and resources to promote intercultural understanding and effective communication among community members. Consider language adaptation, cultural sensitivity, and conflict resolution.

Conclusion

Overcoming communication challenges in multicultural online communities requires a combination of language adaptation, cultural sensitivity, active listening, and educational resources. By implementing these strategies, individuals and communities can bridge cultural divides, foster mutual understanding, and engage in meaningful intercultural communication. As the world becomes more digitally interconnected, these skills are crucial for building inclusive and harmonious online communities.

Strategies for Effective Intercultural Communication on Digital Platforms

In today's interconnected world, digital media platforms have become integral to communication across cultures. However, effective intercultural communication on these platforms can be challenging due to cultural differences, language barriers, and diverse communication styles. This section explores strategies for enhancing intercultural communication on digital platforms, focusing on developing intercultural sensitivity, overcoming communication challenges, and implementing effective communication strategies.

Developing Intercultural Sensitivity in Digital Communication

Intercultural sensitivity refers to the ability to understand and respect cultural differences, perspectives, and communication styles. It is crucial for effective intercultural communication on digital platforms. Here are some strategies to develop intercultural sensitivity:

1. Cultural Awareness: Increase your knowledge and understanding of different cultures, including their values, norms, and communication styles. This can be achieved through reading, attending cultural events, or engaging in conversations with individuals from different cultural backgrounds.

2. Open-mindedness: Be open to different perspectives and avoid making assumptions or stereotypes about other cultures. Approach intercultural communication with curiosity and a willingness to learn.

3. Empathy: Put yourself in the shoes of others and try to understand their feelings, experiences, and challenges. This can help you identify and overcome biases that may hinder effective communication.

4. Active Listening: Practice active listening, which involves giving undivided attention, clarifying understanding, and validating the speaker's perspective. This

INTERCULTURAL COMMUNICATION COMPETENCE IN THE
DIGITAL SPACE   99

demonstrates respect and promotes better understanding between individuals from different cultures.

5. Cultural Sensitivity Training: Consider participating in workshops or training programs that focus on intercultural communication and sensitivity. These programs can provide valuable insights and practical strategies to navigate cultural differences in digital communication.

Overcoming Communication Challenges in Multicultural Online Communities

Multicultural online communities bring together individuals from different cultural backgrounds, which can lead to communication challenges. Here are some strategies to overcome these challenges:

1. Language Assistance: Language barriers can hinder effective communication. Provide language assistance tools such as translation services or language-specific forums to enable individuals to communicate in their preferred language. Additionally, encourage language exchange and learning within the community.

2. Clear and Concise Communication: Strive for clarity and simplicity in your communication, especially when dealing with individuals for whom English may not be their first language. Use plain language, avoid jargon, and provide explanations when necessary.

3. Respectful and Inclusive Language: Use language that promotes inclusivity and avoids cultural or gender biases. Be mindful of idioms, colloquialisms, or cultural references that may be unfamiliar to individuals from different cultures.

4. Visual Communication: Utilize visual elements such as infographics, images, and videos to enhance communication. Visuals can transcend language barriers and facilitate understanding in multicultural online communities.

5. Moderation and Conflict Resolution: Establish clear guidelines for respectful communication and intervene when conflicts or misunderstandings occur. Encourage dialogue, address conflicts promptly, and promote a culture of mutual understanding and respect within the community.

Strategies for Effective Intercultural Communication on Digital Platforms

To promote effective intercultural communication on digital platforms, consider the following strategies:

1. Be Mindful of Communication Styles: Different cultures have distinct communication styles, such as direct or indirect communication. Adapt your communication style to be more aligned with the cultural norms of your intended audience, while avoiding cultural appropriation or insensitive mimicry.

2. Culturally Adaptive User Interfaces: Design user interfaces that are culturally adaptive, allowing users to customize their digital experience based on their cultural preferences. This can include language options, localized content, and culturally relevant visual elements.

3. Use Visual Cues: Utilize visual cues such as emojis or symbols to enhance understanding and convey emotions in a culturally inclusive manner. However, be mindful of potential cultural differences in the interpretation of visual cues.

4. Foster Cross-cultural Collaboration: Encourage collaboration and interaction between individuals from different cultural backgrounds. This fosters understanding, learning, and the sharing of diverse perspectives, leading to more effective intercultural communication.

5. Encourage Feedback and Reflection: Create opportunities for users to provide feedback on the platform's cultural sensitivity and usability. Regularly reflect on the effectiveness of intercultural communication strategies and make necessary improvements.

By implementing these strategies, individuals and digital platforms can enhance intercultural communication, foster mutual respect, and facilitate meaningful connections across cultures on digital media platforms.

Conclusion

Effective intercultural communication on digital platforms is crucial for building bridges between cultures and promoting understanding in our increasingly globalized world. Developing intercultural sensitivity, overcoming communication challenges, and implementing strategies for effective intercultural communication are essential steps toward promoting cultural diversity, inclusivity, and constructing a more connected digital future.

The next chapter delves into the relationship between digital media and identity, exploring how individuals and communities shape their identities in the digital era.

Cultural Perspectives on Digital Media and Identity

Individual Identity and Digital Media

Online Self-presentation and Identity Construction

In the digital age, online self-presentation and identity construction have become crucial aspects of our lives. Through various digital platforms such as social media, individuals have the opportunity to shape and present themselves to a wide audience. This section explores the concept of online self-presentation, its impact on personal identity, the factors influencing it, and the challenges associated with it.

Understanding Online Self-presentation

Online self-presentation refers to the process through which individuals establish and manage their digital personas to others. It involves carefully curating and presenting information, images, and activities that reflect a desired image or identity. The digital context allows individuals to construct different versions of themselves, amplifying certain aspects or downplaying others, depending on the desired impression and the platform's affordances.

The construction of online identity encompasses various elements, including personal information, interests, appearance, and activities shared on digital platforms. It serves as a form of self-expression, enabling individuals to showcase their values, beliefs, and identities to others. However, it is important to note that online self-presentation represents a curated version of oneself rather than a complete reflection of one's true identity.

Factors Influencing Online Self-presentation

Several factors influence how individuals present themselves online and construct their digital identities. These factors can include cultural norms, social influence, personal motivations, and platform affordances.

Cultural Norms: Cultural norms play a significant role in shaping online self-presentation. Different cultures may have distinct expectations regarding appropriate behavior, expression of emotions, and social interactions online. For example, cultures that value collectivism may prioritize group identities and harmonious relationships in their online self-presentation, while cultures valuing individualism may emphasize personal achievements and independence.

Social Influence: Social influence, both offline and online, can impact how individuals present themselves online. Peer pressure, societal expectations, and social comparison can influence the choices individuals make in terms of self-presentation. This can manifest in the types of content shared, the platforms used, and the desire to conform to prevailing online trends or norms.

Personal Motivations: Personal motivations also shape online self-presentation. Individuals may seek attention, validation, or social connection through their digital identities. They might aim to enhance their personal or professional reputation, promote specific causes or interests, or exhibit particular skills or talents. Personal motivations can vary widely, depending on individual goals, values, and needs.

Platform Affordances: The features and affordances of digital platforms influence how individuals present themselves online. Different platforms have distinct functionalities, rules, and user interfaces that shape the possibilities and constraints of self-presentation. For example, image-based platforms like Instagram encourage visual self-presentation, while text-based platforms like Twitter emphasize written expression and concise self-description.

Challenges and Considerations

Online self-presentation also brings forth various challenges and considerations that individuals must navigate to present themselves authentically and responsibly.

INDIVIDUAL IDENTITY AND DIGITAL MEDIA

Authenticity vs. Self-curation: Finding a balance between authenticity and self-curation is a common challenge in online self-presentation. While it is important to present an image that aligns with one's values and aspirations, overly curating an online persona can lead to a sense of inauthenticity and disconnection. Individuals need to reflect on their true selves and be mindful of the image they create.

Privacy and Security Concerns: Online self-presentation comes with privacy and security risks. Sharing personal information and intimate details can compromise one's safety and invite unwanted attention or exploitation. Individuals must be aware of privacy settings, exercise caution while sharing personal information, and understand the potential consequences of oversharing.

Managing Online Reputation: Online self-presentation can have a lasting impact on an individual's reputation. Information shared online can be easily accessible and permanent, affecting personal relationships, career prospects, and social standing. It is crucial to be mindful of the content and activities one engages with online to maintain a positive and consistent online reputation.

Example: The Influencer Phenomenon

The rise of social media has given birth to a new form of online self-presentation: the influencer. Influencers are individuals who have developed a significant online following, often leveraging their digital platforms to shape their personal brand and share sponsored content. Influencers carefully curate their online personas to attract and engage audiences, often portraying an idealized version of their lives.

While influencers can create authentic connections with their followers and provide valuable content, it is essential to critically examine the cultural and societal implications of this phenomenon. The influencer culture blurs the lines between personal and commercial interests, often promoting materialism and unrealistic beauty standards. It raises questions about authenticity, the ethics of sponsored content, and the impact on impressionable audiences.

Resources and Further Reading

- Boyd, D. (2014). It's Complicated: The Social Lives of Networked Teens. Yale University Press.

- Marwick, A., & boyd, d. (2011). To See and Be Seen: Celebrity Practice on Twitter. Convergence: The International Journal of Research into New Media Technologies, 17(2), 139–158.

- Turkle, S. (2011). Alone Together: Why We Expect More from Technology and Less from Each Other. Basic Books.

Exercises

1. Reflect on your own online self-presentation. How do you curate your digital identity on different platforms? What factors influence your choices in self-presentation? Consider cultural norms, personal motivations, social influence, and platform affordances.

2. Choose an influencer on social media and critically analyze their online self-presentation. How do they construct their digital identity? What values and aspirations do they promote? Reflect on the impact their online presence may have on audiences and society.

In this section, we explored the concept of online self-presentation and identity construction. We examined the factors that influence how individuals present themselves online, the challenges they face, and the considerations they must keep in mind. Through an example of the influencer phenomenon, we highlighted the complexities of online self-presentation and its societal implications. It is essential to navigate the digital landscape mindfully, striking a balance between authenticity and self-curation while being aware of privacy, reputation, and ethical concerns.

Self-expression and Digital Media Platforms

Digital media platforms have revolutionized the way individuals express themselves and showcase their identities in the online world. These platforms provide spaces for self-expression, allowing users to create and share content that reflects their thoughts, emotions, and experiences. In this section, we will explore the various aspects of self-expression on digital media platforms, including the opportunities and challenges they present.

The Role of Digital Media Platforms in Self-expression

Digital media platforms, such as social networking sites, blogging platforms, and multimedia sharing platforms, have become powerful tools for self-expression. They allow individuals to communicate their ideas, creativity, and personal stories

INDIVIDUAL IDENTITY AND DIGITAL MEDIA

to a wide audience. These platforms offer features that enable users to post photos, videos, text, and audio content, providing a rich and diverse medium for self-expression.

One of the key advantages of digital media platforms is their accessibility. Anyone with an internet connection can create an account and start sharing their thoughts and experiences. This has democratized self-expression, giving a voice to individuals who may have been marginalized or excluded in traditional media channels. Additionally, digital media platforms often provide privacy settings, allowing users to control who can access and interact with their content, facilitating self-expression in a safe and secure manner.

Creative Expression and Digital Media Platforms

Digital media platforms foster creativity by providing tools and features that allow users to produce and share their artistic creations. For example, photo sharing platforms like Instagram offer various filters and editing options to enhance images, while video sharing platforms like YouTube enable users to upload and edit their videos with professional-like quality. These features not only facilitate self-expression but also encourage individuals to explore and experiment with different forms of creative expression.

Moreover, digital media platforms allow users to receive instant feedback and validation on their creative endeavors. Comments, likes, shares, and followers provide a sense of community and recognition, motivating individuals to continue expressing themselves and improving their creative skills. However, it is important to note that this instant feedback can also create pressure to conform to popular trends and gain social approval, potentially impacting authentic self-expression.

Building and Shaping Online Identity

Digital media platforms play a significant role in shaping individuals' online identities. Users carefully curate their profiles and content to present a particular image of themselves to their online audiences. This process involves selecting and sharing content that aligns with their values, interests, and desired social perception. Online identities are not fixed but rather constantly evolving, as users adapt their presentations to reflect changes in their lives or personal growth.

Online identity construction involves both conscious and unconscious decisions. Users strategically choose what to share based on their desired self-presentation, considering factors such as their target audience, cultural context, and social norms. At the same time, users' online identities are shaped by algorithms and platform affordances, which influence the visibility and reach of their content. This interaction between user agency and platform structures highlights the complex nature of online identity construction.

Challenges and Ethical Considerations

While digital media platforms offer opportunities for self-expression, they also present challenges and ethical considerations. The ease of sharing content online can blur the lines between private and public spheres, raising questions about privacy, consent, and surveillance. Users must navigate the tension between expressing themselves authentically and protecting their personal information.

Digital media platforms also pose risks of online harassment, cyberbullying, and hate speech. Users may face backlash or negative comments that impact their self-esteem and well-being. Additionally, the pursuit of online popularity and validation can lead to unhealthy comparison and self-criticism. It is crucial for individuals and platform designers to actively address these challenges to create safe and inclusive digital environments.

Promoting Authentic Self-expression

To promote authentic self-expression on digital media platforms, it is important to foster a culture of respect, empathy, and inclusivity. Platform designers can facilitate this by implementing features that minimize toxicity, discourage hate speech, and prioritize users' well-being. Furthermore, digital media literacy education can empower users to critically analyze and navigate online platforms, enabling them to make informed choices about their self-expression.

Users can also play an active role in promoting authentic self-expression by embracing diversity and resisting the pressure to conform. Supporting and amplifying marginalized voices and challenging harmful narratives contribute to a more inclusive online environment. By valuing authenticity over popularity, individuals can create a space for genuine self-expression and connection.

Conclusion

Self-expression on digital media platforms offers individuals the opportunity to share their thoughts, ideas, and creativity on a global scale. These platforms empower users to curate their online identities and engage in creative endeavors. However, challenges such as privacy concerns, online harassment, and the pressure to conform exist. By promoting a culture of authenticity, empathy, and inclusivity, digital media platforms can become spaces that foster genuine self-expression and

INDIVIDUAL IDENTITY AND DIGITAL MEDIA

connection, enriching the online experiences of users from diverse cultural backgrounds.

Cultural Identity Formation in Virtual Communities

In today's digital age, virtual communities have become integral to our social lives and cultural interactions. These online spaces provide individuals with the opportunity to form and express their cultural identities in unique and dynamic ways. This section delves into the process of cultural identity formation in virtual communities, exploring how individuals construct, negotiate, and present their cultural identities through digital media.

Defining Cultural Identity

Cultural identity refers to the sense of belonging, shared values, beliefs, behaviors, and customs that are passed down through generations within a particular group. It is shaped by various factors such as ethnicity, nationality, language, religion, and social class. In virtual communities, individuals can explore and express their cultural identities by engaging with others who share similar backgrounds or by interacting with individuals from different cultural contexts.

Construction of Cultural Identity in Virtual Communities

Virtual communities provide a platform for individuals to actively construct their cultural identities. Through online interactions, individuals can share their cultural experiences, beliefs, and practices, which can be empowering and enriching. However, the construction of cultural identity in virtual communities is influenced by several factors:

- **Self-presentation:** Individuals carefully curate their online profiles, selecting information, images, and experiences that align with their cultural identity. For example, a person may post content related to their traditional clothing, music, or cuisine to showcase their cultural heritage.

- **Interaction with others:** Engaging in discussions, sharing stories, and participating in cultural events within virtual communities allow individuals to reinforce their cultural identities. These interactions enable individuals to connect with others who share their cultural background, fostering a sense of belonging and solidarity.

- **Adopting virtual personas:** Some individuals may create or adopt virtual personas, such as avatars or usernames, that reflect specific cultural symbols or identities. These personas can help express and explore cultural aspects that may not be fully realized in their offline lives.

- **Participation in cultural activities:** Virtual communities often offer spaces for individuals to engage in various cultural activities, such as language exchange groups, cultural festivals, or online exhibitions. Active participation in these activities allows individuals to strengthen their cultural identities and broaden their understanding of different cultures.

- **Reception and feedback:** Individuals' cultural identity formation in virtual communities is influenced by how others perceive and respond to their expressions of culture. Positive feedback and validation from others can reinforce a sense of belonging, while negative responses or cultural misunderstandings may lead to identity conflicts and re-evaluation.

Challenges and Opportunities

While virtual communities provide valuable opportunities for cultural identity formation, they also present challenges and complexities:

- **Authenticity and gatekeeping:** Virtual communities may struggle with verifying the authenticity of cultural expressions and identities. Cultural gatekeeping can occur when individuals are excluded based on perceived cultural authenticity or when certain cultural voices dominate the discourse, limiting diverse perspectives.

- **Cultural appropriation:** Virtual communities can foster cultural exchange, but they also pose risks of cultural appropriation. Cultural elements can be misunderstood, taken out of context, or commodified, diminishing their value and contributing to cultural misrepresentation.

- **Negotiating multiple identities:** In virtual communities that bring together people from diverse backgrounds, individuals often navigate the complexities of multiple cultural identities. Balancing and integrating different cultural aspects can be challenging, leading to identity negotiation and potential conflicts.

- **Online anonymity and discrimination:** Anonymity in virtual communities can give individuals the freedom to explore and express their cultural

INDIVIDUAL IDENTITY AND DIGITAL MEDIA

identities without fear of judgment. However, it can also facilitate online discrimination and harassment, as individuals may hide behind anonymity to perpetuate cultural stereotypes or engage in offensive behavior.

Promoting Cultural Understanding and Respect

To foster positive cultural identity formation in virtual communities, it is crucial to promote cultural understanding and respect. Here are some strategies and considerations:

- **Cultural sensitivity and education:** Virtual communities can incorporate cultural sensitivity training and educational resources that emphasize the importance of understanding and respecting diverse cultural identities. This can help mitigate cultural misunderstandings and promote inclusive interactions.

- **Moderation and community guidelines:** Implementing clear guidelines for respectful communication and behavior within virtual communities can create a safe environment for individuals to express their cultural identities. Moderation can prevent the spread of hate speech, discrimination, and cultural appropriation.

- **Facilitating intercultural dialogue:** Virtual communities can facilitate intercultural dialogue by providing spaces for individuals from different cultural backgrounds to engage in meaningful conversations, share experiences, and learn from one another.

- **Promoting cultural exchange:** Encouraging individuals to actively explore different cultures and engage in cross-cultural interactions can foster a sense of empathy, respect, and appreciation for diverse cultural identities.

- **Recognizing and addressing power dynamics:** Virtual communities should actively address power dynamics that may contribute to the marginalization or underrepresentation of certain cultural groups. This can involve amplifying marginalized voices and challenging dominant cultural narratives.

Case Study: The Role of Virtual Communities in Indigenous Cultural Revitalization

For indigenous communities around the world, virtual communities have played a crucial role in cultural revitalization efforts. These communities utilize digital media platforms to connect, share traditional knowledge and practices, and engage in cultural ceremonies and events. For example, the Maasai people of Kenya and Tanzania have formed virtual communities to preserve and celebrate their cultural heritage. Through online storytelling, language revitalization initiatives, and virtual meetings, they have been able to strengthen their cultural identity and inspire younger generations to take pride in their heritage.

Conclusion

Virtual communities offer a vibrant and dynamic space for individuals to construct and express their cultural identities. By actively engaging with others and participating in cultural activities, individuals can reinforce their sense of belonging and connection to their cultural heritage. However, challenges such as cultural appropriation and authenticity also arise, highlighting the importance of promoting cultural understanding and respect. As virtual communities continue to evolve, it is crucial to foster inclusive spaces that celebrate diversity and encourage intercultural dialogue.

Collective Identity and Digital Media

Digital Media and National Identity

Digital media has had a profound impact on the concept of national identity, as it has provided individuals with new means of communication and expression. In this section, we will explore how digital media influences the formation and representation of national identity, and discuss the implications for both individuals and societies.

The Role of Digital Media in National Identity Formation

Digital media platforms, such as social media, websites, and online communities, play a crucial role in shaping national identity. These platforms enable individuals to connect and interact with others who share their national identity, regardless of geographical boundaries. People can participate in online discussions, share their cultural practices, and express their patriotism through digital media.

One way digital media influences national identity formation is through the promotion of cultural heritage. Online platforms provide a space for individuals to showcase their national traditions and customs, thereby strengthening their bond with their cultural roots. For example, individuals can create and share digital content, such as photos, videos, and articles, that celebrate their national festivals, music, dances, and cuisine. This digital representation of cultural heritage reinforces a sense of pride and belonging among individuals, contributing to the formation of national identity.

Moreover, digital media facilitates the dissemination of national narratives and symbols. Governments and other institutions often use digital platforms to promote their national values, history, and achievements. By strategically utilizing digital media, they can shape the collective memory and perception of a nation. For instance, official websites, social media accounts, and online news platforms showcase national icons, landmarks, and historical events, reinforcing the commonalities and shared experiences of citizens.

Challenges and Debates in Digital Media and National Identity

Although digital media provides opportunities for the promotion and preservation of national identity, it also poses challenges and sparks debates.

One challenge is the risk of cultural appropriation in the digital space. As digital media platforms enable global interactions, cultural practices and symbols can be borrowed, imitated, or commodified without proper understanding or respect for their original context. This appropriation may dilute or distort the meaning of cultural elements, potentially eroding national identity. For example, the adoption of traditional clothing or cultural practices by individuals from other cultures as a form of fashion or entertainment can lead to questions of cultural authenticity and misrepresentation.

Another debated issue is the role of digital media in reinforcing or challenging nationalistic narratives. While digital platforms can unite individuals behind a common national identity, they can also facilitate the mobilization of specific ideologies or extremist sentiments. Social media, in particular, has been criticized for its role in spreading nationalist propaganda and promoting hate speech. This raises questions about the influence of digital media on the construction of national identity and its potential to either promote inclusivity or deepen societal divisions.

Case Study: Digital Media and National Identity in Catalonia

An illuminating case study to examine the relationship between digital media and national identity is the separatist movement in Catalonia, a region in Spain. Catalonia has a distinct cultural identity with its own language, traditions, and history. Digital media platforms have played a significant role in fostering and mobilizing support for the Catalan independence movement.

Social media platforms, like Twitter, Facebook, and Instagram, have provided a space for Catalans to express their national identity and advocate for political change. Hashtags related to Catalan independence have trended on Twitter, facilitating the organization of protests, sharing of information, and expression of collective sentiment. Online communities and forums have emerged where supporters of Catalan independence can connect and engage in political discussions, further reinforcing their national identity.

However, the use of digital media in the Catalan independence movement has also been highly contested. The Spanish government has taken measures to suppress the dissemination of pro-independence content online, leading to debates about freedom of speech and the role of digital media in political mobilization. Additionally, fake news and disinformation campaigns have emerged on social media, complicating the formation of a cohesive national identity and contributing to polarization within Catalan society.

Conclusion

Digital media has undoubtedly transformed the formation and representation of national identity. It provides a platform for individuals to express their national pride, celebrate cultural heritage, and connect with like-minded individuals. However, digital media also poses challenges, such as the risk of cultural appropriation and the potential for divisive narratives.

To navigate these challenges and harness the positive potential of digital media for national identity, it is crucial to promote cultural understanding, respect diversity, and foster inclusive digital spaces. Additionally, governments and digital media platforms should work together to combat fake news, hate speech, and other forms of digital manipulation that can harm the construction of national identity.

The future of digital media and national identity will require ongoing research and dialogue to ensure a responsible and balanced approach that empowers individuals while promoting social cohesion.

Digital Media and Ethnic Identity

The intersection between digital media and ethnic identity is a complex and dynamic field of study. As individuals increasingly engage with digital platforms, they simultaneously navigate and negotiate their ethnic identities in this virtual landscape. This section explores the ways in which digital media influences the formation, expression, and representation of ethnic identity. It delves into the challenges and opportunities digital media presents in shaping ethnic identity and

COLLECTIVE IDENTITY AND DIGITAL MEDIA

offers practical strategies for promoting cultural awareness and inclusivity in digital media design.

Understanding Ethnic Identity

Ethnic identity refers to a person's sense of belonging to a particular ethnic group, which includes shared cultural values, traditions, language, and history. It is a multifaceted construct that evolves over time and is shaped by various factors, including social interactions, historical contexts, and personal experiences.

Digital Media and Ethnic Identity Formation

Digital media plays a significant role in the formation of ethnic identity by providing platforms for individuals to connect with others who share similar cultural backgrounds. Social media platforms, online communities, and digital storytelling enable individuals to express their ethnic identity, preserve cultural heritage, and build solidarity with others.

For example, young members of a diaspora community may use social media to reconnect with their ancestral culture, share experiences, and learn about their roots. They can engage in conversations, exchange ideas, and celebrate their cultural practices, reinforcing their ethnic identity in the process.

On the other hand, digital media can also influence the construction of inauthentic or superficial ethnic identities. Cultural appropriation, where elements of a culture are commodified or misappropriated without understanding or respect, can distort and dilute the essence of ethnic identity. It is important to critically examine the representation and portrayal of ethnic identities in digital media to ensure authenticity and avoid perpetuating stereotypes.

Challenges and Opportunities

While digital media provides opportunities for individuals to explore and express their ethnic identities, it also presents challenges. One challenge is the potential for cultural essentialism, where ethnic identity is reduced to a set of stereotypes or fixed characteristics. This can lead to the marginalization or exclusion of certain ethnic groups and hinder the development of a more inclusive digital space.

Another challenge is the digital divide, which refers to the unequal access to digital technologies and skills among different ethnic groups. Limited access to digital media can impede the representation and visibility of marginalized ethnic communities, perpetuating power imbalances and further marginalizing them.

114 *CULTURAL PERSPECTIVES ON DIGITAL MEDIA AND IDENTITY*

However, digital media also offers solutions to these challenges. Digital storytelling initiatives can empower individuals to reclaim their narratives, challenge stereotypes, and foster understanding between different ethnic groups. Collaborative projects that involve multiple ethnic communities can promote cultural exchange and appreciation, facilitating the formation of diverse and inclusive digital spaces.

Promoting Inclusivity in Digital Media Design

Designers and developers have a crucial role in creating inclusive digital media platforms that foster the expression and representation of diverse ethnic identities. Here are some strategies for promoting inclusivity in digital media design:

1. User Research: Conducting thorough user research to understand the specific needs, preferences, and cultural contexts of diverse ethnic groups can inform the design process and ensure that digital platforms resonate with their target audience.

2. Representation: Ensuring diverse ethnic representation in digital media content can help challenge stereotypes and promote belonging and inclusivity. Including a range of voices, perspectives, and experiences helps to create a more nuanced and authentic portrayal of ethnic identities.

3. Accessibility: Designing digital media platforms with accessibility in mind ensures that individuals with diverse abilities and linguistic backgrounds can fully engage with the content. Providing multilingual options, closed captions, and accessible interfaces promotes inclusivity and equal access.

4. Co-creation: Involving members of various ethnic communities in the design process can help create digital media that accurately reflects their experiences, needs, and aspirations. Collaboration ensures that design decisions are informed by cultural knowledge and sensitivity.

5. Cultural Responsiveness: Continuously adapting and updating digital media platforms to accommodate the evolving nature of ethnic identities promotes cultural responsiveness. Staying attuned to emerging cultural trends, social issues, and community feedback helps maintain relevance and inclusivity.

By implementing these strategies, digital media designers can contribute to a more inclusive and empowering online environment that respects and celebrates diverse ethnic identities.

The Power of Digital Media in Ethnic Identity Formation

Digital media has the power to both reinforce and challenge ethnic identity formation. It can be a tool for cultural preservation, collective empowerment, and

COLLECTIVE IDENTITY AND DIGITAL MEDIA

cross-cultural understanding. However, it also poses risks, such as cultural appropriation and the perpetuation of stereotypes. To harness the positive potential of digital media in shaping ethnic identity, it is essential to adopt an inclusive and culturally sensitive approach in its design, content creation, and representation.

Conclusion

The digital era has transformed the landscape of ethnic identity formation, offering new possibilities and challenges. As digital media continues to evolve, it is imperative to acknowledge and address the complexities associated with the intersection of digital media and ethnic identity. Promoting cultural inclusivity, challenging stereotypes, and fostering collaboration are crucial steps toward creating a more equitable and empathetic virtual space. By embracing the power of digital media, we can enhance the understanding and appreciation of diverse ethnic identities in our interconnected world.

Further Reading

1. Ang, I. (2001). On Not Speaking Chinese: Living Between Asia and the West. Routledge.

2. Hess, J. E., & Worthington Jr, R. L. (2016). Culturally adapted mental health interventions: A meta-analytic review. Psychotherapy, 53(4), 361-378.

3. Nakamura, L., & Chow-White, P. (2012). Race after the Internet. Routledge.

4. Recuero, R. (2014). Social media in Brazil: Activism, politics, and everyday culture. Routledge.

5. Wang, Y., & Wei, S. (2019). Transcultural communication on digital platforms: Asian diasporic YouTube celebrities. Journal of International and Intercultural Communication, 12(1), 22-41.

Cultural Movements and Identity Politics on Digital Platforms

Cultural movements and identity politics play a significant role in shaping the dynamics of digital platforms. In this section, we explore how these movements and politics manifest on digital platforms, the challenges they face, and the impact they have on individuals and society as a whole.

Understanding Cultural Movements

Cultural movements, also known as social movements or cultural revolutions, arise when a group of individuals with shared beliefs, values, and goals come together to create social change. These movements can be centered around various issues, such as civil rights, feminism, environmentalism, LGBTQ+ rights, and more. In the context of digital platforms, cultural movements often involve collective action and mobilization through online communities, social media, and other digital tools.

Digital Platforms as Catalysts for Cultural Movements

Digital platforms, including social media, online forums, and blogging platforms, have provided a space for cultural movements to flourish and gain momentum. These platforms offer an accessible means for individuals to express their thoughts, connect with like-minded individuals, and organize collective action across geographical boundaries. The ease of sharing information and ideas on digital platforms has fundamentally transformed the way cultural movements operate.

For example, the #MeToo movement, which shed light on the prevalence of sexual harassment and assault, gained traction through social media platforms like Twitter and Facebook. What started as a hashtag quickly evolved into a global movement, with individuals sharing their personal stories and using social media as a tool for advocacy, awareness, and support.

Challenges Faced by Cultural Movements on Digital Platforms

While digital platforms have provided new opportunities for cultural movements, they also present unique challenges. One of the major challenges is the digital divide, which refers to the unequal access to digital technologies and internet connectivity. This divide can limit the participation of marginalized communities in cultural movements and perpetuate existing power imbalances.

Additionally, cultural movements on digital platforms often face resistance and backlash from individuals or groups with opposing views. Online harassment, trolling, and the spread of misinformation can hinder the progress of these movements and create a hostile environment for participants.

Identity Politics and Intersectionality

Identity politics refers to the ways political and social movements are shaped by the intersecting identities of individuals, such as race, gender, religion, sexuality, and

COLLECTIVE IDENTITY AND DIGITAL MEDIA

socio-economic status. On digital platforms, identity politics often come into play as individuals navigate their multiple identities and engage in online discussions.

Intersectionality, a concept coined by scholar Kimberlé Crenshaw, emphasizes the interconnected nature of various forms of oppression and discrimination. It recognizes that individuals' experiences are shaped not only by a single aspect of their identity but by the intersection of multiple identities and systems of power. Intersectionality is particularly relevant in understanding the dynamics of cultural movements on digital platforms, as it highlights the complexity of issues and the need for inclusive and intersectional approaches to activism.

The Impact of Cultural Movements on Digital Platforms

Cultural movements on digital platforms can have far-reaching impacts on individuals, communities, and society. They can raise awareness about social issues, challenge dominant narratives, influence public opinion, and inspire policy changes. By amplifying marginalized voices and providing a platform for underrepresented perspectives, cultural movements on digital platforms have the potential to drive social change and promote inclusivity.

However, it is important to recognize that not all cultural movements on digital platforms have a positive impact. Some movements may perpetuate harmful ideologies, engage in online harassment, or spread misinformation. Critical analysis and mindful engagement with cultural movements on digital platforms are necessary to navigate the complexities and ensure positive outcomes.

Examples of Cultural Movements on Digital Platforms

To illustrate the wide range of cultural movements on digital platforms, let's examine two prominent examples: Black Lives Matter and the Indigenous Rights Movement.

The Black Lives Matter movement emerged in response to police violence and systemic racism against Black individuals. Through social media campaigns, hashtags, and online activism, the movement has brought attention to issues of racial injustice, prompting public conversations, policy reforms, and increased accountability. Online communities and digital platforms have provided spaces for organizing protests, sharing educational resources, and uplifting Black voices.

The Indigenous Rights Movement has also found strength and visibility through digital platforms. Indigenous activists worldwide have utilized social media to raise awareness about land rights, cultural preservation, and political sovereignty. Online platforms have facilitated the connection between Indigenous

118 CULTURAL PERSPECTIVES ON DIGITAL MEDIA AND IDENTITY

communities, enabling them to share stories, traditions, and struggles while mobilizing support and solidarity.

Resources for Cultural Movements on Digital Platforms

Those interested in engaging with cultural movements on digital platforms can access a variety of resources to enhance their understanding and participation. Online forums and communities focused on specific issues or identities provide spaces for sharing experiences, learning from others, and organizing action. Activist toolkits and guides are available to educate individuals on effective digital advocacy strategies, ensuring ethical and impactful engagement.

Organizations dedicated to social justice, such as Amnesty International, Human Rights Watch, and grassroots activist groups, often utilize digital platforms to disseminate information, mobilize supporters, and provide resources for individuals interested in joining cultural movements. These resources can empower individuals to engage in meaningful digital activism and contribute to positive social change.

Tricks, Caveats, and Unconventional Approaches

One unconventional approach to cultural movements on digital platforms is the use of gamification techniques to engage participants and promote collaboration. Gamification involves applying game elements, such as rewards, challenges, and leaderboards, to non-game contexts. By incorporating gamified elements into digital activism campaigns, cultural movements can encourage active participation, amplify reach, and foster a sense of community among participants.

However, it is important to be mindful of potential pitfalls associated with gamification. Oversimplification of complex issues, reliance on shallow engagement, and the risk of tokenization are some of the caveats that need to be considered. Gamification should be used as a complementary strategy, not as a replacement for genuine dialogue and action.

Exercises

1. Choose a cultural movement that interests you and research its presence on digital platforms. Evaluate the impact of digital tools on the movement's success and challenges it may face. Consider how identities and intersectionality shape the movement's narratives.

COLLECTIVE IDENTITY AND DIGITAL MEDIA

2. Identify a cultural movement on a digital platform that has faced backlash or controversy. Analyze the reasons behind the backlash and discuss strategies that could have been employed to address the concerns raised.

3. Reflect on your own digital activism practices or experiences. Consider how your own identities and intersectionalities influence your involvement in cultural movements on digital platforms. Share your reflections with a trusted friend or online community.

Conclusion

Cultural movements and identity politics have become central phenomena on digital platforms, allowing individuals to mobilize, advocate for change, and challenge dominant narratives. Understanding the complexities of cultural movements on digital platforms is crucial for promoting inclusive and ethical engagement. By navigating the challenges and harnessing the potential of these movements, individuals and communities can contribute to a more equitable and just society.

Cultural Perspectives on Digital Media and Power

Digital Media and Cultural Hegemony

Global Media Corporations and Cultural Influence

Global media corporations play a significant role in shaping cultural perspectives on digital media. These corporations have the power to influence and impact cultural values, norms, and behaviors through their control of media platforms, content, and distribution channels. In this section, we will explore the ways in which global media corporations exert cultural influence and discuss the implications of this influence on digital media.

The Concentration of Media Ownership

One key aspect of global media corporations is the concentration of media ownership, where a few major companies dominate the media landscape. This concentration of ownership can have a profound impact on cultural diversity and representation in digital media. When a limited number of companies control a significant portion of media outlets, they have the ability to determine which cultural perspectives are prominently featured and which are marginalized.

For example, consider the role of major media conglomerates like Disney, Comcast, and Time Warner in shaping cultural influence through their ownership of various television networks, film studios, and digital streaming platforms. These corporations have the power to promote certain cultural narratives, values, and representations while suppressing others. This concentration of ownership raises concerns about the potential homogenization of cultural perspectives in digital media.

Cultural Imperialism and Cultural Hybridity

The influence of global media corporations has been criticized for promoting cultural imperialism, which refers to the dominance of one culture over others through the spread of media content. Cultural imperialism can lead to the erosion of local cultural traditions and the dominance of Western or globalized cultural perspectives.

However, it is important to consider that the influence of global media corporations is not solely driven by an imposition of dominant cultures. Cultural hybridity, the blending of different cultural influences, can also be observed in digital media. Cultural hybridity occurs when different cultural perspectives interact and combine to create new and unique cultural expressions.

An example of cultural hybridity in digital media can be seen in the rise of K-pop (Korean pop) and its global popularity. Korean music and entertainment companies have successfully utilized digital media platforms to reach a global audience, resulting in the fusion of Korean and Western cultural elements. This example illustrates how global media corporations can facilitate the exchange and blending of diverse cultural perspectives.

Challenges of Cultural Influence

The cultural influence of global media corporations presents both opportunities and challenges. On one hand, it can contribute to cultural diversity by exposing audiences to different cultural perspectives and promoting cross-cultural understanding. On the other hand, it can perpetuate cultural stereotypes, reinforce inequality, and marginalize certain cultural groups.

For instance, the representation of certain racial, ethnic, or gender identities in media can perpetuate stereotypes and biases. The underrepresentation or misrepresentation of diverse cultural perspectives can lead to a limited understanding and appreciation of different cultures.

Promoting Cultural Diversity and Representation

To address the challenges associated with global media corporations and cultural influence, efforts are being made to promote cultural diversity and representation in digital media. One approach is to increase the participation and representation of marginalized cultural groups in media production and decision-making processes. This can help ensure that a wide range of cultural perspectives are included and accurately portrayed.

DIGITAL MEDIA AND CULTURAL HEGEMONY

123

Additionally, supporting independent and local media outlets can help counterbalance the dominance of global media corporations. By providing platforms and resources for diverse voices, these outlets can contribute to a more inclusive and equitable media landscape.

Regulation and Policy Considerations

Regulation and policy frameworks also play a crucial role in addressing the influence of global media corporations on cultural perspectives. Governments can enact policies that promote diversity, cultural representation, and media pluralism. They can also implement regulations to prevent monopolistic practices and encourage fair competition among media corporations.

Furthermore, the ethical responsibilities of global media corporations should be emphasized. These corporations have an ethical obligation to promote cultural understanding, respect diverse perspectives, and avoid perpetuating harmful stereotypes or biases. Ethical guidelines and educational initiatives can help encourage responsible media practices that prioritize cultural diversity and representation.

Conclusion

Global media corporations hold significant influence over cultural perspectives in the digital media landscape. Their concentration of ownership and global reach allow them to shape narratives, promote certain cultural perspectives, and impact cultural diversity. However, it is important to recognize the potential for cultural hybridity and the role of regulation and ethical considerations in promoting cultural diversity and representation.

As we navigate the future of digital media, it is essential to critically examine the cultural influence of global media corporations and work towards a more inclusive and equitable media ecosystem that respects and values diverse cultural perspectives. By doing so, we can foster a digital media landscape that reflects the richness and complexity of our global society.

Digital Divide and Cultural Marginalization

The digital divide refers to the gap between those who have access to digital technologies and those who do not. It is a global issue that encompasses both technological access and the ability to effectively use and benefit from digital tools. Cultural marginalization refers to the exclusion or marginalization of certain cultural groups or communities, often resulting from systemic discrimination and unequal power dynamics.

In the context of digital media, the digital divide and cultural marginalization intersect, reinforcing each other to perpetuate inequalities in access, representation, and participation. This section explores the ways in which the digital divide contributes to cultural marginalization, and how cultural perspectives can shed light on these issues.

Digital Divide: Access and Infrastructure

The digital divide manifests in different forms, including disparities in access to technology and infrastructure. In many regions, marginalized communities, such as rural areas, low-income neighborhoods, and indigenous populations, lack reliable internet connectivity and access to necessary hardware and software. This lack of access limits their ability to engage in digital communication and participate fully in the digital world.

Example: In rural areas of developing countries, inadequate infrastructure and limited connectivity options make it difficult for residents to access the internet. This limitation restricts their ability to participate in online activities, access educational resources, and benefit from digital services that are increasingly essential in various aspects of life.

Cultural Marginalization: Representation and Participation

Cultural marginalization goes beyond access issues and encompasses issues of representation and participation. Marginalized cultural groups often find themselves underrepresented or misrepresented in digital media platforms and content. This limited representation perpetuates stereotypes and reinforces existing power structures.

Example: The underrepresentation of indigenous cultures in mainstream digital media platforms can lead to the perpetuation of stereotypes and the erasure of their unique perspectives. Inaccurate portrayals can further marginalize these communities, as their voices and cultural practices are misrepresented or dismissed.

Intersectionality and Complex Inequalities

The digital divide and cultural marginalization are intersectional issues, meaning that multiple dimensions of inequality intersect to create complex challenges.

DIGITAL MEDIA AND CULTURAL HEGEMONY

Factors such as race, ethnicity, gender, socioeconomic status, and geographic location play a crucial role in determining an individual's access to digital technologies and their ability to fully participate in digital media.

Example: An indigenous woman living in a remote area not only faces challenges related to the digital divide but also encounters intersecting forms of discrimination and marginalization. She may experience limited access to technology, gender-based discrimination, and the erasure of her cultural identity in digital media platforms. These intersecting factors compound the challenges she faces, making it harder for her to overcome the cultural and digital barriers she encounters.

Addressing the Digital Divide and Cultural Marginalization

Addressing the digital divide and cultural marginalization requires a multi-faceted approach that considers the interaction between technology, culture, and social structures. Here are some strategies and considerations for bridging these gaps:

Policy Interventions: Governments, international organizations, and stakeholders should develop policies and initiatives that prioritize providing equitable access to digital technologies and infrastructure. This includes investing in broadband expansion, reducing costs, and promoting community-driven solutions.

Cultural Representation and Empowerment: Efforts should be made to increase the representation of marginalized cultural groups across digital media platforms. This can be achieved by involving these communities in the creation and production of content, challenging stereotypes, and promoting diverse narratives.

Digital Literacy and Skills Training: Providing digital literacy programs and skills training can empower marginalized communities to effectively use digital tools and navigate online spaces. This includes fostering critical thinking, media literacy, and privacy and security awareness.

Community Engagement and Collaboration: Building partnerships and collaborations between communities, organizations, and governments can help develop localized solutions that address the specific needs and challenges faced by marginalized groups. This can include community-led initiatives, mentorship programs, and knowledge-sharing platforms.

Ethical Considerations: It is essential to approach digital media interventions with ethical considerations, ensuring that cultural practices, knowledge, and intellectual property are respected and not exploited.

Conclusion

The digital divide and cultural marginalization are complex and interrelated issues that require interdisciplinary solutions. By addressing the disparities in access, representation, and participation in digital media, we can strive towards a more inclusive and equitable digital landscape. Bridging the gaps between technological access and cultural empowerment is crucial for fostering social justice and amplifying marginalized voices in the digital age.

Representation and Power in Digital Media

Representation and power play a crucial role in the realm of digital media. In this section, we will explore how digital media enables the representation of individuals, communities, and ideologies, and the power dynamics that are intertwined with these representations. We will examine the ways in which digital media platforms can shape and influence our understandings of identity, politics, culture, and society.

The Politics of Representation

Representation in digital media refers to how individuals and groups are portrayed and depicted in online spaces. It encompasses issues of visibility, voice, and agency. However, representation is not a neutral act; it is deeply political, as it determines who is seen, heard, and valued within a given context. Digital media platforms provide opportunities for multiple voices and perspectives to be heard, but they also perpetuate power dynamics and structural inequalities.

One of the key challenges in representation is the issue of underrepresentation and misrepresentation. Marginalized groups such as women, people of color, LGBTQ+ individuals, and individuals with disabilities have historically been underrepresented or misrepresented in mainstream media. This lack of representation perpetuates stereotypes and reinforces the hegemonic power of dominant groups. In the digital era, social media platforms have given marginalized groups the opportunity to create their own representations and challenge dominant narratives. However, the algorithms and mechanisms that shape online spaces can still reproduce biases and exclusionary practices.

Intersectionality and Digital Media

Intersectionality is a framework that recognizes the interconnected nature of social categories such as gender, race, class, sexuality, and ability. These aspects of identity intersect and shape the experiences of individuals and communities. In the context of digital media, intersectionality highlights the importance of considering multiple dimensions of identity in analyzing representation and power dynamics.

For example, an analysis of representation in online gaming communities should consider how gender, race, and class intersect to shape the experiences of different gamers. Similarly, an examination of social media activism should take into account how different dimensions of identity influence the visibility and impact of online activism efforts. Intersectionality provides a lens through which we can better understand the complexities of representation and power in digital media.

Power Dynamics in Digital Media

Power dynamics are inherent in digital media platforms. These platforms shape the distribution of resources, influence, and visibility. They can amplify certain voices and marginalize others. Understanding power in digital media requires considering both explicit and implicit power structures.

Explicit power structures refer to the formal hierarchies and institutions that govern digital media platforms. For example, the decision-making processes and content moderation policies of social media companies can have a profound impact on representation and power dynamics. The algorithms that shape our social media feeds also play a significant role in determining what content is seen and by whom.

Implicit power structures, on the other hand, are less visible and often hidden within the design and functionality of digital media platforms. They can perpetuate biases and uphold existing power structures without explicit intention. An example of implicit power in digital media is the lack of diverse representation in stock photos or the limited options for gender on online forms. These seemingly small design decisions can have real-world consequences and contribute to the exclusion of certain groups.

Empowering Marginalized Voices

While digital media platforms can reproduce power imbalances, they also have the potential to empower marginalized voices and challenge existing power structures. Social media has become a crucial tool for activists and marginalized communities to share their stories and advocate for social change.

128 CULTURAL PERSPECTIVES ON DIGITAL MEDIA AND POWER

Digital media allows individuals and communities to bypass traditional gatekeepers and reach wider audiences with their perspectives and experiences. Organizations and individuals can use platforms like Twitter, Instagram, and YouTube to create counter-narratives and challenge dominant ideologies. Hashtag movements such as #BlackLivesMatter and #MeToo have gained global attention and catalyzed social and political movements.

However, it is important to recognize that digital media activism also has its limitations. While marginalized groups can utilize these platforms to amplify their voices, they are still operating within structures and systems that can silence or ignore their messages. Additionally, online activism can sometimes be performative or superficial, lacking the meaningful action necessary to create lasting change.

Ethical Considerations

When examining representation and power in digital media, it is essential to consider the ethical implications of these dynamics. As consumers and creators of digital media content, we have a responsibility to challenge existing power imbalances and promote equitable representations.

Digital media practitioners should prioritize inclusivity and diversity in their content creation and distribution strategies. This includes actively seeking out and amplifying marginalized voices, representing the complexities of identities and experiences, and avoiding harmful stereotypes and tropes.

Moreover, digital media companies and platforms should be transparent about their practices and algorithms. They should actively work towards reducing biases and addressing the power imbalances that exist within their systems. Policies and guidelines for content moderation should be developed in collaboration with diverse communities to ensure fair and equitable representation.

Case Study: Representation and Power in Online Advertising

A case study that exemplifies the power dynamics and representation challenges in digital media is online advertising. Advertisements play a significant role in shaping cultural narratives and influencing consumer behavior. However, they often reinforce stereotypes and exclude certain groups from representation.

One example is the representation of women in advertising. Historically, women have been objectified and portrayed in narrow and unrealistic ways in ads. This perpetuates harmful gender norms and contributes to the marginalization and disempowerment of women. Similarly, people of color, LGBTQ+ individuals,

POLITICS, PROPAGANDA, AND DIGITAL MEDIA

and individuals with disabilities are often underrepresented or depicted stereotypically in online ads.

To address these issues, advertisers and marketers need to critically examine their practices and challenge existing power structures. This can be done through inclusive casting, diverse representation, and the deconstruction of harmful stereotypes. Advertisers should also prioritize authentic storytelling and engage in meaningful conversations with the communities they are representing.

Conclusion

Representation and power in digital media are complex and interconnected. By understanding the politics of representation, the intersectionality of identity, and the power dynamics at play, we can work towards more inclusive and equitable digital spaces. Empowering marginalized voices and challenging existing power structures should be at the forefront of our efforts. In addition, ethical considerations and responsible practices are essential for promoting fair and representative digital media environments. It is through these efforts that we can foster a more diverse, inclusive, and empowering digital future.

Politics, Propaganda, and Digital Media

Social Media and Political Mobilization

Social media has dramatically impacted the way individuals and communities engage with political issues and mobilize for change. With its ability to reach millions of people in real-time, social media platforms such as Facebook, Twitter, and Instagram have become powerful tools for political mobilization. This section explores the impact of social media on political activism, the strategies used by activists, and the challenges and opportunities that arise in this digital age of political mobilization.

The Role of Social Media in Political Activism

Social media platforms have become important spaces for political discussions, activism, and mobilization. They provide individuals with a platform to express their views, share information, and engage with others who share similar political interests. The widespread adoption of social media has made it easier than ever for individuals to connect with like-minded people, organize protests and rallies, and raise awareness about pressing political issues.

130   CULTURAL PERSPECTIVES ON DIGITAL MEDIA AND POWER

One of the key strengths of social media in political mobilization is its ability to amplify marginalized voices and empower individuals who may have traditionally been excluded from the political discourse. Social media provides a platform for grassroots activists and citizen journalists to share their stories and perspectives, allowing for a more diverse range of voices to be heard.

Strategies for Political Mobilization on Social Media

Political activists have utilized various strategies to mobilize supporters and drive social and political change on social media platforms. Some of the most common strategies include:

1. **Information Sharing**: Social media platforms allow activists to quickly and easily share information about political issues, events, and campaigns. Activists can share articles, videos, infographics, and other forms of content to inform and engage their audience.

2. **Hashtag Campaigns**: Hashtags have become powerful tools for organizing and mobilizing social and political movements. Activists create and promote hashtags related to their cause, which allows for easy discovery of relevant content and helps to build a sense of community among supporters.

3. **Live Streaming**: Platforms like Facebook Live, Instagram Live, and Twitter's Periscope enable activists to broadcast events, protests, and rallies in real-time. Live streaming allows for immediate engagement with supporters and helps to create a sense of urgency and solidarity.

4. **Memes and Satire**: Memes and satire can be effective tools for political mobilization, as they can quickly spread and capture attention. Humor can be used to critique political leaders, policies, or ideologies, and engage a wider audience in the discourse.

5. **Network Building**: Activists utilize social media platforms to connect with and build networks of supporters. By engaging with followers, responding to comments, and actively participating in discussions, activists can cultivate a loyal and engaged online community.

These strategies, along with many others, have been instrumental in mobilizing supporters, raising awareness, and effecting change through social media.

Challenges and Opportunities

While social media has provided new opportunities for political mobilization, it also presents a range of challenges. One major challenge is the spread of misinformation or "fake news." Social media platforms have struggled to regulate the spread of false or misleading information, which can undermine the credibility of political movements and lead to public confusion.

Another challenge is the potential for online harassment and the silencing of marginalized voices. Although social media has provided a platform for empowerment, it has also become a space where individuals face cyberbullying, trolling, and harassment. This can discourage individuals from participating in political discourse and undermine the inclusivity of online spaces.

Additionally, social media algorithms can create echo chambers, where users are only exposed to content that aligns with their existing beliefs. This can limit the diversity of perspectives and hinder constructive dialogue among individuals with differing political views.

Despite these challenges, social media also offers opportunities for political mobilization. It allows individuals to engage in activism from the comfort of their own homes, providing accessibility to those who may face physical limitations or geographical barriers. It can also facilitate cross-cultural collaborations and global movements, as social media platforms transcend national borders.

Case Study: The Arab Spring

The Arab Spring is a prominent example of the power of social media in political mobilization. In 2010 and 2011, a wave of protests and uprisings swept across several countries in the Middle East and North Africa region, demanding political reform and regime change. Social media, particularly platforms like Facebook and Twitter, played a crucial role in organizing and coordinating these protests.

Platforms like Facebook allowed activists to spread information, mobilize supporters, and organize protests and demonstrations. Twitter, with its real-time nature, facilitated the rapid diffusion of information and updates on the protests, providing a platform for citizen journalism and enabling activists to garner international attention and support.

The Arab Spring demonstrated how social media can bypass traditional media channels, break down barriers to communication, and empower individuals to challenge existing power structures. However, it also highlighted some of the challenges and limitations of relying solely on social media for political mobilization, as the ultimate outcomes of the uprisings varied across different countries.

Conclusion

Social media has revolutionized the way political activism is organized and mobilized. It has empowered individuals, amplified marginalized voices, and provided a platform for cross-cultural collaborations and global movements. However, social media also poses challenges, such as the spread of fake news, online harassment, and the creation of echo chambers. Understanding the dynamics of social media in political mobilization is crucial for activists, policymakers, and researchers alike, as it shapes the future of political engagement and social change.

Digital Media and Fake News

The emergence of digital media has brought about numerous changes in the way news is produced, disseminated, and consumed. One of the major concerns in this digital age is the proliferation of fake news. Fake news refers to false or misleading information presented as if it were true news. It is often created and spread through digital media platforms, with the intent to deceive or manipulate audiences. The phenomenon of fake news has serious implications for individuals, societies, and even democratic processes. In this section, we will explore the relationship between digital media and fake news, examining its causes, impacts, and potential solutions.

Causes of Fake News in Digital Media

The spread of fake news is a complex issue, and its causes can be attributed to various factors within the digital media landscape. One of the primary causes is the ease and speed of information dissemination enabled by digital technologies. With the advent of social media platforms and online news portals, anyone can publish content and share it with a potentially global audience. This has created a fertile ground for the rapid dissemination of false information.

Another factor contributing to the spread of fake news is the lack of gatekeeping and fact-checking mechanisms in digital media. Traditional media outlets have editorial processes in place to verify the accuracy and credibility of news before it is published. However, in the digital realm, there are fewer checks and balances, allowing fake news to circulate unchecked. The absence of a centralized authority to regulate and verify the authenticity of information further exacerbates the problem.

POLITICS, PROPAGANDA, AND DIGITAL MEDIA

Additionally, the algorithms and algorithms employed by social media platforms play a role in the spread of fake news. These algorithms are designed to personalize the content presented to users based on their preferences and previous interactions. While this personalization enhances user experience, it also creates echo chambers, where individuals are exposed only to content that aligns with their existing beliefs and biases. This can lead to the reinforcement and spread of false narratives, as individuals are less likely to encounter opposing viewpoints and fact-checking information.

Impacts of Fake News on Society

The spread of fake news has significant implications for individuals, societies, and democratic processes. Firstly, the dissemination of false information can lead to misinformation and misunderstanding among the public. This can have serious consequences, especially in areas such as public health, where misinformation can lead to the adoption of harmful behaviors or the rejection of critical interventions.

Fake news also has the potential to exacerbate societal divisions and polarization. The echo chambers created by personalized algorithms can reinforce existing biases and ideologies, leading to the amplification of fake news within specific communities. This can further contribute to the fragmentation of societies and a breakdown in public discourse.

Moreover, fake news can undermine trust in traditional media and democratic institutions. When individuals are constantly exposed to false information, they may become skeptical of all sources of news and information, including legitimate journalism. This erosion of trust can weaken the democratic fabric of societies, as informed decision-making relies on access to accurate and reliable information.

Addressing Fake News in Digital Media

Addressing the issue of fake news requires a multi-faceted approach involving various stakeholders, including media organizations, technology companies, and individuals. Below are some strategies and solutions that can help combat fake news in the digital media landscape:

1. Promote media literacy: Educating individuals about media literacy is crucial in enabling them to critically evaluate news and information. Teaching individuals how to distinguish between credible and fake sources, fact-check information, and identify bias can empower them to make informed decisions in the digital sphere.

2. Strengthen fact-checking: Media organizations and technology companies should invest in robust fact-checking mechanisms. This can involve the

establishment of dedicated fact-checking teams, partnerships with credible institutions, and the development of automated tools to identify and flag fake news.

3. Enhance algorithm transparency: Social media platforms should strive to be more transparent about their algorithms and how they determine the content shown to users. By providing clearer explanations and options for users to control their content preferences, platforms can reduce the likelihood of echo chambers and expose users to a broader range of perspectives.

4. Encourage responsible sharing: Individuals should be encouraged to verify the accuracy of information before sharing it. Simple practices such as reading beyond headlines, cross-referencing multiple sources, and assessing the credibility of the author or platform can help prevent the inadvertent spread of fake news.

5. Support digital media literacy research: Continued research into digital media literacy is essential for understanding and addressing the challenges posed by fake news. Interdisciplinary collaborations between researchers in media studies, psychology, computer science, and other relevant fields can contribute to the development of effective interventions and policies.

It is worth noting that the fight against fake news is an ongoing and evolving battle. As technology continues to advance, so do the tactics employed by perpetrators of fake news. Therefore, continuous vigilance and adaptation to changing circumstances are necessary to effectively combat this issue.

In conclusion, the rise of digital media has given rise to the problem of fake news. This section has explored the causes of fake news in the digital media landscape, discussed its impacts on individuals and societies, and highlighted potential strategies to address and mitigate this issue. By promoting media literacy, strengthening fact-checking mechanisms, enhancing algorithm transparency, encouraging responsible sharing, and supporting research in digital media literacy, we can collectively work towards creating a more informed and resilient digital media ecosystem.

Online Public Sphere and Digital Democracy

The online public sphere has emerged as a significant platform for democratic discourse and engagement in the digital age. It provides individuals with the opportunity to voice their opinions, participate in public discussions, and shape public opinion. Digital democracy, on the other hand, refers to the use of digital technologies to enhance democratic processes, including voting, decision-making, and participation.

POLITICS, PROPAGANDA, AND DIGITAL MEDIA

The Role of the Online Public Sphere in Democratic Discourse

The online public sphere has transformed traditional notions of public discourse and civic engagement. It has enabled individuals from diverse backgrounds and perspectives to come together and engage in discussions on various social and political issues. Online platforms, such as social media, forums, and blogs, have provided a space for citizens to express their opinions, share information, and debate ideas.

One of the key benefits of the online public sphere is its ability to overcome barriers of time and space. People can engage in discussions and debates in real-time, regardless of their geographical location. This allows for a more inclusive and participatory form of public discourse, as individuals who may not have had the opportunity to participate in traditional public arenas now have a platform to express their views.

Furthermore, the online public sphere has the potential to foster deliberation and the exchange of diverse perspectives. By enabling individuals to engage with others who hold different opinions, it promotes a more inclusive and pluralistic democratic culture. However, it is important to note that the online public sphere also poses challenges and requires careful consideration.

Challenges and Limitations of the Online Public Sphere

While the online public sphere has expanded the possibilities for democratic discourse, it is not without its challenges. One of the key challenges is the issue of digital divide, which refers to the unequal access to digital technologies and the internet. This divide can exacerbate existing social inequalities, as those who lack access to online platforms are excluded from participating fully in the online public sphere.

Moreover, the online public sphere is susceptible to the spread of misinformation and echo chambers. The rapid dissemination of information online can lead to the proliferation of false or misleading content, which can undermine the quality of public discourse and decision-making. Additionally, individuals tend to gravitate towards like-minded communities online, creating echo chambers where their beliefs and opinions are reinforced without exposure to alternative viewpoints.

Another challenge is the issue of online harassment and the suppression of diverse voices. The anonymity provided by online platforms can lead to the targeting and silencing of individuals who express dissenting views or belong to

136 CULTURAL PERSPECTIVES ON DIGITAL MEDIA AND POWER

marginalized communities. This undermines the principles of inclusivity and freedom of expression that underpin democratic discourse.

The Potential of Digital Democracy

Digital democracy encompasses a range of strategies and technologies aimed at enhancing democratic processes. These include online voting systems, participatory budgeting, e-petitions, and crowdsourcing platforms. These tools have the potential to increase citizen engagement, facilitate transparency, and streamline decision-making processes.

One of the key advantages of digital democracy is its ability to overcome traditional barriers to participation. Online voting systems, for instance, can make it easier for individuals to exercise their right to vote, particularly for those who face mobility or accessibility challenges. This can lead to increased voter turnout and a more representative democratic system.

Furthermore, digital democracy can foster greater transparency and accountability. Online platforms that enable public access to government data and decision-making processes promote openness and enable citizens to hold their governments accountable. Similarly, participatory budgeting platforms allow citizens to take part in the allocation of public funds, ensuring greater transparency and fairness in resource distribution.

However, it is important to recognize that digital democracy is not a panacea for all democratic challenges. It requires thoughtful design and implementation to address the limitations and potential risks associated with digital technologies. Moreover, it is crucial to ensure that digital democracy initiatives are inclusive and accessible to all citizens, regardless of their digital literacy or access to technology.

Case Study: The Role of Social Media in Political Mobilization

Social media has played a significant role in political mobilization and activism around the world. The Arab Spring protests, for example, were largely organized and coordinated through social media platforms such as Twitter and Facebook. These platforms facilitated the rapid spread of information and allowed activists to mobilize quickly and effectively.

However, the role of social media in political mobilization is not without its complexities. While it can serve as a powerful tool for organizing collective action, it can also be used for the spread of misinformation and the manipulation of public opinion. The Cambridge Analytica scandal, for instance, revealed how social media data can be exploited for political purposes, potentially undermining the integrity of democratic processes.

Conclusion

The online public sphere and digital democracy have reshaped democratic discourse and engagement in the digital age. The online public sphere provides a platform for individuals to voice their opinions and participate in public discussions, while digital democracy initiatives aim to enhance democratic processes through the use of digital technologies.

However, the online public sphere and digital democracy are not without their challenges and limitations. Issues such as the digital divide, the spread of misinformation, online harassment, and the manipulation of public opinion need to be carefully addressed to ensure the effectiveness and inclusivity of digital democracy. Furthermore, it is crucial to continually evaluate and adapt digital democracy initiatives to keep pace with technological advancements and changing societal needs.

Cultural Perspectives on Digital Media and Creativity

Digital Media as Cultural Artifacts

Digital Media and Cultural Heritage Preservation

In this section, we will explore the relationship between digital media and the preservation of cultural heritage. Cultural heritage refers to the tangible and intangible artifacts, traditions, and knowledge inherited from past generations, which provide valuable insights into our history, identity, and aspirations. Digital media, with its unique capabilities, has revolutionized the way we preserve, document, and disseminate cultural heritage, ensuring its longevity and accessibility for future generations.

The Significance of Cultural Heritage Preservation

Preserving cultural heritage is crucial for several reasons. Firstly, it allows us to understand and appreciate our roots, fostering a sense of identity, belonging, and pride in our cultural diversity. Secondly, cultural heritage provides a valuable source of knowledge, enabling us to learn from the past and make informed decisions in the present. Additionally, cultural heritage tourism contributes to economic development and sustains local communities. Finally, cultural heritage represents our shared humanity and serves as a bridge between different civilizations, promoting tolerance, empathy, and mutual understanding.

Challenges in Cultural Heritage Preservation

Preserving cultural heritage is not without its challenges. Traditional methods of preservation, such as physical artifacts and oral traditions, are vulnerable to

144 CULTURAL PERSPECTIVES ON DIGITAL MEDIA AND CREATIVITY

degradation, loss, and destruction due to natural disasters, human conflicts, and the passage of time. Moreover, cultural heritage sites may be inaccessible or at risk, making it difficult for people to experience and appreciate them. Inadequate funding, limited resources, and a lack of technological expertise further exacerbate these challenges.

Digital Media and Cultural Heritage Preservation

Digital media has emerged as a powerful tool for cultural heritage preservation, offering innovative solutions to overcome these challenges. Here, we explore some key applications of digital media in the preservation and dissemination of cultural heritage.

Digital Documentation and Conservation Digital media allows cultural heritage objects, artifacts, and sites to be digitally documented, creating accurate and detailed representations. 3D scanning technologies, such as laser scanning and photogrammetry, capture the intricate details of sculptures, buildings, and archaeological sites. The resulting digital models serve as virtual records, ensuring their preservation even if the physical objects are damaged or lost. Furthermore, digital conservation techniques, such as image processing and data visualization, can help restore and enhance deteriorated artifacts, making them accessible to a wider audience.

Virtual Reality and Augmented Reality Virtual Reality (VR) and Augmented Reality (AR) technologies offer immersive experiences that enable users to explore and interact with cultural heritage sites and artifacts from anywhere in the world. VR recreates real or fictional environments, allowing users to virtually walk through historical sites or participate in cultural performances. AR overlays virtual content onto the real world, enhancing the visitor's perception and understanding of cultural heritage. These technologies can provide a more engaging and educational experience, especially for those who are unable to visit physical sites due to geographical, physical, or financial constraints.

Digital Archives and Libraries Digital media enables the creation of vast archives and libraries, preserving and organizing cultural heritage materials in a digital format. Digitized manuscripts, photographs, audio recordings, and videos can be stored and easily accessed by researchers, scholars, and the general public. With advanced search functionalities and metadata tagging, these digital archives become invaluable resources, fostering research, collaboration, and cultural

DIGITAL MEDIA AS CULTURAL ARTIFACTS

exchange. Furthermore, digital libraries facilitate the preservation of traditional knowledge, languages, and practices that might otherwise be forgotten or marginalized.

Digital Storytelling and Interactive Exhibitions   Digital media offers new ways to share cultural heritage stories and engage audiences. Digital storytelling combines multimedia elements, such as audio, video, images, and animations, to convey narratives and provide context to cultural artifacts. Interactive exhibitions, both online and in physical spaces, allow visitors to explore cultural heritage at their own pace, providing detailed information, interactive activities, and personalized learning experiences. These approaches enhance visitor engagement, encourage knowledge retention, and promote cultural understanding.

Digital Media and Cultural Heritage Preservation Ethics

Using digital media for cultural heritage preservation raises ethical considerations that must be carefully addressed. It is crucial to involve local communities and stakeholders in decision-making processes to ensure cultural sensitivity, respect, and consent. Intellectual property rights, copyright laws, and data ownership should be appropriately managed to protect the rights of indigenous communities and creators. Moreover, data security, privacy, and preservation standards must be upheld to prevent unauthorized access, loss, or misuse of cultural heritage materials. The ethical framework should prioritize the equitable and inclusive representation of diverse cultural identities and narratives, avoiding bias, stereotypes, and cultural appropriation.

Current Challenges and Future Directions

Despite the significant potential of digital media in cultural heritage preservation, several challenges persist. Limited access to technology, particularly in developing regions, widens the digital divide and hinders equal participation in cultural heritage preservation efforts. Technological obsolescence poses a risk to the sustainability of digital preservation initiatives, necessitating ongoing vigilance and adaptation. Furthermore, issues of funding, capacity building, and long-term maintenance remain challenging in the digital preservation landscape.

Looking ahead, future research and practice should focus on addressing these challenges and exploring emerging technologies and methodologies. Artificial intelligence and machine learning can assist in automating the preservation processes, analyzing large datasets, and providing contextual insights. Blockchain technology holds promise in ensuring the integrity and provenance of digital cultural heritage assets. Collaborative partnerships between governments, cultural institutions, academia, and communities can foster knowledge sharing, capacity building, and the establishment of best practices.

Conclusion

Digital media plays a crucial role in the preservation, documentation, and dissemination of cultural heritage. Through digital documentation, virtual reality experiences, digital archives, and interactive exhibitions, cultural heritage becomes accessible to a wider and more diverse audience. However, ethical considerations, access disparities, and technological challenges need to be carefully navigated to ensure the sustainability, inclusivity, and integrity of digital cultural heritage preservation efforts. By embracing innovative technologies and fostering collaborative approaches, we can safeguard our shared cultural heritage for generations to come.

Digital Media and Cultural Expressions

Digital media has revolutionized the way we create and consume cultural expressions. It has provided individuals and communities with unprecedented opportunities to showcase their cultural heritage, artistic talents, and creative ideas. In this section, we will explore the relationship between digital media and cultural expressions, examining how digital platforms have transformed traditional art forms, facilitated the emergence of new cultural practices, and fostered cultural exchange on a global scale.

The Transformation of Traditional Art Forms

Digital media has breathed new life into traditional art forms, enabling artists to experiment with new techniques and reach wider audiences. For example, traditional music has been revolutionized by digital platforms, allowing musicians to record and distribute their work more easily and connect with listeners from around the world. Artists can now collaborate remotely, blending different musical styles and cultural influences to create unique and innovative compositions.

Visual arts have also been transformed by digital media. Artists can now create digital paintings, sculptures, and installations using software and digital tools. These digital artworks can be easily shared and exhibited online, transcending geographical boundaries and reaching a global audience. Moreover, digital technologies have enabled the fusion of different art forms, such as combining

DIGITAL MEDIA AS CULTURAL ARTIFACTS

traditional painting techniques with digital animation or incorporating interactive elements in installations.

The Emergence of New Cultural Practices

In addition to transforming traditional art forms, digital media has also given rise to new cultural practices that were not possible before. For instance, the rise of user-generated content platforms has empowered individuals to become creators and curators of cultural content. People can now produce and share videos, podcasts, blogs, and social media posts that reflect their cultural interests, perspectives, and experiences.

Online communities and virtual spaces have become hubs of cultural exchange and creativity. Platforms like Reddit, Twitter, and Instagram have allowed individuals from diverse backgrounds to form communities based on shared cultural interests. These communities become spaces where cultural expressions are shared, discussed, and celebrated. Online events, such as virtual festivals and art exhibitions, have emerged as new avenues for showcasing cultural expressions and fostering intercultural dialogue.

Fostering Cultural Exchange on a Global Scale

Digital media has dramatically expanded the reach and impact of cultural expressions by facilitating cross-cultural exchange on a global scale. Artists can now easily share their work with audiences from different countries and continents, transcending linguistic and geographical barriers. This has led to the emergence of a vibrant global digital cultural ecosystem, characterized by the exchange and hybridization of cultural ideas, practices, and aesthetics.

Social media platforms, in particular, have played a pivotal role in connecting individuals, communities, and cultures. Artists can use platforms like Facebook, Instagram, and TikTok to showcase their work, build a following, and engage with an international audience. Through hashtags, collaborations, and viral trends, cultural expressions can quickly spread and gain recognition worldwide.

However, the globalization of cultural expressions through digital media also presents challenges. Cultural appropriation, the unauthorized adoption or exploitation of elements from one culture by members of another culture, can occur more easily in the digital realm. It is important to promote cultural sensitivity, respect, and understanding to avoid the commodification or misrepresentation of cultural expressions in digital spaces.

148 CULTURAL PERSPECTIVES ON DIGITAL MEDIA AND CREATIVITY

Case Study: Digital Storytelling

One example of how digital media has revolutionized cultural expressions is digital storytelling. Traditional storytelling has long been a powerful means of transmitting cultural values, history, and knowledge. With digital media, storytelling has been taken to new heights, allowing storytellers to incorporate multimedia elements such as text, images, audio, and video.

Digital storytelling can be seen in various forms, such as interactive storytelling apps, web-based narratives, and immersive virtual reality experiences. These platforms enable storytellers to engage their audience in new and interactive ways, blurring the boundaries between the storyteller and the audience. Through user participation and customization, digital storytelling allows for a more personalized and immersive cultural experience.

For example, the Maori people of New Zealand have embraced digital storytelling to preserve and share their cultural heritage. The online platform "Māori Maps" utilizes digital media to map out ancestral sites, legends, and stories, allowing users to explore and learn about Maori culture. This digital approach ensures the accessibility and continuity of cultural knowledge for future generations while reaching a global audience.

Ethical Considerations in Digital Cultural Expressions

As digital media continues to shape cultural expressions, it is important to address ethical considerations associated with this transformation. Cultural expressions are deeply rooted in specific contexts, histories, and communities, and their digital representation should respect these origins.

One ethical concern is the potential for digital media to perpetuate cultural stereotypes or distort cultural narratives. It is important to empower individuals and communities to control the narrative of their own cultural expressions in digital spaces. This can be achieved through increased representation, inclusion, and collaboration with cultural insiders in the production and curation of digital content.

Another ethical consideration is the protection of intellectual property rights and the fair compensation of artists and creators. The ease of copying and distributing digital content poses challenges for artists who rely on their creativity and cultural expressions for their livelihood. Developing fair and sustainable models for digital cultural production that respect and compensate artists is essential for the continued vitality of cultural expressions.

DIGITAL MEDIA AS CULTURAL ARTIFACTS 145

Conclusion

Digital media has transformed cultural expressions, offering new possibilities for creativity, collaboration, and cultural exchange. Traditional art forms have been reinvented, new cultural practices have emerged, and global connections have been forged. However, ethical considerations must be taken into account to ensure the respectful and inclusive representation of cultural expressions in the digital space. As we look to the future, the continued exploration of digital media's potential in cultural expressions promises exciting possibilities for the preservation, innovation, and celebration of diverse cultures.

Digital Media and Cultural Production

In this section, we will explore the relationship between digital media and cultural production. Cultural production refers to the creation and dissemination of cultural content, such as art, music, literature, films, and other creative expressions. With the advent of digital media, the landscape of cultural production has undergone significant transformations. We will examine the impact of digital media on cultural production, the challenges and opportunities it presents, and the ways in which digital media has reshaped the creative process.

The Impact of Digital Media on Cultural Production

Digital media has revolutionized cultural production by providing new avenues for creativity, distribution, and consumption. It has democratized the production process, allowing individuals and communities to create and share their cultural expressions on a global scale. In the past, cultural production was often restricted to a select few who had access to resources and platforms. However, digital media has opened up new possibilities for marginalized groups and underrepresented voices to participate in cultural production.

One major impact of digital media on cultural production is the blurring of boundaries between creators and consumers. In the digital age, audiences have become active participants in the production process. Through social media, blogs, and other online platforms, individuals can create and share their own cultural content, such as fan art, remixes, and parodies. This participatory culture has allowed for greater diversity and creativity in cultural production.

Furthermore, digital media has facilitated the remix and reinterpretation of existing cultural content. Sampling, mashups, and other forms of digital manipulation have become integral to the creative process. Artists can draw inspiration from a wide range of sources, remixing and recontextualizing them to

146 CULTURAL PERSPECTIVES ON DIGITAL MEDIA AND CREATIVITY

create something new. This has led to the emergence of new artistic genres and forms, such as digital collage and glitch art.

Challenges and Opportunities in Digital Cultural Production

While digital media has created abundant opportunities for cultural production, it has also posed unique challenges. One of the main challenges is the issue of intellectual property rights. With the ease of copying and sharing digital content, it has become more difficult for creators to protect their work from unauthorized use or plagiarism. Copyright laws and enforcement mechanisms have struggled to keep pace with the rapidly evolving digital landscape, leading to ongoing debates and legal battles regarding digital piracy and fair use.

Another challenge is the issue of cultural commodification. Digital media has facilitated the commercialization of cultural products, as they can be easily bought, sold, and consumed online. This has raised concerns about cultural appropriation, where dominant cultures appropriate and exploit the cultural expressions of marginalized communities for profit. It is essential to recognize and respect the cultural origins and significance of creative works, especially when they are repurposed or commodified in the digital realm.

Despite these challenges, digital media also presents numerous opportunities for cultural production. The accessibility and affordability of digital tools have democratized the creative process, allowing individuals with limited resources to produce high-quality content. Digital platforms have also provided artists with new ways to reach global audiences and cultivate niche communities. Through crowdfunding and online marketplaces, creators can directly connect with their fans and monetize their work without the need for traditional intermediaries.

Digital Media and Collaboration in Cultural Production

Digital media has also facilitated collaboration and collective creativity in cultural production. Artists, musicians, writers, and other creators can collaborate across geographical boundaries and share their work instantaneously. Online platforms, such as GitHub for software development or SoundCloud for music production, have enabled collective creation and feedback in real-time.

Moreover, digital media has allowed for the preservation and archiving of cultural heritage. Digital libraries, museums, and archives have digitized and made accessible a vast range of cultural artifacts, ensuring their longevity and availability to future generations. This digitization process not only facilitates preservation but also enables new forms of engagement and reinterpretation of cultural heritage.

Examples of Digital Cultural Production

To illustrate the concepts discussed, let's look at a few examples of digital cultural production. One notable example is the rise of digital literature or electronic literature. Digital platforms have allowed authors and poets to experiment with interactive storytelling, incorporating multimedia elements such as sound, images, and interactive graphics into their works. The digital format provides a unique reading experience, where the reader becomes an active participant in the narrative.

Another example is the influence of digital media on music production. Digital audio workstations (DAWs) and software instruments have transformed the way music is created and produced. Artists can now compose, record, and mix their music entirely in the digital realm, eliminating the need for expensive recording studios and physical instruments. This has democratized music production, allowing aspiring musicians to create professional-quality compositions from the comfort of their own homes.

Lastly, the world of digital art has witnessed a surge in creativity and innovation. Artists can experiment with new mediums such as virtual reality (VR) and augmented reality (AR) to create immersive and interactive experiences for the audience. These technologies enable viewers to engage with artworks in ways that were previously unimaginable, blurring the boundaries between the physical and digital realms.

Conclusion

Digital media has had a profound impact on cultural production, reshaping the creative process and transforming the way cultural content is created, shared, and consumed. It has provided new opportunities for diverse voices to be heard and has facilitated collaboration and collective creativity. However, it has also posed challenges related to copyright, cultural appropriation, and the commodification of cultural products. As we move forward, it is crucial to navigate these challenges ethically and to harness the potential of digital media to foster inclusive, diverse, and innovative cultural production.

148 CULTURAL PERSPECTIVES ON DIGITAL MEDIA AND CREATIVITY

Exercises

1. Choose a cultural artifact from your country and imagine how it could be transformed by digital media. Describe the potential changes in its production, distribution, and consumption, and discuss the implications for its cultural significance.

2. Conduct research on a contemporary digital artist or musician who uses digital media in their creative process. How does their work challenge traditional notions of cultural production? Analyze the impact of their digital media practices on their artistic output and audience engagement.

3. Explore the legal and ethical considerations surrounding digital cultural production, such as copyright infringement and cultural appropriation. Discuss the importance of recognizing and respecting cultural origins and the potential consequences of appropriating cultural expressions.

4. Create a digital artwork using any digital media tools at your disposal. Reflect on your creative process and how digital media influenced your artistic choices. Consider the affordances and limitations of digital media in comparison to traditional art forms.

5. Investigate the role of digital media in the preservation and reinterpretation of cultural heritage. Choose a cultural artifact or historical event and discuss the ways in which digital media can contribute to its preservation, accessibility, and understanding.

Further Reading

- Manovich, L. (2001). The Language of New Media. MIT Press.
- Jenkins, H. (2006). Convergence Culture: Where Old and New Media Collide. New York University Press.
- Kurgan, L. (2013). Close Up at a Distance: Mapping, Technology, and Politics. Zone Books.
- Baym, N. K. (2015). Personal Connections in the Digital Age. Polity Press.
- Lessig, L. (2008). Remix: Making Art and Commerce Thrive in the Hybrid Economy. Penguin Books.

Digital Media and Cultural Consumption

In this section, we will explore the relationship between digital media and cultural consumption. Cultural consumption refers to the ways in which individuals engage with and interact with cultural artifacts, practices, and expressions within a specific cultural context. With the advent of digital media, the landscape of cultural consumption has significantly transformed, offering new possibilities and challenges.

Digital Media and Cultural Representation

One of the key aspects of cultural consumption is the representation of culture in digital media. Digital platforms have provided space for diverse cultural expressions and narratives that were previously marginalized or underrepresented. For example, online streaming platforms have enabled the global distribution of movies and TV shows from different cultural backgrounds, allowing audiences to engage with a wide range of content from around the world. This increased accessibility and exposure to various cultures through digital media has resulted in a more diverse and inclusive cultural landscape.

However, it is important to consider the power dynamics at play in the representation of culture in digital media. Global media corporations still dominate the production and distribution of digital content, which can lead to the perpetuation of cultural stereotypes and biases. For instance, certain cultures may be exoticized or portrayed in a simplified and one-dimensional manner to cater to Western audiences. This raises ethical questions about cultural appropriation and the need for responsible content creation in the digital space.

Cultural Consumption Patterns in the Digital Age

The rise of digital media has also had a significant impact on cultural consumption patterns. Traditionally, cultural consumption was largely influenced by geographic location and physical access to cultural resources. However, digital media has disrupted these norms by making cultural content more readily available and accessible. People can now consume cultural artifacts and practices from anywhere in the world with just a few clicks.

Furthermore, digital media has facilitated new forms of cultural consumption, such as participatory culture and user-generated content. Social media platforms, for example, have empowered individuals to actively engage in cultural production and sharing. Users can create and share their own cultural expressions, such as music, art, and fashion, thereby blurring the boundaries between consumers and producers of culture.

However, the digital age has also brought challenges in terms of evaluating the authenticity and quality of cultural consumption. With the ease of access to a vast amount of digital content, individuals may face information overload and struggle to discern the cultural value and significance of different artifacts and practices.

150 CULTURAL PERSPECTIVES ON DIGITAL MEDIA AND CREATIVITY

Additionally, the democratization of cultural consumption through digital media has led to the proliferation of low-quality and potentially harmful content, making it necessary to develop critical literacy skills to navigate the digital cultural landscape.

Digital Media and Cultural Preservation

Digital media has also played a crucial role in the preservation and dissemination of cultural heritage. Traditional cultural artifacts, such as ancient texts, artwork, and music, can be digitally archived and made accessible to a global audience. This digital preservation allows for the safeguarding of cultural diversity and the transmission of cultural knowledge across generations.

Moreover, digital media provides new opportunities for cultural institutions, such as museums and libraries, to engage with audiences and enhance their cultural consumption experiences. Virtual tours, interactive exhibits, and immersive technologies enable individuals to explore cultural institutions and artifacts remotely, breaking down geographical barriers.

However, the digital preservation of cultural heritage comes with its own set of challenges. Issues such as copyright infringement, ownership rights, and the potential loss of material authenticity need to be carefully addressed. Additionally, the digital divide, with unequal access to digital technologies, can exacerbate cultural inequalities in terms of the preservation and consumption of cultural artifacts.

Examples and Exercises

To further understand the intersection of digital media and cultural consumption, let's consider a few examples:

Example 1: Global Music Streaming Platforms Global music streaming platforms, such as Spotify and Apple Music, have revolutionized the way people consume music. These platforms offer a vast catalog of music from different cultures and genres, allowing users to explore and discover new artists and styles from around the world. Discuss the cultural significance of these platforms in promoting cultural diversity and facilitating global cultural consumption.

Example 2: Social Media Influencer Marketing In recent years, social media influencers have become powerful cultural producers and influencers. Research how social media influencers impact cultural consumption patterns, particularly in

DIGITAL MEDIA AND CREATIVE INDUSTRIES

terms of fashion, beauty, and lifestyle trends. Discuss the potential for cultural appropriation and the influence of economic factors on cultural consumption in this context.

Exercise: Analyzing Cultural Consumption Patterns   Conduct a survey among your peers to analyze their cultural consumption patterns in the digital age. Ask questions about their preferences in terms of music, movies, TV shows, and online content. Analyze the data to identify any cultural biases or trends and discuss the implications of these findings on digital media and cultural consumption.

Resources and Further Reading

To delve deeper into the topic of digital media and cultural consumption, here are some recommended resources:

- Book: "Cultural Consumption in Everyday Life" by Lidia Pârțachi

- Journal Article: "Digital Media and the Cultural Consumption of Migration" by Maralee Mayberry

- Documentary: "The Internet's Own Boy: The Story of Aaron Swartz" (2014) directed by Brian Knappenberger, exploring the impact of digital media on information access and cultural consumption.

Conclusion

Digital media has significantly shaped cultural consumption, offering both opportunities and challenges. It has expanded access to diverse cultural content, facilitated active participation in cultural production, and enabled the preservation and dissemination of cultural heritage. However, it also raises concerns about cultural representation, authenticity, and the quality of cultural consumption. Understanding and critically analyzing these dynamics is essential for navigating the digital cultural landscape and promoting cultural diversity and inclusivity.

Digital Media and Creative Industries

Cultural Entrepreneurship and Digital Media

Cultural entrepreneurship refers to the process of utilizing cultural resources, such as artistic creations, traditions, or heritage, to create economically viable ventures.

It involves the application of entrepreneurial principles and practices in the cultural sector. With the rise of digital media, cultural entrepreneurship has gained new dimensions and opportunities. This section will explore the relationship between cultural entrepreneurship and digital media, highlighting the challenges and opportunities it presents.

The Intersection of Culture and Entrepreneurship

Culture plays a vital role in shaping entrepreneurial activities. Cultural entrepreneurs leverage cultural assets, knowledge, and practices to create innovative and sustainable businesses. They are driven by a passion for cultural expression and aim to generate economic value while preserving and promoting cultural heritage.

Entrepreneurship, on the other hand, involves the identification and exploitation of opportunities. It is characterized by risk-taking, creativity, and resourcefulness. Digital media has opened up new channels for cultural entrepreneurship to flourish, allowing cultural entrepreneurs to reach wider audiences and engage with diverse communities.

Digital Media as a Platform for Cultural Entrepreneurship

Digital media platforms, such as social networks, websites, and online marketplaces, have transformed the way cultural entrepreneurship operates. They provide a global reach, allowing cultural entrepreneurs to connect with audiences worldwide. Here are some key aspects of digital media that have shaped cultural entrepreneurship:

- **Global Market Access:** Digital media platforms enable cultural entrepreneurs to market their products and services to a global audience. They can showcase their cultural offerings, including artwork, traditional crafts, or performances, to potential customers across borders and cultural contexts.

- **Direct-to-Consumer Model:** Digital media eliminates intermediaries between cultural entrepreneurs and their customers. This direct-to-consumer model enables cultural entrepreneurs to bypass traditional distribution channels, reducing costs and increasing profit margins. They can establish their online presence, interact directly with customers, and build brand loyalty.

- **Crowdfunding and Collaborative Funding:** Digital media platforms have facilitated alternative financing models for cultural entrepreneurs.

Crowdfunding platforms, for instance, allow cultural entrepreneurs to showcase their projects and raise funds from supporters worldwide. Collaborative funding models encourage collective participation and engagement, fostering a sense of community around cultural ventures.

- **Data Analytics and Market Insights:** Digital media provides cultural entrepreneurs with valuable insights into consumer behavior and preferences through data analytics. They can track user engagement, measure the effectiveness of marketing campaigns, and make data-driven decisions to optimize their business strategies.

Challenges and Opportunities

While digital media offers numerous opportunities for cultural entrepreneurship, it also presents various challenges. Cultural entrepreneurs need to navigate these challenges to succeed in the digital landscape. Here are some key considerations:

- **Digital Divide:** Access to digital media infrastructure and skills is not evenly distributed globally. Cultural entrepreneurs from marginalized communities or regions with limited internet connectivity face barriers in participating in digital cultural entrepreneurship. Bridging the digital divide is crucial to ensure equal opportunities for cultural entrepreneurs worldwide.

- **Intellectual Property Protection:** Digital media poses challenges in protecting intellectual property rights. Cultural entrepreneurs may face issues related to copyright infringement, unauthorized reproduction or distribution of their cultural products. Developing robust legal frameworks and digital rights management systems is essential to safeguard the creative works of cultural entrepreneurs.

- **Digital Marketing and Branding:** Effectively promoting cultural products and services in the saturated digital marketplace can be challenging. Cultural entrepreneurs need to develop digital marketing and branding strategies that authentically represent their cultural values and resonate with their target audiences. They should leverage storytelling techniques, visual media, and social media influencers to create compelling digital narratives.

- **Cultural Appropriation:** Cultural entrepreneurs must navigate the fine line between appreciating and appropriating cultural elements. The digital sphere is susceptible to cultural misrepresentation or commodification. Cultural entrepreneurs should be mindful of ethical considerations, respect

CULTURAL PERSPECTIVES ON DIGITAL MEDIA AND CREATIVITY

the intellectual and cultural rights of communities, and engage in fair and responsible cultural exchanges.

Case Study: Cultural Entrepreneurship in the Digital Age

To illustrate the concepts discussed, let's consider the case of a cultural entrepreneur named Maria, who belongs to an indigenous community known for their traditional pottery. Maria decides to leverage digital media to promote and sell her pottery creations globally.

Maria establishes an e-commerce website showcasing her pottery products, including detailed descriptions and high-quality images. She creates social media accounts and actively engages with users, sharing the stories behind her creations and collaborating with influencers who appreciate indigenous craftsmanship. Maria also joins online communities of cultural entrepreneurs, exchanging ideas, and learning from peers.

To address the challenge of intellectual property protection, Maria acquires copyright registrations for her unique designs. She integrates watermarks on her digital images to prevent unauthorized use and educates her customers about the cultural significance of her pottery, fostering a sense of respect and appreciation.

To overcome the digital divide, Maria partners with local organizations to provide digital literacy training to artisans in her community. She advocates for improved internet connectivity in her region, enabling other cultural entrepreneurs to embrace digital opportunities.

By leveraging the power of digital media, Maria successfully establishes her brand internationally. Her sustainable business model promotes cultural heritage, empowers her community, and generates economic value.

Conclusion

Cultural entrepreneurship in the digital age opens up new avenues for preserving, promoting, and monetizing cultural assets. Digital media platforms empower cultural entrepreneurs to reach global audiences, build authentic connections, and create sustainable ventures. However, cultural entrepreneurs need to navigate challenges such as the digital divide, intellectual property protection, and cultural appropriation ethically. By leveraging digital media effectively and embracing innovative strategies, cultural entrepreneurs can contribute to the preservation and revitalization of diverse cultural traditions while generating economic value.

Cultural Policy in the Digital Era

Cultural policy plays a crucial role in shaping the development and dissemination of digital media in the modern age. With the advent of the digital era, new challenges and opportunities have emerged in the cultural landscape. This section explores the intersection of cultural policy and digital media, highlighting the key issues, principles, and strategies for effective policy-making in the digital era.

Understanding Cultural Policy

Cultural policy refers to a set of guidelines, regulations, and practices that governments, organizations, and communities employ to promote and support cultural activities and expressions. It encompasses a wide range of areas, including arts, heritage, media, and education. In the digital era, cultural policy must adapt to the rapid changes brought about by technology and digital media.

The Digital Age and Cultural Policy

The digital age has revolutionized the way we create, consume, and distribute cultural content. The widespread availability of digital technologies has made it easier for individuals to create and share their work, breaking down traditional barriers to entry. However, this has also led to challenges such as copyright infringement, cultural appropriation, and the digital divide.

Principles of Cultural Policy in the Digital Era

In formulating cultural policy in the digital era, several principles should be considered to ensure a holistic and inclusive approach. These principles include:

1. **Access and Digital Inclusion:** Cultural policy should aim to bridge the digital divide by ensuring equal access to digital media and technologies. This includes addressing issues such as affordability, digital literacy, and infrastructure development.

2. **Cultural Diversity and Pluralism:** Cultural policy should promote and celebrate cultural diversity, recognizing the value of different cultural expressions and perspectives. It should strive to provide equal opportunities for all cultural communities to participate and contribute to the digital cultural sphere.

156ULTURAL PERSPECTIVES ON DIGITAL MEDIA AND CREATIVITY

3. **Collaborative Governance:** Cultural policy-making should involve collaboration and dialogue between government agencies, cultural institutions, artists, and communities. This participatory approach ensures that policies are responsive to the needs and aspirations of diverse stakeholders.

4. **Sustainability and Resilience:** Cultural policy should support the sustainability and resilience of cultural industries and practices. This includes fostering economic growth, protecting cultural heritage, and adapting to technological advancements.

Challenges in Cultural Policy

Cultural policy in the digital era faces several challenges that require careful consideration and innovative solutions. These challenges include:

1. **Copyright and Intellectual Property:** Digital media has made it easier to copy and distribute cultural works, leading to increased challenges related to copyright infringement and intellectual property rights. Cultural policy should strike a balance between protecting the rights of creators and enabling access to cultural content.

2. **Cultural Appropriation:** The digital era has also brought to the forefront the issue of cultural appropriation, where elements of one culture are adopted by another without proper acknowledgment or respect. Cultural policy should address this issue by promoting cultural understanding, dialogue, and respectful collaboration.

3. **Digital Divide:** The digital divide refers to the gap between those who have access to digital technologies and those who do not. Cultural policy should focus on reducing this divide by providing affordable and accessible connectivity, digital skills training, and support for marginalized communities.

Strategies for Effective Cultural Policy

To address these challenges, several strategies can be employed in the formulation and implementation of cultural policy in the digital era:

1. **Education and Awareness:** Cultural policy should focus on raising awareness about the value of cultural expressions and promoting responsible

DIGITAL MEDIA AND CREATIVE INDUSTRIES

digital media consumption. This can be achieved through educational initiatives, public campaigns, and media literacy programs.

2. **Partnerships and Collaboration:** Collaboration between government agencies, cultural institutions, private sector organizations, and civil society is key to effective cultural policy-making. Partnerships can leverage expertise, resources, and diverse perspectives to develop comprehensive and sustainable policies.

3. **Regulation and Standards:** Cultural policy should establish clear regulations and standards to address issues such as copyright infringement, cultural appropriation, and online safety. These regulations should strike a balance between enabling creativity and protecting the rights and interests of cultural producers and consumers.

Case Study: Cultural Policy in Singapore

Singapore serves as an interesting case study in cultural policy in the digital era. The country has implemented various initiatives to promote and support digital media and creativity while addressing the challenges posed by technological advancements.

One such initiative is the Media Development Authority (MDA), which has been restructured as the Infocomm Media Development Authority (IMDA) to reflect the changing digital landscape. The IMDA promotes digital and media literacy, supports the development of local content creators, and ensures the responsible and ethical use of digital media.

Another notable example is the National Library Board (NLB), which has transformed its services to adapt to the digital era. The NLB provides access to digital resources, offers digital literacy programs, and supports local authors and publishers through its digital publishing initiatives.

These case studies demonstrate the importance of proactive cultural policy in harnessing the potential of digital media while addressing the challenges and ensuring inclusivity and sustainability.

Conclusion

Cultural policy in the digital era plays a critical role in shaping the development and dissemination of digital media. By embracing principles such as access, cultural diversity, collaborative governance, and sustainability, cultural policy can effectively address the challenges and harness the opportunities of the digital age. Through strategic approaches such as education, partnerships, and regulation, cultural

CULTURAL PERSPECTIVES ON DIGITAL MEDIA AND CREATIVITY

policy can ensure the responsible and inclusive growth of digital media and its positive impact on cultural expressions and communities.

Intellectual Property and Digital Media

In the digital age, the creation, distribution, and consumption of media have undergone significant transformations. With the rise of digital media, issues related to intellectual property have become increasingly complex and contentious. Intellectual property refers to legal rights that are granted to individuals or organizations for their creative and intellectual works, such as inventions, literary and artistic works, designs, and symbols. In the context of digital media, intellectual property plays a crucial role in protecting the rights of creators and ensuring fair use and access.

Understanding Intellectual Property

Intellectual property comprises several distinct categories, including copyright, patents, trademarks, and trade secrets. Each category serves different purposes and provides creators with different forms of protection.

1. Copyright: Copyright is primarily concerned with protecting original works of authorship, such as books, music, films, and computer programs. It grants the creator exclusive rights to reproduce, distribute, display, and perform their work, as well as to create derivative works based on their original creation. Copyright protection helps incentivize creativity by ensuring that creators can profit from their work and have control over how it is used by others. In the digital age, copyright has become more challenging to enforce due to the ease of copying and distributing digital content.

2. Patents: Patents are granted to inventors in order to encourage innovation by granting them exclusive rights to their inventions for a limited period of time. In the realm of digital media, patents can be relevant to software algorithms, technical innovations in hardware, and other technological advancements. Patents encourage inventors to disclose their inventions to the public, enabling others to build upon their work once the patent expires.

3. Trademarks: Trademarks protect distinctive signs, symbols, or logos that distinguish the goods or services of one entity from those of others. In the digital realm, trademarks are particularly relevant in branding, advertising, and e-commerce. Trademark protection ensures that consumers can identify and differentiate between products or services.

DIGITAL MEDIA AND CREATIVE INDUSTRIES 159

4. Trade Secrets: Trade secrets refer to valuable and confidential information that provides a competitive advantage to a business. This can include formulas, manufacturing processes, customer lists, and marketing strategies. Trade secret protection enables businesses to maintain their market position by preventing competitors from gaining access to valuable information.

Challenges and Issues

The digital environment brings unique challenges and issues concerning intellectual property. These challenges arise due to the ease of reproducing and distributing digital content, the global nature of the internet, and the rapid advancements in technology. Some of the key challenges in the context of intellectual property and digital media include:

1. Piracy and Copyright Infringement: The ease of copying and distributing digital content has led to widespread piracy and copyright infringement. Unauthorized downloading, sharing, and streaming of copyrighted materials have resulted in significant losses for content creators and media industries. The enforcement of copyright laws in the digital age has become increasingly complex, requiring international cooperation and innovative mechanisms to combat piracy effectively.

2. New Modes of Creativity and Remix Culture: The digital age has also given rise to new modes of creativity, such as remixes, mashups, and fan fiction. These forms of creativity often involve the use of existing copyrighted works, raising questions about the boundaries of fair use and derivative works. Balancing the rights of content creators and the freedom of expression and creativity of individuals is an ongoing challenge.

3. Digital Rights Management (DRM): Content creators and distributors often employ DRM technologies to protect their digital content from unauthorized use. DRM systems, such as encryption and access control mechanisms, aim to prevent piracy and ensure that content is used in accordance with the rights holder's permissions. However, DRM has been a subject of debate due to its potential to restrict consumers' rights, impede fair use, and hinder innovation.

4. Cross-border Issues and Jurisdictional Challenges: The internet knows no borders, and digital media can be accessed from anywhere in the world. This raises jurisdictional challenges when it comes to enforcing intellectual property rights. Different countries have different laws and regulations

160 CULTURAL PERSPECTIVES ON DIGITAL MEDIA AND CREATIVITY

regarding intellectual property, and coordinating efforts to combat infringement globally can be complex.

Solutions and Best Practices

Addressing the challenges and issues related to intellectual property in the context of digital media requires a multi-faceted approach involving legal frameworks, technological solutions, and ethical considerations. Some solutions and best practices that have emerged in recent years include:

1. Digital Watermarking and Fingerprinting: Digital watermarking and fingerprinting technologies embed unique identifiers into digital content, allowing content owners to track and identify unauthorized copies or use. These technologies can assist in copyright enforcement and act as a deterrent against piracy.

2. Creative Commons Licensing: Creative Commons licenses provide a flexible and standardized way for content creators to grant permissions for others to use their work. These licenses allow creators to retain some rights while enabling others to share, remix, or build upon their work under certain conditions. Creative Commons licenses have been instrumental in fostering a culture of open access and collaboration.

3. Strengthening International Intellectual Property Laws: Cooperation and coordination among nations are crucial to effectively combat intellectual property infringements in the digital age. International agreements and treaties, such as the WIPO Copyright Treaty, aim to harmonize copyright laws and facilitate enforcement globally.

4. Fair Use and User Rights: Balancing the interests of content creators and users' rights is fundamental in the digital realm. Fair use provisions, where applicable, allow limited use of copyrighted work without permission from the rights holder. Encouraging a broader understanding of fair use is essential for fostering creativity and innovation.

5. Education and Awareness: Raising awareness about intellectual property issues, copyright law, and ethical use of digital media is vital. Educating individuals, particularly students, about their rights and responsibilities as consumers and creators of digital content can help reduce unintentional infringement and promote a culture of respect for intellectual property.

Case Study: The Music Industry

A notable case study in the intersection of intellectual property and digital media is the music industry. The advent of digital technologies, such as MP3 encoding and peer-to-peer file sharing, revolutionized the way music was produced, distributed, and consumed. The industry initially struggled to adapt to the new digital landscape, as unauthorized sharing and downloading of music became rampant. However, the music industry has since undergone significant transformations, embracing new business models and technological innovations to protect their intellectual property and meet the changing demands of consumers.

One successful approach has been the development of legal digital music platforms, such as iTunes and Spotify. These platforms offer convenient and affordable access to a vast library of music, providing consumers with a legal alternative to piracy. Additionally, some artists have explored innovative licensing models, such as Creative Commons, to promote their work while still retaining certain rights.

Despite these advances, challenges persist, particularly in the enforcement of copyright and the fair compensation of artists. Continued efforts are needed to strike a balance between protecting the rights of content creators and ensuring that consumers have access to diverse and affordable digital media.

Conclusion

The intersection of intellectual property and digital media presents both opportunities and challenges. While digital technologies have revolutionized the creation, distribution, and consumption of media, they have also disrupted traditional models of intellectual property protection. Finding solutions that balance the rights of creators and users, foster innovation, and respect cultural diversity is critical in shaping the future of intellectual property in the digital age. By embracing ethical practices, embracing technological advancements, and strengthening legal frameworks, we can navigate the intricacies of intellectual property in the digital realm and promote a vibrant and inclusive digital media landscape.

Cultural Perspectives on Digital Media and Education

Cultural Contexts of Digital Education

Digital Divide and Educational Inequality

The digital divide refers to the gap between those who have access to digital technology and those who do not. This divide is not only limited to access to hardware and internet connectivity but also encompasses the skills and knowledge required to effectively navigate and utilize digital media. In the context of education, the digital divide can significantly contribute to educational inequality.

Understanding the Digital Divide

In today's digital age, access to technology has become increasingly important for educational success. Students who have access to digital devices, such as computers and tablets, and reliable internet connection have a greater advantage in terms of accessing information, engaging in online learning platforms, and collaborating with peers. On the other hand, students without such access face numerous challenges that can hinder their educational progress.

The digital divide is a complex issue influenced by various factors including socioeconomic status, geographic location, and infrastructure. Low-income communities and marginalized populations are disproportionately affected by the digital divide, exacerbating existing educational inequalities. Students from disadvantaged backgrounds often lack the necessary resources to acquire digital devices, subscribe to internet services, or receive adequate training in digital literacy skills.

Impact on Educational Inequality

The digital divide perpetuates educational inequality by limiting the opportunities available to students from marginalized communities. Here are several key ways in which the digital divide affects educational outcomes:

1. Limited access to information: Students without digital technology may struggle to access up-to-date information and resources available online. This can put them at a disadvantage compared to their peers who can easily access a vast range of educational materials.

2. Unequal learning opportunities: Online learning platforms and educational resources are becoming increasingly common in modern education. Students who lack access to digital technology may miss out on these opportunities, leading to a disparity in educational experiences.

3. Reduced digital literacy skills: Digital literacy skills are essential in the digital age, encompassing the ability to conduct online research, critically evaluate information, and utilize various digital tools. Students without access to digital technology may lack the opportunity to develop these vital skills, further widening the gap between them and their digitally literate peers.

4. Limited collaboration and communication: Digital media provides platforms for collaboration and communication among students and educators. Students without access to these tools may face challenges in participating in online discussions, group projects, or receiving instant feedback from their teachers.

Addressing the Digital Divide

Addressing the digital divide requires efforts from various stakeholders, including governments, educational institutions, and community organizations. Here are some strategies to reduce educational inequality caused by the digital divide:

1. Access to hardware and internet: Ensuring that all students have access to digital devices and internet connectivity is crucial. Governments can implement policies to provide subsidies or grants for students from low-income backgrounds, while institutions can offer computer labs and internet access in schools and libraries.

2. Digital literacy training: Alongside access to technology, it is necessary to provide training and support in developing digital literacy skills. Offering workshops, training programs, or online courses can help students and educators become proficient in utilizing digital tools effectively.

3. Curriculum integration: Integrating digital literacy skills into the curriculum can help bridge the gap. Teachers can incorporate digital media into their teaching

CULTURAL CONTEXTS OF DIGITAL EDUCATION

methods, fostering digital creativity and critical thinking skills among students.

4. Community partnerships: Collaborating with community organizations and businesses can expand access to technology and provide resources to underserved populations. Initiatives such as providing discounted or free internet service in public spaces or offering refurbished devices can make a significant impact.

Case Study: One Laptop per Child

One notable initiative that aimed to address the digital divide in education is the One Laptop per Child (OLPC) project. The OLPC project aimed to provide low-cost laptops to children in developing countries, enabling them to access educational resources and learn essential digital skills. This project demonstrated the potential of technology in bridging educational gaps and empowering students in underserved communities.

Conclusion

The digital divide plays a significant role in perpetuating educational inequality. Bridging this divide requires concerted efforts to provide equal access to digital technology and ensure that students from marginalized communities have the opportunity to develop essential digital literacy skills. By addressing the digital divide, we can work towards creating a more equitable educational system that empowers all students to thrive in the digital age.

Cultural Factors in Digital Literacy

Digital literacy is the ability to use, understand, and evaluate digital technologies in an informed and critical manner. It encompasses a range of skills, including basic computer literacy, information literacy, media literacy, and critical thinking. However, digital literacy is not solely a technical skill; it is also influenced by cultural factors that shape how individuals engage with and make sense of digital technologies.

Cultural Dimensions of Digital Literacy

Cultural factors play a crucial role in shaping digital literacy. Different cultures have varying attitudes, values, and practices regarding technology use, which can affect how individuals acquire and engage with digital skills. Understanding these cultural dimensions is essential for promoting effective digital literacy education.

CULTURAL PERSPECTIVES ON DIGITAL MEDIA AND EDUCATION

Attitudes towards Technology Cultural attitudes towards technology can influence the level of digital literacy within a society. For example, in some cultures, there may be a belief that digital technologies are disruptive or detrimental to traditional practices. This can create barriers to embracing digital literacy and hinder the adoption of new technologies. On the other hand, cultures that embrace technological innovation may foster a more positive attitude towards digital literacy, leading to higher levels of engagement and proficiency.

Digital Divide and Access The digital divide refers to the unequal access to digital technologies and the internet based on factors such as socioeconomic status, geography, and cultural factors. Cultural norms and values can affect disparities in digital access and skills. For instance, technological advancements may be more readily embraced in societies that prioritize and invest in digital infrastructure and education. Addressing the digital divide requires an understanding of cultural barriers that contribute to unequal access and working toward bridging those gaps.

Cultural Considerations for Digital Literacy Education

To promote digital literacy in culturally diverse contexts, it is important to consider cultural factors in the design and implementation of digital literacy education programs. Here are some strategies and considerations:

Culturally-Responsive Pedagogy Culturally-responsive pedagogy recognizes and values the cultural backgrounds, experiences, and identities of learners. In the context of digital literacy education, culturally-responsive pedagogy involves tailoring instructional approaches to learners' cultural contexts and integrating culturally relevant examples and materials. This approach promotes engagement, relevance, and inclusivity, helping learners to connect their cultural identities with digital literacy skills.

Local Language and Content Language is an important aspect of cultural identity. Digital literacy education should consider the language preferences and proficiency of learners. Providing instructional materials and resources in learners' native languages can enhance comprehension and engagement. Incorporating culturally-relevant content and examples also helps learners connect digital skills to their own cultural contexts, making the learning experience more meaningful and relevant.

CULTURAL CONTEXTS OF DIGITAL EDUCATION

Participatory Learning   Engaging learners actively in the learning process can enhance their digital literacy skills.   Adopting a participatory learning approach allows learners to apply digital skills in authentic contexts and encourages collaboration and knowledge-sharing. This approach recognizes that learners bring diverse knowledge and experiences to the learning environment, fostering a sense of ownership and empowerment.

Case Study: Cultural Factors in Digital Literacy Education in Rural Communities

In rural communities, cultural factors can significantly influence digital literacy education.   Limited access to resources, traditional lifestyles, and lower levels of technology adoption may pose challenges to digital literacy initiatives. However, cultural strengths and values can also be leveraged to enhance digital literacy education in these contexts.

For example, in some rural communities deeply rooted in oral traditions, incorporating storytelling and oral history can serve as a bridge between the traditional and digital worlds. Digital literacy programs can teach community members how to use digital tools to document and share their cultural stories, preserving their heritage while acquiring new digital skills.

Additionally, recognizing the importance of local customs, traditions, and indigenous knowledge can help design digital literacy programs that resonate with rural communities. This inclusivity and cultural sensitivity can foster a sense of pride and ownership among learners, motivating them to embrace digital literacy as a means of preserving and promoting their cultural heritage.

Conclusion

Cultural factors significantly influence digital literacy, shaping individuals' attitudes, access, and engagement with digital technologies. Recognizing and addressing these cultural dimensions is essential for promoting effective and inclusive digital literacy education.   By incorporating culturally-responsive pedagogical approaches, providing local language and content, and leveraging participatory learning methods, educators can create more meaningful and relevant digital literacy experiences for diverse learners. Understanding and catering to the cultural factors in digital literacy education empowers individuals to fully participate in the digital age, while preserving and celebrating their cultural identities.

Culturally-responsive Pedagogy and Digital Learning

Culturally-responsive pedagogy is an approach to education that recognizes and values the diverse cultural backgrounds and experiences of students. It aims to create an inclusive and empowering learning environment that acknowledges the contributions of all students and promotes their academic success. In the context of digital learning, culturally-responsive pedagogy seeks to leverage digital technologies to support culturally relevant teaching and learning experiences. This section explores the principles, strategies, and challenges of culturally-responsive pedagogy in the digital age.

Principles of Culturally-responsive Pedagogy

Culturally-responsive pedagogy is based on several foundational principles that guide the design and implementation of instructional strategies. These principles include:

1. Cultural awareness: Educators need to develop an understanding of their students' cultural backgrounds, including their values, beliefs, and traditions. This awareness helps teachers recognize the diversity of experiences and perspectives that students bring to the classroom.

2. Equity and inclusion: Culturally-responsive pedagogy aims to create an equitable and inclusive learning environment where every student feels valued and respected. It challenges the notion of a "one-size-fits-all" approach to education and recognizes the importance of accommodating different learning styles and cultural practices.

3. Culturally-relevant curriculum: The curriculum should be designed to reflect and incorporate the cultural experiences and perspectives of the students. It should include materials and resources that are culturally diverse, relevant, and representative of the students' backgrounds.

4. Student-centered learning: Culturally-responsive pedagogy emphasizes engaging students in the learning process and empowering them to take an active role in their education. It fosters student agency, self-reflection, and critical thinking skills.

Strategies for Culturally-responsive Digital Learning

Integrating digital technologies into culturally-responsive pedagogy offers unique opportunities to engage students and facilitate their learning. Here are some strategies for implementing culturally-responsive digital learning:

CULTURAL CONTEXTS OF DIGITAL EDUCATION

1. Multimodal and multimedia resources: Use a variety of digital resources, such as videos, interactive websites, and audio recordings, that represent diverse cultural perspectives and experiences. This allows students to engage with content in different ways and encourages their active participation.

2. Collaborative online discussions: Create online discussion platforms, such as forums or chat rooms, where students can share their perspectives, engage in dialogue, and learn from one another. Encourage students to reflect on their own cultural backgrounds and create a respectful and inclusive space for diverse viewpoints.

3. Culturally-relevant project-based learning: Design project-based learning activities that connect students' cultural identities and experiences with real-world problems or challenges. For example, students could research and propose solutions to issues related to cultural preservation, environmental sustainability, or social justice.

4. Digital storytelling: Encourage students to create digital stories that reflect their cultural experiences, values, or traditions. This can be done through multimedia presentations, blogs, or podcast episodes. Provide opportunities for students to share their stories with their peers and wider audiences to foster understanding and appreciation of different cultures.

Challenges and Considerations

Implementing culturally-responsive pedagogy in the digital age also presents challenges and considerations that educators need to address. Some of these challenges include:

1. Access and connectivity: Not all students have equal access to digital technologies and the internet, which can create inequities in accessing culturally-responsive digital learning resources. Educators need to consider strategies to ensure all students have equitable access and connectivity.

2. Digital divide: The digital divide refers to the unequal distribution of digital technologies and skills based on socioeconomic factors. Educators should be aware of this divide and provide support and resources to bridge the gap and ensure all students can participate fully in digitally-enhanced culturally-responsive learning.

3. Cultural sensitivity: While digital technologies can enhance learning experiences, it is essential to ensure digital resources and tools are culturally sensitive and do not perpetuate stereotypes or biases. Educators should critically evaluate and select digital resources that accurately represent diverse cultural perspectives.

170 CULTURAL PERSPECTIVES ON DIGITAL MEDIA AND EDUCATION

4. Ethical considerations: As with any digital learning environment, educators need to address ethical considerations, such as privacy, security, and digital citizenship. It is crucial to teach students about responsible and ethical digital practices, including respect for cultural diversity and intellectual property rights.

Example: Culturally-responsive Digital Learning in a Global History Course

In a global history course, an educator implements culturally-responsive digital learning strategies to engage students in exploring different historical perspectives. The educator incorporates the following activities:

1. Virtual museum tour: Students explore virtual museums that showcase artifacts and artworks from various cultures and historical periods. They critically analyze the exhibits and discuss the cultural, social, and historical contexts of these artifacts.

2. Online discussion board: The educator creates an online discussion board where students can share personal stories, family traditions, or historical events from their own cultural backgrounds. Students engage in respectful dialogue and expand their understanding of diverse cultural perspectives.

3. Digital storytelling project: Students research historical events from multiple cultural perspectives and create digital stories that represent these perspectives. They use multimedia tools to bring their stories to life, incorporating images, videos, and narration.

Through these activities, students develop a deeper understanding of global history by recognizing and appreciating the diverse cultural perspectives that shape historical events. They engage in critical thinking, collaboration, and self-expression, while also promoting cultural awareness and inclusivity.

Resources and Further Readings

- Banks, J. A. (2015). Cultural diversity and education: Foundations, curriculum, and teaching (6th ed.). Routledge.

- Ladson-Billings, G. (1995). Toward a theory of culturally relevant pedagogy. American Educational Research Journal, 32(3), 465-491.

- Digital Promise: Culturally Responsive Teaching and Learning. Retrieved from: `https://digitalpromise.org/initiative/culturally-responsive-teaching-and-learning/`

- Edutopia: Culturally Responsive Teaching. Retrieved from: https://www.edutopia.org/article/ culturally-responsive-teaching-resources
- ISTE: Culturally Responsive Teaching and Learning. Retrieved from: https://www.iste.org/explore/ Culturally-Responsive-Teaching-and-Learning

Challenges and Opportunities of Digital Media in Education

Cultural Appropriation in Educational Technology

Cultural appropriation is a complex issue that has gained significant attention in recent years. It refers to the adoption or use of elements from another culture by members of a dominant culture, often without understanding or respecting the original context and meaning. In the context of educational technology, cultural appropriation occurs when technologies are developed and used in ways that exploit or misrepresent the cultural traditions and knowledge of marginalized groups. It can perpetuate stereotypes, reinforce power imbalances, and hinder educational equity.

One example of cultural appropriation in educational technology is the use of culturally specific imagery and symbols without proper understanding or context. For instance, using sacred indigenous symbols or images in a gamified learning app without recognizing their cultural significance or seeking permission from the respective community can be deeply disrespectful. It reduces cultural symbols to mere decorative elements, eroding their value and meaning.

Another example is the development of language learning applications that tokenize and commodify languages and cultures. Some apps may prioritize widely spoken or economically valuable languages over marginalized or endangered languages. By doing so, they perpetuate existing power dynamics and reinforce the dominance of certain cultures while marginalizing others.

To address issues of cultural appropriation in educational technology, it is essential to adopt a culturally responsive approach. This approach involves recognizing and valuing the diverse cultural backgrounds of learners, integrating cultural knowledge and perspectives into educational content and technology, and promoting respectful engagement with cultures.

Educational technology designers and developers can begin by conducting thorough research and consultation with communities when incorporating cultural elements into their products. This includes seeking permission, collaborating with community members, and ensuring accurate representation and interpretation of cultural symbols, languages, and traditions.

Furthermore, it is crucial to prioritize the inclusion of diverse perspectives and voices in the design and development process. This can be achieved by involving representatives from marginalized communities in decision-making, consulting with cultural experts, and engaging in ongoing dialogue to address concerns and opportunities for improvement.

To foster a culturally responsive educational technology environment, it is essential to provide training and professional development for educators. They need to develop cross-cultural competence and understanding to create inclusive and respectful learning environments that honor diversity and promote cultural exchange.

In addition to addressing cultural appropriation, it is crucial to consider issues of access and equity in the development and implementation of educational technology. The digital divide, which refers to disparities in access to and use of technology, often disproportionately affects marginalized communities. Therefore, developers should strive to design technologies that are accessible and affordable to all learners, regardless of their cultural or socioeconomic background.

In conclusion, cultural appropriation in educational technology poses significant challenges to creating inclusive and equitable learning environments. By adopting a culturally responsive approach, involving marginalized communities, and prioritizing accessibility, we can work towards developing educational technologies that honor cultural diversity while promoting educational equity. It is crucial to consider the power dynamics and implications of our design choices and ensure that our technologies are respectful, accurate, and inclusive.

Digital Media and Multimodal Learning

Digital media has revolutionized the way we learn and interact with information. In the context of education, digital media offers a multitude of opportunities for engaging and immersive learning experiences. One such approach is multimodal learning, which combines various modes of communication, such as text, images, audio, and video, to enhance the learning process. In this section, we will explore the concept of multimodal learning in digital media and discuss its benefits, challenges, and potential applications.

CHALLENGES AND OPPORTUNITIES OF DIGITAL MEDIA IN EDUCATION

Understanding Multimodal Learning

Multimodal learning recognizes that individuals have different learning styles and preferences. Some learners may benefit more from visual stimuli, while others may prefer auditory or kinesthetic experiences. By incorporating multiple modes of communication, multimodal learning seeks to cater to diverse learning needs and maximize learning outcomes.

In the digital media context, multimodal learning involves integrating different forms of media to deliver educational content. This can include presenting information through videos, interactive simulations, infographics, animations, and collaborative online platforms. The goal is to create a rich learning environment that engages learners through multiple senses and channels of communication.

Benefits of Multimodal Learning in Digital Media

Multimodal learning offers several benefits for learners in the digital age. Here are some key advantages:

- **Enhanced Engagement:** Multimodal learning promotes active engagement by providing interactive and dynamic learning experiences. Learners can actively participate in activities, simulations, and experiments, which can increase their motivation and interest in the subject matter.

- **Improved Comprehension:** Different modes of communication reinforce learning by appealing to different senses and cognitive processes. Visual aids help learners visualize complex concepts, while audio components provide additional explanations and reinforce key ideas. This multi-sensory approach enhances comprehension and retention.

- **Catering to Diverse Learning Styles:** Multimodal learning accommodates various learning preferences, allowing learners to engage with content through their preferred modality. Visual learners can benefit from diagrams and charts, while auditory learners can listen to podcasts or lectures. This personalized approach enhances the learning experience for all students.

- **Promoting Creativity and Critical Thinking:** Incorporating multimedia elements challenges learners to think creatively and critically. They can analyze, synthesize, and evaluate information from different sources, stimulating higher-order thinking skills. This promotes a deeper understanding of the subject matter.

174 *CULTURAL PERSPECTIVES ON DIGITAL MEDIA AND EDUCATION*

- **Accessible Learning Opportunities:** Digital media and multimodal learning provide accessible learning opportunities for diverse learners. Digital content can be easily modified to accommodate learners with disabilities, such as providing transcripts for audio content or alternative text for images. This promotes inclusivity and ensures that all learners have equal access to educational resources.

Challenges of Multimodal Learning in Digital Media

While multimodal learning offers numerous benefits, educators and learners may encounter challenges when implementing this approach. Here are some key challenges and considerations:

- **Technical Infrastructure:** Multimodal learning heavily relies on digital technology and infrastructure. Educational institutions need to ensure that they have the necessary equipment, software, and internet connectivity to support multimedia-rich learning experiences. Lack of access to technology can hinder the implementation of multimodal learning.

- **Content Creation and Curation:** Creating and curating high-quality multimodal content requires time, expertise, and resources. Educators need to possess digital literacy skills and multimedia production knowledge to design effective learning materials. Additionally, there is a need to select and assess appropriate digital resources to ensure their relevance and accuracy.

- **Digital Divide:** The digital divide, referring to the gap between those who have access to digital technology and those who do not, can create inequalities in multimodal learning. Learners from disadvantaged backgrounds may not have the same access to digital devices or internet connectivity, limiting their ability to engage in multimodal learning experiences. Bridging the digital divide is essential to ensure equitable access to education.

- **Information Overload:** With the vast amount of digital media available, learners may face information overload and find it challenging to navigate through the abundance of resources. Educators play a crucial role in guiding learners and helping them develop critical digital literacy skills to evaluate the quality and relevance of digital content.

Applications of Multimodal Learning in Digital Media

Multimodal learning is applicable across various educational disciplines and contexts. Here are a few examples of how multimodal learning can be utilized in different domains:

- **STEM Education:** In science, technology, engineering, and mathematics (STEM) education, multimodal learning can be used to create interactive simulations, virtual experiments, and data visualizations. These immersive experiences enable learners to explore complex concepts, conduct virtual experiments, and analyze real-world data.

- **Language Learning:** Multimodal learning is particularly effective in language learning, where learners can benefit from a variety of media, such as videos, audio clips, and interactive exercises. Digital tools and platforms can facilitate language practice, provide instant feedback on pronunciation and grammar, and offer culturally authentic materials for language immersion.

- **Arts Education:** In arts education, multimodal learning allows learners to delve into different artistic expressions, including visual arts, music, dance, and theater. Digital media enables learners to explore various art forms, appreciate cultural diversity, and even create their own digital artworks using multimedia software.

- **Social Sciences and Humanities:** Multimodal learning can be applied in social sciences and humanities to facilitate critical analysis of historical events, literature, and cultural phenomena. Learners can engage with multimedia resources, such as documentaries, interviews, and interactive timelines, to gain a deeper understanding of complex social issues.

Conclusion

Multimodal learning in digital media offers a powerful approach to engage and support learners in diverse educational contexts. By integrating different modes of communication, educators can create immersive and interactive learning experiences that cater to individual learning preferences and promote deeper understanding. While challenges exist, leveraging digital media and multimodal learning can effectively enhance teaching and learning practices for a wide range of disciplines. It is crucial for educators and institutions to embrace this approach and explore its potential for creating inclusive, engaging, and impactful learning environments.

Digital Media and Cross-cultural Collaborative Learning

Cross-cultural collaborative learning refers to the process of bringing together individuals from different cultural backgrounds to engage in educational activities and achieve shared learning goals. In the context of digital media, cross-cultural collaborative learning harnesses the power of technology to connect learners from diverse cultural contexts and facilitate meaningful interactions and knowledge exchange. This section explores the role of digital media in cross-cultural collaborative learning, the challenges and opportunities it presents, and strategies for effective implementation.

The Role of Digital Media in Cross-cultural Collaborative Learning

Digital media plays a crucial role in facilitating cross-cultural collaborative learning by providing platforms and tools for communication, collaboration, and knowledge sharing. It allows learners from different cultural backgrounds to overcome geographical barriers and engage in virtual interactions, enabling them to gain insights into different perspectives, learn from one another, and develop critical thinking and problem-solving skills.

One of the key benefits of using digital media in cross-cultural collaborative learning is the opportunity for cultural exchange. Through online platforms such as video conferencing, discussion forums, and social media groups, learners can share their cultural experiences, beliefs, and traditions, thereby broadening their understanding of different cultures and fostering appreciation for diversity.

Digital media also enhances collaborative learning by enabling learners to work together on projects and assignments in real-time, regardless of their geographical locations. For example, students from different countries can collaborate on a research project by using cloud-based tools for document sharing, task allocation, and project management. This collaborative approach promotes teamwork, intercultural communication skills, and a deeper understanding of different cultural perspectives.

Furthermore, digital media offers a wide range of multimedia resources, such as online videos, interactive simulations, and educational games, that can be used to enhance cross-cultural collaborative learning. These resources not only cater to different learning styles but also provide opportunities for learners to explore and engage with culturally diverse content, fostering their global awareness and intercultural competence.

Challenges and Opportunities of Digital Media in Cross-cultural Collaborative Learning

While digital media offers numerous opportunities for cross-cultural collaborative learning, it also presents challenges that need to be addressed for effective implementation. Some of the major challenges are:

1. **Technological barriers:** Access to technology and reliable internet connectivity can vary across different cultural contexts. In some cases, learners may not have access to the necessary tools or skills to fully engage in digital media-based collaborative learning. It is essential to ensure equitable access to technology and provide necessary support to all learners, irrespective of their cultural backgrounds.

2. **Language and communication barriers:** Language differences can pose challenges in cross-cultural collaborative learning. Learners may have varying levels of proficiency in a shared language, leading to miscommunication and misunderstanding. It is important to establish clear communication guidelines and provide language support to ensure effective communication and understanding among participants.

3. **Cultural differences:** Cultural norms and values can influence the way learners interact and collaborate. Misunderstandings or conflicts may arise due to differences in communication styles, decision-making processes, or perceptions of authority. Cultural sensitivity and awareness training can help participants navigate these differences and promote a harmonious learning environment.

Despite these challenges, digital media also presents unique opportunities for cross-cultural collaborative learning:

1. **Enhanced cultural understanding:** Digital media allows learners to engage directly with people from different cultural backgrounds, exposing them to diverse perspectives, beliefs, and values. This exposure promotes cultural understanding and empathy, enabling learners to develop a global mindset and appreciate different ways of thinking.

2. **Authentic learning experiences:** Through digital media, learners can access authentic resources and engage in real-life scenarios that reflect the cultural contexts they are studying. This authenticity enhances the quality of cross-cultural collaborative learning, enabling learners to apply their knowledge and skills in meaningful ways.

3. **Increased motivation and engagement:** Digital media provides interactive and personalized learning experiences that can increase learners' motivation and engagement. Collaborating with peers from different cultures, exploring multimedia resources, and utilizing innovative tools fosters an active learning environment that promotes curiosity and critical thinking.

178 *CULTURAL PERSPECTIVES ON DIGITAL MEDIA AND EDUCATION*

Strategies for Effective Cross-cultural Collaborative Learning using Digital Media

To ensure effective cross-cultural collaborative learning using digital media, educators and instructional designers can employ various strategies. Here are some key strategies to consider:

1. **Establish clear learning goals and expectations:** Clearly define the learning goals and expectations of the cross-cultural collaborative learning experience. This includes outlining the specific knowledge, skills, and intercultural competencies that learners are expected to develop.

2. **Foster inclusive and culturally responsive environments:** Create an inclusive learning environment that values and respects the cultural identities, experiences, and perspectives of all participants. Encourage open dialogue, active listening, and empathy to foster cross-cultural understanding and collaboration.

3. **Provide language support:** To overcome language barriers, offer language support resources, such as translation tools, bilingual dictionaries, or language learning platforms. Encourage participants to use simple and concise language while promoting a culture of patience and understanding.

4. **Facilitate structured interactions:** Incorporate structured activities and discussions that encourage cross-cultural interactions and promote collaboration. For example, learners can engage in virtual group projects, online debates, or reflective discussions to exchange ideas and reflect on their own cultural perspectives.

5. **Encourage reflection and self-assessment:** Provide opportunities for learners to reflect on their cross-cultural learning experiences. Encourage self-assessment and self-reflection on personal biases, stereotypes, and assumptions. This enables learners to develop a critical awareness of their own cultural values and biases.

6. **Leverage digital tools and platforms:** Utilize a variety of digital tools and platforms to support cross-cultural collaborative learning. This may include video conferencing tools, online collaboration platforms, social media groups, or virtual reality simulations. Choose tools that are user-friendly, accessible, and align with the learning goals.

7. **Promote intercultural competence:** Incorporate activities and assignments that explicitly promote the development of intercultural competence. This may include research projects on cultural traditions, comparative analysis of cultural practices, or online discussions on global issues. Encourage learners to critically examine cultural perspectives and challenge their own assumptions.

8. **Provide ongoing support and feedback:** Regularly assess and provide

CHALLENGES AND OPPORTUNITIES OF DIGITAL MEDIA IN EDUCATION

feedback on learners' progress in cross-cultural collaborative learning. Offer ongoing support and guidance to address any challenges or concerns that learners may face. This can be done through individual or group mentoring, virtual office hours, or peer-to-peer support networks.

In summary, digital media has the potential to facilitate cross-cultural collaborative learning by connecting learners from diverse cultural backgrounds, providing platforms for communication and collaboration, and offering multimedia resources for knowledge sharing. However, challenges such as technological barriers, language differences, and cultural variations need to be addressed for effective implementation. By employing strategies that foster inclusive environments, provide language support, facilitate structured interactions, and promote intercultural competence, educators can harness the power of digital media to create engaging and transformative cross-cultural collaborative learning experiences.

Practical Strategies for Cultural Perspectives on Digital Media

Promoting Cultural Awareness in Digital Media Design

User Interface Design and Cultural Considerations

User interface design plays a crucial role in shaping the user experience of digital media. It determines how users interact with and navigate through digital platforms, influencing their satisfaction, engagement, and overall perception of the product. However, user interface design cannot be considered in isolation from cultural factors. Cultural considerations must be taken into account to create interfaces that are culturally sensitive and inclusive.

The Role of Culture in User Interface Design

Culture influences individuals' perception, behavior, and preferences. It shapes their values, beliefs, and customs, which in turn impact the way they engage with digital media. User interface designers need to be mindful of the cultural nuances that exist among different user groups to ensure that their designs are effective and inclusive.

Cultural dimensions, such as individualism-collectivism, power distance, uncertainty avoidance, and masculinity-femininity, provide valuable insights into how culture influences user behavior and interaction. For example, individuals from collectivist cultures may prioritize social connections and group harmony, whereas those from individualistic cultures may emphasize personal goals and autonomy. This disparity has implications for how user interfaces can be designed to accommodate different cultural values and needs.

Designing Culturally-Sensitive User Interfaces

To develop user interfaces that are culturally sensitive, designers should consider the following strategies:

1. Cultural Research and User Profiling Conducting cultural research and user profiling helps designers gain a deeper understanding of the target audience. This involves studying cultural norms, values, and practices and identifying user preferences and expectations. Through user profiling, designers can create personas that represent the diverse cultural backgrounds of their users, ensuring that the interface caters to their specific needs.

2. Visual Design and Representation Visual design elements, such as colors, icons, and images, can carry cultural connotations and meanings. Designers must be aware of these cultural associations and select visuals that are appropriate and resonate with the target audience. For example, certain colors may symbolize different emotions or concepts in different cultures. Using culturally appropriate visuals helps create a sense of familiarity and relatability for users.

3. Language Localization Language plays a crucial role in user interface design. To accommodate users from different linguistic backgrounds, designers should prioritize language localization. This involves translating the interface content, adapting it to fit the linguistic and cultural nuances of the target audience. It is important to ensure that translations are accurate and culturally appropriate, taking into account idiomatic expressions, cultural references, and sensitivities.

4. Navigation and Layout Navigation and layout should be intuitive and user-friendly, considering cultural differences in information processing and cognitive styles. For instance, in cultures that read from right to left, designers should adapt the interface layout accordingly. Similarly, navigation patterns may differ based on cultural expectations. Understanding how different cultures approach information organization and sequencing can greatly enhance user experience.

5. Accessibility and Inclusivity User interface design should prioritize accessibility and inclusivity, considering users with different abilities, including those with visual or hearing impairments. Designers should follow best practices to ensure that the interface is perceivable, operable, understandable, and robust for all users. This may involve providing alternative text for visual elements, captions for videos, or adjustable text size and color contrast options.

Case Study: Cross-Cultural User Interface Design in Online Shopping

Let's consider a case study of a user interface for an online shopping platform targeting users from different cultures.

Problem The design team wants to create a user interface that caters to diverse cultural backgrounds, ensuring a seamless online shopping experience for users worldwide.

Solution To design a culturally-sensitive user interface, the team follows a systematic approach:

1. Cultural Research: The team conducts thorough research on cultural preferences, including factors such as color symbolism, product categorization, and payment methods. They identify cultural variations in shopping behaviors and expectations.

2. User Profiling: Based on the research findings, the team creates detailed user profiles representing different cultural backgrounds. These profiles encompass factors such as age, gender, cultural values, and technological literacy, helping to understand users' needs better.

3. Visual Design: Taking into account cultural associations with colors and symbols, the team selects a color scheme and visual elements that are appealing and culturally appropriate for each target audience. They ensure that product images and representations reflect the diversity of the user base.

4. Language Localization: The team translates all interface content into the languages of their target markets. They partner with native speakers to ensure accurate translations that consider cultural nuances and contexts.

5. Navigation and Layout: The team designs navigation and layout that accommodate the reading direction and information hierarchy expected by users from different cultures. They prioritize ease of use and intuitive navigation, making sure that users can find products and complete purchases seamlessly.

6. Accessibility and Inclusivity: The team ensures that the interface is accessible to users with disabilities. They incorporate screen reader compatibility, adjustable font sizes, and high color contrast options to accommodate diverse user needs.

By following this culturally-sensitive design approach, the team creates a user interface that respects and reflects the cultural diversity of their target audience, enhancing the overall shopping experience.

Resources and Further Reading

1. Cultural User Interface Design by Luz Elena Arroyo-López, Juan Antonio Coad-Trainer, and Tito Rojas-Morales.

2. Designing for Culture: Creating User Interfaces for International Markets by Alistair Duggin.

3. "Cross-Cultural Interface Design Guidelines" by International Organization for Standardization (ISO) and International Electrotechnical Commission (IEC).

4. "Cultural Differences in Designing User Interfaces" by Masaaki Kurosu.

5. The Non-Designer's Design Book by Robin Williams (includes general design principles applicable to user interface design).

Key Takeaways

- Culture significantly influences user behavior and preferences, making it essential to consider cultural factors in user interface design. - Cultural research and user profiling help create interfaces that are tailored to the needs and expectations of diverse cultural backgrounds. - Visual design, language localization, navigation, and layout should all be approached with cultural sensitivity in mind. - Accessibility and inclusivity should be prioritized to ensure equitable access to digital platforms for all users. - Case studies and real-world examples can provide valuable insights into the practical application of culturally-sensitive design principles.

Exercises

1. Conduct a cultural analysis of a popular social media platform and identify examples of how the user interface reflects cultural considerations.

2. Choose two different cultures and compare their cultural values and communication styles. Discuss how these differences might impact user interface design.

3. Design a user interface for an e-learning platform that accommodates the needs of both individualistic and collectivist cultures. Consider visual design, language localization, and navigation patterns.

4. Research and analyze a case study of a user interface design that failed to consider cultural sensitivity. Identify the challenges faced and propose solutions for improvement.

5. Reflect on your own cultural background and preferences. How might your cultural values and practices influence your expectations and preferences for user interfaces?

Localization and Culturalization of Digital Products

Localization and culturalization are essential processes in adapting digital products to different cultural contexts. While often used interchangeably, localization and culturalization refer to distinct aspects of adapting digital media to specific cultural settings. Localization involves the translation of content, user interface, and other components to fit the language and cultural preferences of the target audience. Culturalization, on the other hand, goes beyond translation and involves adapting the content, design, and functionality to align with the cultural values, norms, and expectations of the target audience. In this section, we will explore the importance of localization and culturalization in digital product development, discuss challenges and strategies, and provide practical guidelines for achieving effective results.

The Importance of Localization and Culturalization

Localization and culturalization are crucial for ensuring the usability, acceptability, and effectiveness of digital products in different cultural contexts. When a digital product is not properly adapted to a specific culture, users may face difficulties in understanding the content, navigating the interface, or engaging with the functionalities. Such barriers can significantly hinder user adoption and engagement, reducing the product's overall effectiveness.

Localization and culturalization also play a vital role in promoting inclusivity and accessibility. By tailoring digital products to cater to local language, cultural preferences, and user expectations, developers can create a more inclusive and user-friendly experience. This approach helps to bridge the digital divide and ensures equitable access to technology for diverse cultural communities.

Furthermore, localization and culturalization contribute to the success of digital products in global markets. By addressing cultural nuances and preferences, organizations can enhance user satisfaction and gain a competitive edge. It allows companies to establish a stronger presence in different cultural contexts, build trust among local users, and increase market penetration.

Challenges in Localization and Culturalization

Localization and culturalization of digital products present various challenges that organizations must address to achieve effective results. These challenges include linguistic, cultural, technical, and legal considerations.

From a linguistic perspective, translating digital content requires careful attention to idiomatic expressions, linguistic nuances, and cultural references that may not have direct equivalents in the target language. Literal translation often leads to misunderstandings or misinterpretations, which can negatively affect user experience and engagement.

Cultural considerations involve adapting the content and design to align with the cultural values, norms, and sensitivities of the target audience. This requires a deep understanding of the culture, including social customs, etiquette, symbolism, and taboos. Failure to address these cultural nuances can result in offensive or inappropriate content that may damage the reputation of the digital product and the organization behind it.

Technical challenges arise when adapting user interfaces, functionalities, and navigational structures to the specific requirements of different cultural contexts. This includes considerations for text direction, input methods, date formats, currency symbols, and measurement units. Additionally, addressing technical challenges related to font support, encoding, and compatibility across different platforms and devices is crucial for ensuring seamless user experience.

Legal considerations are vital in the process of localization and culturalization. Organizations need to ensure compliance with local laws, regulations, and industry standards related to data privacy, accessibility, and digital content. Violations of legal requirements can lead to severe consequences, including lawsuits, financial penalties, and reputational damage.

Strategies for Effective Localization and Culturalization

To overcome the challenges mentioned above and achieve effective localization and culturalization of digital products, organizations can follow several strategies:

1. **Cultural Research:** Conduct in-depth research on the target culture, including its values, beliefs, behaviors, and communication styles. This research will provide insights into cultural expectations and help identify areas that require adaptation.

2. **Collaboration with Native Speakers:** Engage native speakers and cultural experts throughout the localization and culturalization process. Their input and feedback will ensure cultural authenticity and accuracy.

3. **Content Adaptation:** Go beyond literal translation by adapting the content to fit the cultural context. This involves modifying idiomatic expressions, analogies, and humor to resonate with the target audience while avoiding offensive or culturally sensitive content.

4. **Design Localization:** Tailor the design elements, color schemes, visuals, and UI/UX components to appeal to the target culture. This includes considering cultural symbols, aesthetics, and visual preferences to create a familiar and engaging experience.

5. **Functional Adaptation:** Customize the functionalities and features of the digital product to meet the specific needs and expectations of the target culture. This may include incorporating local payment methods, integrating region-specific social media platforms, or offering contextually relevant content.

6. **User Testing:** Conduct extensive user testing with representatives from the target culture to gather feedback and identify areas that require improvement. This iterative process ensures that the digital product aligns with user expectations and cultural preferences.

7. **Continuous Improvement:** Regularly update and optimize the localized digital product based on user feedback, cultural shifts, technological advancements, and legal requirements. Localization and culturalization should be ongoing processes to adapt to evolving cultural contexts.

Case Study: Localization of a Social Media Platform

To illustrate the importance of localization and culturalization, let's consider the case of a social media platform expanding into a new cultural market. The platform aims to attract users from a specific country with its unique language, traditions, and cultural context.

In the process of localization, the social media platform first conducts cultural research to understand the target culture's social norms, communication styles, and existing social media habits. Through this research, the platform identifies key cultural considerations, such as the preference for hierarchical communication, the importance of privacy, and the popularity of regional influencers.

Based on the research findings, the platform adapts its user interface by incorporating the language and linguistic expressions commonly used in the target country. It also ensures that the design elements, such as color schemes and visuals, resonate with the cultural aesthetics and preferences of the users.

In terms of functional adaptation, the platform integrates local payment methods, supports region-specific social media platforms, and tailors the content recommendation algorithms to promote popular local influencers and relevant cultural content.

Throughout the localization process, the platform collaborates with native speakers and cultural experts to ensure cultural authenticity and accuracy. It also conducts extensive user testing with representatives from the target culture to gather feedback and fine-tune the localized experience.

By following these strategies and investing in effective localization and culturalization, the social media platform successfully establishes a strong presence in the new cultural market. It gains popularity among local users, fosters a sense of belonging, and enhances user engagement through a culturally tailored experience.

Conclusion

Localization and culturalization are integral aspects of digital product development. By adapting digital products to different cultural contexts, organizations can enhance user experience, promote inclusivity, and gain a competitive edge in global markets. However, localization and culturalization present unique challenges that require careful consideration and strategic approaches. By conducting cultural research, collaborating with native speakers, adapting content and design, and engaging in continuous improvement, organizations can overcome these challenges and create digital products that successfully resonate with diverse cultural audiences.

Inclusive Design and Accessible Digital Media

In this section, we will explore the principles and practices of inclusive design and accessible digital media. Inclusive design refers to the process of creating products, systems, and services that can be used by people with a wide range of abilities, disabilities, and cultural backgrounds. Accessible digital media, on the other hand, involves designing content and technology in a way that allows people with disabilities to perceive, understand, navigate, and interact with digital media effectively.

Importance of Inclusive Design and Accessible Digital Media

Inclusive design and accessible digital media are essential to ensure equal access and participation in the digital age. With the ever-increasing reliance on digital technologies for communication, education, entertainment, and commerce, it is critical to consider the needs of all individuals, including those with disabilities.

By adopting inclusive design principles and making digital media accessible, we can break down barriers and empower individuals with disabilities to fully engage with digital content. This not only enhances their quality of life and supports their independence but also promotes their inclusion and diversity in the digital society.

Principles of Inclusive Design

Inclusive design follows several key principles:

1. **Diverse User Representation:** Design should consider the needs, preferences, and capabilities of a wide range of users, accounting for various abilities, disabilities, ages, cultural backgrounds, and language skills.

2. **Flexibility and Customization:** Design should allow users to customize and adapt digital media to their individual needs and preferences. This includes adjustable color schemes, font sizes, contrast levels, and alternative input methods.

3. **Simplicity and Clarity:** Design should be simple, intuitive, and easy to understand. Clear and concise language, logical navigation, and consistent interaction patterns are essential for promoting accessibility.

4. **Perceptibility and Feedback:** Design should ensure that content is perceivable through multiple senses, such as visual, auditory, and tactile modalities. Providing feedback and guidance is crucial to assist users in understanding their actions and the system's response.

5. **Error Prevention and Recovery:** Design should minimize the occurrence of errors and provide effective mechanisms for users to correct or recover from mistakes. Clear error messages, undo functionalities, and the prevention of critical errors are important considerations.

6. **Inclusive Collaboration:** Design should be developed through inclusive and diverse collaborative processes. Involving people with disabilities and diverse perspectives in the design and testing phases ensures that their needs are understood and addressed appropriately.

Accessible Digital Media Guidelines

To ensure accessibility in digital media, various guidelines and standards have been developed. The Web Content Accessibility Guidelines (WCAG) are widely recognized and provide a comprehensive framework for web accessibility. WCAG covers a wide range of aspects, including perceivability, operability, understandability, and robustness of digital content.

Some key guidelines for accessible digital media include:

+ Providing alternative text descriptions for images, videos, and other non-text content to ensure they can be understood by individuals who are visually impaired or using screen readers.

+ Designing web pages and applications that can be navigated using a keyboard alone, as some individuals may have difficulty using a mouse or other pointing devices.

+ Using clear and consistent heading structures, lists, and captions to facilitate content comprehension for individuals using screen readers or text-to-speech technologies.

+ Ensuring the color contrast between text and background meets accessibility standards, as low contrast makes it challenging for individuals with low vision or color blindness to read the content.

+ Providing transcripts and captions for audio and video content to enable individuals with hearing impairments to understand the information conveyed.

Challenges and Solutions

While inclusive design and accessible digital media are crucial, they do present challenges in practice. Some common challenges include:

+ **Technical Constraints:** Designing for accessibility requires an understanding of various technologies, standards, and coding techniques. Ensuring compatibility across different platforms and devices can be complex.

+ **Awareness and Education:** Many designers and developers may not be aware of accessibility guidelines or the needs of individuals with disabilities. Promoting awareness and providing training on inclusive design practices can help overcome this challenge.

+ **Testing and Evaluation:** Ensuring the accessibility of digital media requires thorough testing with users who have different disabilities. Conducting usability tests and gathering feedback from diverse users can help identify and resolve accessibility issues.

To address these challenges and promote inclusive design and accessible digital media, designers and developers can follow these solutions:

- **Accessibility Tools and Technologies**: Utilize accessibility tools, such as screen readers or color contrast analyzers, to evaluate and ensure compliance with accessibility standards. Incorporate assistive technologies, like voice input or alternative input methods, to enhance accessibility.

- **User-Centered Design Process**: Involve individuals with disabilities throughout the design process to gain insights into their needs and challenges. Conduct user testing and obtain feedback to iteratively improve the accessibility and usability of digital media.

- **Collaboration and Knowledge Sharing**: Engage with the accessibility community, including organizations, forums, and conferences, to share knowledge and best practices. Collaborate with stakeholders, accessibility experts, and people with disabilities to facilitate inclusive design practices.

Best Practices and Resources

To ensure inclusive design and accessible digital media, several best practices can be followed:

- Consider accessibility from the early stages of the design process and involve users with disabilities as active participants.

- Use semantic HTML markup that is compatible with assistive technologies and screen readers.

- Design for device independence and responsive layouts to accommodate various screen sizes and user preferences.

- Provide clear instructions, error messages, and help documentation to guide users with disabilities.

- Regularly test and evaluate digital media for accessibility compliance and address any identified issues promptly.

Additionally, there are several resources available to support inclusive design and accessible digital media:

PRACTICAL STRATEGIES FOR CULTURAL PERSPECTIVES ON
DIGITAL MEDIA

- ✦ Web Content Accessibility Guidelines (WCAG): The WCAG provides detailed guidelines for web accessibility and is a valuable resource for designers and developers. It can be accessed at `https://www.w3.org/WAI/standards-guidelines/wcag/`.

- ✦ Assistive Technology: Understanding the capabilities and limitations of assistive technologies, such as screen readers, voice recognition software, and alternative input devices, is essential for designing accessible digital media. Resources on assistive technology can be found at `https://www.assistivetechnology.org/`.

- ✦ Accessibility Evaluation Tools: Various tools are available to evaluate the accessibility of digital media. Examples include the Wave Accessibility Evaluation Tool (`https://wave.webaim.org/`) and the aXe accessibility testing toolkit (`https://www.deque.com/axe/`).

- ✦ Inclusive Design Guidelines: Organizations such as the Inclusive Design Research Centre offer guidelines and resources for inclusive design. An example is the Inclusive Design Guide (`https://guide.inclusivedesign.ca/`).

Conclusion

Inclusive design and accessible digital media are vital for ensuring equal access and participation in the digital space. By embracing the principles of inclusive design, following accessibility guidelines, and addressing challenges through collaboration and user-centered design, we can create digital media that is accessible to all individuals, regardless of their abilities or disabilities. The resources and best practices provided here serve as a foundation for designing digital media that promotes diversity, inclusivity, and equitable access for everyone.

Ethical Guidelines for Digital Media Practices

Cultural Appropriation and Digital Media Ethics

Cultural appropriation refers to the adoption or use of elements from another culture, often by members of a dominant culture, without proper understanding and respect for the original cultural context. In the digital media landscape, cultural appropriation can manifest in various ways, such as using cultural symbols, images, music, or fashion without proper acknowledgment or permission.

ETHICAL GUIDELINES FOR DIGITAL MEDIA PRACTICES

9.2.1.1 Understanding Cultural Appropriation

To understand cultural appropriation, it is essential to recognize the power dynamics at play. Dominant cultures often appropriate elements of marginalized or oppressed cultures, perpetuating stereotypes, erasing cultural significance, and reinforcing power imbalances. Digital media platforms, with their global reach and instantaneous dissemination, have made cultural appropriation more visible and widespread than ever before.

Cultural appropriation can occur both explicitly and implicitly. Explicit appropriation involves conscious and intentional borrowing, often for profit or personal gain, while implicit appropriation may occur unknowingly or unintentionally due to ignorance or lack of cultural sensitivity.

9.2.1.2 Ethical Implications of Cultural Appropriation

Ethical issues arise when cultural appropriation occurs in digital media. Using cultural elements without respect for their history and significance can lead to misrepresentation, distortion, and commodification of cultural practices. This undermines the identities and experiences of the cultures being appropriated, reinforcing harmful stereotypes and contributing to cultural erasure.

Cultural appropriation can result in economic exploitation by profiting from the cultural elements without benefiting the communities from which they originate. Moreover, it can perpetuate power imbalances by reinforcing the dominant culture's control over the narrative and representation of marginalized cultures.

9.2.1.3 Protecting Cultures and Respecting Intellectual Property

Respecting cultural appropriation in digital media involves establishing ethical guidelines for content creators, platforms, and users. Some strategies to protect cultures and respect intellectual property include:

1. Research and Education: Content creators should conduct thorough research to understand the cultural significance and contextual meaning of the elements they intend to use. Education about cultural diversity and sensitivity is crucial to avoid unintentional appropriation.

2. Collaboration and Attribution: Collaboration with members of the culture being portrayed can provide valuable insights and ensure accurate representation. Proper attribution should be given to the source culture, acknowledging and honoring its contributions.

3. Permission and Consent: Seeking permission and obtaining proper consent from the cultural community before using their symbols, traditions, or expressions is essential. This promotes mutual respect and reduces the risk of appropriation.

4. Fair Compensation: When cultural elements are used for commercial purposes, fair compensation should be provided to the originating culture to support their community and preserve their traditions.

5. Cultural Exchange: Encouraging a genuine exchange of ideas, knowledge, and experiences between cultures promotes understanding and appreciation without appropriation. Establishing platforms that facilitate respectful dialogue can bridge the gap between cultures.

9.2.1.4 Examples and Case Studies

To illustrate the concept of cultural appropriation in digital media, let's consider a few examples:

Example 1: Fashion Industry and Indigenous Cultures The fashion industry has often faced criticism for appropriating traditional designs, fabrics, and symbols from indigenous cultures without proper acknowledgment or benefit to the communities. This undermines the cultural significance of these elements and reduces them to mere fashion trends. Digital media platforms have amplified these discussions and facilitated conversations on cultural misappropriation.

Example 2: Use of Sacred Symbols in Digital Art Artists who incorporate sacred symbols or religious iconography from different cultures into their digital artwork without understanding the cultural and spiritual context can be seen as appropriating those symbols. This not only disrespects the original meaning but can also offend and alienate communities that hold those symbols sacred.

9.2.1.5 Resources and Best Practices

Various resources and best practices can assist content creators and digital media practitioners in addressing cultural appropriation:

1. UNESCO Guidelines on the Use of Cultural Expressions: These guidelines provide a policy framework for respecting cultural diversity and promoting the rights of creators and communities involved in cultural expressions.

2. Creative Commons Licenses: Using Creative Commons licenses allows content creators to indicate how others can use their work while respecting cultural attribution and intellectual property rights.

3. Ethical Style Guide: Developing an ethical style guide specifically tailored to digital media can help content creators navigate potential cultural appropriation pitfalls. This guide can include principles, examples, and guidelines on respectful representation.

4. Indigenous Intellectual Property Rights Organizations: Collaboration with organizations representing indigenous communities, such as the World Intellectual Property Organization's Traditional Knowledge Division, can provide guidance on respectful use of indigenous cultural expressions.

9.2.1.6 Exercises

1. Research and select a case study of cultural appropriation in digital media. Analyze the ethical implications and propose alternative practices that respect the culture in question. 2. Develop a content creation guideline for a digital platform

ETHICAL GUIDELINES FOR DIGITAL MEDIA PRACTICES 195

to ensure respectful representation and avoid cultural appropriation. 3. Create a digital media campaign that raises awareness about cultural appropriation, targeting a specific audience or community.

Remember, when engaging with cultural appropriation, it is essential to approach the topic with sensitivity, awareness, and a willingness to learn and respect the cultures involved. Respecting the origins and cultural significance of elements used in digital media can contribute to a more inclusive and ethically responsible digital landscape.

Responsible Content Creation and Digital Media Ethics

Responsible content creation and digital media ethics are crucial aspects of cultural perspectives on digital media. In a digital landscape where information spreads rapidly and has far-reaching impacts, it is important for content creators to exercise responsibility and adhere to ethical standards. This section explores the principles and guidelines for responsible content creation and the ethical considerations associated with digital media.

Principles of Responsible Content Creation

Responsible content creation encompasses several principles that guide creators in producing content that is accurate, fair, and respectful:

1. **Accuracy:** It is essential for content creators to strive for accuracy by conducting thorough research, fact-checking, and verifying the information presented in their content. Inaccurate information can lead to the spread of falsehoods and the erosion of trust in digital media.

2. **Fairness:** Content creators should aim for fairness in their content by presenting multiple perspectives, representing diverse voices, and avoiding biased or discriminatory language or depictions. Fair content contributes to a more inclusive and respectful digital media environment.

3. **Integrity:** Creators should maintain integrity in their content by being transparent about their sources, conflicts of interest, and any biases they may have. Transparency helps build trust with the audience and fosters accountability in digital media.

4. **Respect:** It is important for content creators to treat all individuals and groups with respect and dignity. This includes respecting privacy rights,

cultural sensitivities, and avoiding content that promotes hate speech or discrimination.

5. **Responsibility:** Content creators should acknowledge their responsibility to the audience and society at large. This involves considering the potential impact of their content, particularly regarding sensitive topics, and taking measures to minimize harm.

6. **Authenticity:** Authenticity is crucial for content creators to establish credibility and trust with their audience. Creating genuine and original content helps cultivate a positive reputation and fosters meaningful engagement.

Adhering to these principles ensures that digital media content is informative, fair, respectful, and trustworthy.

Ethical Considerations in Digital Media

Ethics play a fundamental role in digital media, shaping the boundaries of acceptable content creation, distribution, and consumption. Several ethical considerations arise in the context of digital media:

1. **Plagiarism and Copyright Infringement:** Content creators must respect intellectual property rights by properly attributing sources and obtaining necessary permissions for using copyrighted material. Plagiarism and copyright infringement undermine the integrity of digital media.

2. **Fake News and Misinformation:** Responsible content creation involves combating fake news and misinformation by verifying sources, cross-checking information, and ensuring that content is based on credible and reliable sources. Content creators have a role in promoting accurate information and combatting the spread of misinformation.

3. **Privacy and Data Protection:** Content creators must respect individuals' privacy rights and handle personal data responsibly. This includes obtaining informed consent for collecting and using personal information and taking measures to protect data from unauthorized access.

4. **Stereotyping and Representation:** Content creators should avoid perpetuating harmful stereotypes or misrepresenting individuals or communities. They should strive for accurate and respectful portrayal, embracing diversity and inclusive representation.

ETHICAL GUIDELINES FOR DIGITAL MEDIA PRACTICES

5. **Transparency and Disclosure:** Authenticity and transparency are crucial ethical considerations. Content creators should disclose any potential conflicts of interest, sponsored content, or advertising, ensuring that their audience can make informed decisions.

Addressing these ethical considerations fosters a more ethical digital media environment that upholds integrity, respects privacy, promotes accurate information, and encourages responsible content creation.

Examples of Responsible Content Creation

To illustrate responsible content creation and digital media ethics, let's consider two examples:

Example 1: A fashion influencer on social media wants to promote sustainable and ethical fashion. They ensure that the content they create follows responsible practices by:

- Researching and verifying the ethical practices of the brands they collaborate with before endorsing their products.

- Disclosing any sponsored content or partnerships, ensuring transparency with their audience.

- Encouraging their followers to make conscious and sustainable fashion choices through educational content and sharing resources.

- Creating diverse and inclusive content that represents different body types, ethnicities, and cultural backgrounds.

Example 2: A news organization aims to provide accurate and unbiased news coverage. They uphold responsible content creation by:

- Conducting thorough research and fact-checking before publishing news articles or sharing information.

- Presenting diverse perspectives on complex issues to ensure fair representation.

- Clearly distinguishing between news and opinion pieces to maintain transparency with their audience.

- Promptly correcting any errors or inaccuracies that may arise in their content.

+ Engaging in open dialogue with their audience and addressing feedback or concerns appropriately.

These examples demonstrate how responsible content creation aligns with ethical considerations, promoting accuracy, fairness, integrity, and respect in digital media.

Tools and Resources for Responsible Content Creation

Content creators can utilize various tools and resources to support responsible content creation and digital media ethics:

+ **Fact-checking tools:** Tools like FactCheck.org, Snopes, and Google Fact Check Explorer can assist in verifying information and combatting misinformation.

+ **Style and ethics guides:** Many news organizations and professional associations provide style guides and ethics codes that outline best practices and ethical standards for content creation.

+ **Image and video verification tools:** Tools such as TinEye, Google Reverse Image Search, and InVID can help verify the authenticity and original source of images and videos.

+ **Privacy protection tools:** Encrypted messaging apps, secure browsing tools, and privacy protection plugins help ensure data privacy and protect personal information.

By leveraging these tools and resources, content creators can enhance responsible content creation and promote ethical practices in digital media.

Exercises

1. Choose a news article and evaluate it based on the principles of responsible content creation. Identify any potential ethical considerations and suggest improvements.

2. Research and analyze a case study where digital media content creators faced ethical dilemmas. Discuss the implications of their actions and propose alternative paths they could have taken.

ETHICAL GUIDELINES FOR DIGITAL MEDIA PRACTICES

3. Create a social media campaign promoting responsible content creation and digital media ethics. Outline the key messages, target audience, and strategies for maximum impact.

Engaging in exercises like these encourages critical thinking and practical application of responsible content creation and digital media ethics principles.

Conclusion

Responsible content creation and digital media ethics are integral to maintaining integrity, accuracy, and fairness in the digital media landscape. Adhering to the principles of responsible content creation, addressing ethical considerations, and utilizing relevant tools and resources can contribute to a more trustworthy and inclusive digital media environment. By promoting responsible content creation, content creators play a vital role in shaping the cultural perspectives on digital media and ensuring its positive impact on society.

Privacy and Security Considerations in Cultural Contexts

Privacy and security are essential considerations in the digital age, and their importance is magnified when viewed through the lens of cultural perspectives. Different cultures have unique norms, values, and expectations regarding privacy and security, which can significantly influence digital media practices and behavior. In this section, we will explore the intersection of privacy, security, and culture in the context of digital media, and discuss practical strategies for ensuring privacy and security in culturally sensitive ways.

Cultural Variations in Privacy and Security Concerns

Privacy and security concerns are not universal. They vary across cultures due to cultural, social, and historical factors. Cultural values and norms shape individuals' attitudes towards privacy and influence their behavior in digital spaces. For example, in collectivist cultures, where group cohesion and social harmony are highly valued, privacy may be perceived differently compared to individualistic cultures that prioritize personal autonomy and freedom.

In some cultures, sharing personal information, opinions, and experiences openly on digital media platforms is the norm. These cultures may have less stringent privacy concerns and place a greater emphasis on collective identity and social connectedness. On the other hand, certain cultures value privacy and personal boundaries to a greater extent, and individuals from these cultures may be more cautious about sharing personal information online.

The cultural variations in privacy and security concerns have implications for digital media design and practices. It is important for designers and developers to take into account cultural differences and ensure that privacy settings and security measures are customizable and adaptable to individual preferences.

Challenges in Privacy and Security in Cultural Contexts

Ensuring privacy and security in cultural contexts comes with its own set of challenges. Cultural norms and expectations may clash with the technological features and functionalities of digital media platforms. For example, in some cultures, sharing personal photos or videos with a limited circle of friends and family is the norm, whereas digital media platforms often encourage public sharing and engagement.

One challenge is the potential for cultural appropriation and misuse of personal data. Cultural appropriation occurs when individuals or groups appropriate elements of another culture without proper understanding, respect, or permission. In the context of digital media, this can manifest as the unauthorized use of cultural symbols, traditions, or expressions. Privacy considerations should extend to protecting cultural heritage or sensitive aspects of a culture from exploitation or misrepresentation.

Another challenge is the digital divide, which refers to the gap in access to and knowledge about digital technologies. In some cultural contexts, certain groups may have limited access to digital media platforms or face barriers in understanding privacy and security settings. Bridging this divide requires not only technological solutions but also educational and awareness-building efforts that are sensitive to cultural differences.

Strategies for Privacy and Security in Cultural Contexts

To address the challenges and ensure privacy and security in cultural contexts, several strategies can be implemented:

1. **Cultural Sensitivity in Design:** Designers and developers should consider cultural norms and values when creating digital media platforms. This involves allowing customization of privacy settings, providing language options, and incorporating culturally appropriate symbols or representations.

2. **User Education and Awareness:** Promoting digital literacy and creating awareness about privacy and security practices are crucial. Information should be

provided in a culturally sensitive manner and tailored to different cultural contexts. This may involve collaborating with local communities, organizations, or cultural ambassadors.

3. Transparency and Consent: Privacy policies and terms of service should be clear and easily understood. Digital media platforms should seek explicit consent when collecting and using user data, and users should have the option to opt-out or modify their privacy settings.

4. Collaborative Approaches: Engaging users from different cultural backgrounds in the design and development process can help identify potential cultural biases and ensure inclusivity. This can be achieved through user feedback, user testing, and conducting research studies within diverse cultural contexts.

5. Regulation and Policy: Governments and policymakers play a significant role in ensuring privacy and security in cultural contexts. Developing and enforcing regulations that protect user privacy and mitigate cultural risks is crucial. Collaboration between policymakers, digital media companies, and cultural experts can help strike a balance between cultural sensitivity and user protection.

Real-world Example: Privacy and Social Media in Japan

In Japan, privacy and security concerns in digital media are heavily influenced by cultural norms of modesty and discretion. The cultural concept of "honne" and "tatemae," which refers to the contrast between a person's true feelings (honne) and the behaviors they publicly exhibit (tatemae), has an impact on how Japanese individuals present themselves online.

Japanese social media platforms often prioritize privacy and allow users to control who can view their content. Many Japanese users prefer closed online communities, such as Mixi or Ameba, where they can share content exclusively with friends and acquaintances. Public sharing of personal information or opinions may be considered inappropriate or unnecessary in Japanese cultural contexts.

This cultural emphasis on privacy has also influenced privacy laws in Japan. The Act on the Protection of Personal Information, enacted in 2005, sets standards for the handling of personal data and emphasizes user consent and transparency.

Understanding cultural nuances and preferences like those in Japan is crucial for digital media companies to design platforms that respect privacy and security while providing engaging experiences.

Further Resources

For further exploration of privacy and security considerations in cultural contexts, consider the following resources:

- Book: "Privacy in Context: Technology, Policy, and the Integrity of Social Life" by Helen Nissenbaum

- Article: "Cultural Considerations in Public Privacy Mechanisms" by Karen Renaud

- Article: "Cultural Considerations in Privacy and Security" by Akio Fujiyoshi

- Website: Electronic Privacy Information Center (www.epic.org)

Conclusion

Privacy and security considerations in digital media cannot be divorced from cultural contexts. Understanding cultural perspectives and adapting digital media practices accordingly is vital to respect individuals' privacy preferences and protect their information. By accounting for cultural variations, recognizing challenges, and implementing culturally sensitive strategies, digital media can foster a more inclusive and secure online environment.

Conclusion: The Future of Cultural Perspectives on Digital Media

Emerging Trends in Cultural Perspectives on Digital Media

Artificial Intelligence and Cultural Communication

Artificial Intelligence (AI) is revolutionizing various aspects of our lives, including communication. It holds immense potential for enhancing cultural communication by bridging gaps, enabling cross-cultural understanding, and facilitating inclusive and dynamic interactions. In this section, we will explore the intersection of AI and cultural communication, discussing the underlying principles, applications, challenges, and future trends.

Principles of Artificial Intelligence

Before delving into the role of AI in cultural communication, let's briefly discuss the principles that underpin AI systems. AI refers to the development of computer systems that can perform tasks that typically require human intelligence. Machine Learning (ML), a subset of AI, enables computers to learn from data and improve their performance over time.

ML algorithms are trained on enormous amounts of data to recognize patterns, make predictions, and generate insights. Deep Learning (DL), a subfield of ML, utilizes neural networks with multiple layers to simulate human brain functioning and achieve more sophisticated tasks. Natural Language Processing

CONCLUSION: THE FUTURE OF CULTURAL PERSPECTIVES ON DIGITAL MEDIA

(NLP) is another vital component of AI, enabling computers to understand, analyze, and generate human language.

Applications of AI in Cultural Communication

AI has diverse applications in cultural communication, fostering understanding and collaboration across different cultures. One key area where AI has made significant contributions is language translation. Advanced translation algorithms powered by AI, such as Google Translate, facilitate multilingual communication by quickly and accurately translating texts or speech in real-time. This technology has immense potential in breaking down language barriers and promoting cross-cultural interactions.

Moreover, AI-powered chatbots and virtual assistants play a crucial role in facilitating cultural communication. These intelligent systems can engage in conversations, provide information, and assist users from various cultural backgrounds. They adapt their responses based on user preferences and context, creating more personalized and culturally sensitive interactions.

AI also plays a vital role in content curation and recommendation. Streaming platforms like Netflix and Spotify leverage AI algorithms to analyze users' cultural preferences, suggesting relevant movies, music, and other content. This not only enhances user experience but also promotes cultural diversity and exposure to different cultural perspectives.

Challenges and Ethical Considerations

While AI technology holds immense potential, there are challenges and ethical considerations associated with its application in cultural communication. One of the significant concerns is biased algorithms. AI systems trained on biased or limited datasets can perpetuate societal biases and stereotypes, leading to cultural misrepresentation or exclusion. This calls for the development of fair and inclusive AI models that consider diverse cultural perspectives.

Another challenge is the loss of human touch in communication. While AI-powered chatbots and virtual assistants can provide efficient and accurate responses, they lack the emotional intelligence and cultural nuances inherent in human communication. Overreliance on AI systems may lead to a diminished understanding and appreciation of diverse cultural practices and norms. Therefore, it is crucial to strike a balance between AI-enabled communication and human interaction.

EMERGING TRENDS IN CULTURAL PERSPECTIVES ON DIGITAL MEDIA

Privacy and data security also pose ethical dilemmas in the context of AI in cultural communication. AI systems collect and process vast amounts of user data, raising concerns about data privacy and potential misuse. It is essential to implement robust privacy policies and ethical guidelines to safeguard user information and ensure transparency in data handling practices.

Future Trends in AI and Cultural Communication

The future of AI in cultural communication holds exciting possibilities. Emerging technologies like augmented reality (AR) and virtual reality (VR) can enhance cultural experiences by creating immersive and interactive environments. For instance, AR and VR applications can enable users to explore cultural landmarks, museums, or historical sites virtually, providing a unique and engaging cultural learning experience.

Furthermore, AI-powered social robots are likely to play a more prominent role in cultural communication. These robots can navigate diverse cultural contexts, understanding and respecting cultural norms, and assisting with language translation or cultural information. They have the potential to bridge cultural gaps, particularly in multicultural settings.

Additionally, AI algorithms can be trained to analyze cultural preferences, behaviors, and trends, providing valuable insights for businesses, policymakers, and researchers. Cultural analytics, powered by AI, can enable a deeper understanding of cultural dynamics, aiding in the development of more culturally responsive products, services, and policies.

Conclusion

AI is revolutionizing cultural communication, offering new opportunities and challenges. With the advancements in AI technologies, we have the potential to bridge cultural gaps, foster cross-cultural understanding, and promote inclusive and dynamic interactions. However, it is crucial to navigate ethical considerations and ensure that AI systems are developed with cultural sensitivity, transparency, and fairness. As we move forward, it is essential to embrace the potential of AI while preserving the human touch and cultural richness that underpins effective communication.

Virtual Reality and Immersive Cultural Experiences

Virtual Reality (VR) technology has rapidly advanced in recent years, providing new ways for individuals to immerse themselves in digital environments and experiences. This section explores the intersection of virtual reality and cultural perspectives, highlighting the potential for VR to enhance our understanding and appreciation of diverse cultures.

Understanding Virtual Reality

Before delving into immersive cultural experiences, let's first establish a foundational understanding of virtual reality. VR refers to the use of computer technology to create a simulated environment that can be experienced and interacted with by an individual. This environment can be completely artificial or a replication of the real world.

VR typically involves the use of head-mounted displays (HMDs) that provide a stereoscopic view and track the user's head movements to create a sense of presence within the virtual environment. Users can explore and interact with this environment through hand controllers, body tracking, and even haptic devices that provide tactile feedback.

Immersive Cultural Experiences

Virtual reality opens up exciting possibilities for experiencing and understanding different cultures. Through immersive VR experiences, individuals can be transported to unfamiliar places, engage with diverse cultural traditions, and gain deeper insights into the lived experiences of others.

1. **Cultural Heritage Preservation:** VR can play a crucial role in preserving cultural heritage by digitally recreating historical sites, monuments, and artifacts that may have been damaged or destroyed. For example, the Palmyra in Syria, a UNESCO World Heritage site damaged by conflict, can be reconstructed virtually, allowing people to explore and learn about its rich history and significance.

2. **Virtual Museums and Exhibitions:** VR technology enables the creation of virtual museums and exhibitions, providing access to cultural artifacts and artworks from around the world. Users can navigate through virtual galleries, examine artifacts up close, and even listen to audio guides that provide cultural context and historical information.

3. **Cultural Immersion and Virtual Travel:** VR enables individuals to "travel" to different countries and immerse themselves in the local culture without leaving their homes. Virtual travel experiences can include visiting landmarks, attending cultural festivals, participating in traditional ceremonies, or exploring natural

EMERGING TRENDS IN CULTURAL PERSPECTIVES ON DIGITAL MEDIA

wonders. This not only enriches one's understanding of different cultures but also fosters a sense of empathy and connection.

4. **Language and Communication:** VR can be utilized as a tool for language learning and cross-cultural communication. Language learners can practice conversational skills with virtual native speakers, providing a safe and immersive environment to improve fluency. Additionally, VR can be used to simulate intercultural communication scenarios, helping individuals develop cultural sensitivity and effective communication skills.

Challenges and Considerations

While virtual reality offers immense potential for immersive cultural experiences, several challenges and considerations need to be addressed:

1. **Authenticity and Representation:** VR experiences should strive for authenticity and accuracy in representing cultural traditions, practices, and artifacts. Collaborating with cultural experts and communities is essential to ensure respectful and accurate portrayals.

2. **Ethical Dilemmas:** The creation and dissemination of VR content may raise ethical dilemmas, particularly concerning the ownership, control, and appropriation of cultural knowledge and artifacts. It is important to engage in ethical discussions and establish guidelines for responsible VR content creation and use.

3. **Accessibility and Inclusivity:** VR technology should be accessible to people from diverse backgrounds, including those with disabilities. Considerations such as adjustable settings for motion sickness, multilingual support, and physical accessibility can enhance inclusivity in immersive experiences.

4. **Digital Divide:** The digital divide, referring to the gap in access to technology, must be addressed to ensure equitable distribution and participation in VR experiences. Efforts should be made to make VR technology and content accessible and affordable to marginalized communities.

Case Study: "Through the Eyes of Another"

To illustrate the potential of virtual reality for immersive cultural experiences, let's explore the case study of "Through the Eyes of Another." This VR experience allows users to step into the shoes of individuals from different cultural backgrounds, enabling them to see the world from diverse perspectives.

Users can choose to embody the experiences of a Maasai tribesperson in Kenya, a young refugee in a war-torn country, or an indigenous artist in the Amazon rainforest. Through a combination of stunning visuals, spatial audio, and

CONCLUSION: THE FUTURE OF CULTURAL PERSPECTIVES ON DIGITAL MEDIA

interactive elements, users can engage with the daily lives, challenges, and triumphs of these individuals.

The immersive nature of VR enables users to empathize with the characters and gain a deeper understanding of their cultural contexts. The experience prompts reflection on one's own identity, biases, and cultural assumptions, fostering greater cultural sensitivity and appreciation.

Resources and Further Exploration

For those interested in delving deeper into the intersection of virtual reality and cultural experiences, here are some suggested resources:

1. *Virtual Reality and Cultural Preservation*: A scholarly article by Zhang et al. (2018) that explores the use of VR in cultural heritage preservation.

2. *Virtual Museums: Advantages, Disadvantages, and Future Perspectives*: A research paper by Prendinger and Metais (2014) that examines the potential of VR in the museum context.

3. *Beyond the Frame: Virtual Reality and Cultural Heritage*: A TEDx talk by Jenna Ng that discusses the transformative power of VR in experiencing cultural heritage.

4. *Virtual Reality for Language Learning*: A book by Chun and Plass (2016) that explores the application of VR in language learning and intercultural communication.

Virtual reality has the power to bridge the gaps of time, distance, and cultural understanding. By providing immersive cultural experiences, VR has the potential to foster empathy, preserve cultural heritage, and promote cross-cultural dialogue. As technology continues to evolve, it is crucial to approach these immersive experiences with respect, ethical considerations, and cautious exploration of their impact on society.

Big Data and Cultural Analytics

Big data and cultural analytics are two interconnected fields that have gained significant importance in the digital era. With the vast amount of data generated through digital media, there is a growing need to analyze and understand the cultural implications of this data. This section explores the concept of big data, its relevance to cultural perspectives on digital media, and the application of cultural analytics to uncover insights from this data.

Understanding Big Data

Big data refers to extremely large and complex datasets that cannot be effectively processed with traditional data processing applications. It is characterized by four key dimensions: volume, variety, velocity, and veracity. The volume refers to the immense amount of data generated, while variety indicates the diverse formats and sources of data. Velocity refers to the high speed at which data is generated, and veracity refers to the quality and reliability of the data.

In the context of digital media, big data encompasses various types of data, including social media posts, online transactions, user-generated content, website clicks, and sensor data. The availability of this data presents exciting opportunities to gain insights into cultural patterns, behaviors, and trends.

Relevance to Cultural Perspectives on Digital Media

Big data has the potential to significantly impact cultural perspectives on digital media. By analyzing large-scale datasets, researchers and practitioners can identify patterns and trends in cultural behavior and preferences. This can help uncover hidden biases, preferences, and cultural nuances that influence digital media consumption and production.

Cultural perspectives on digital media can be enriched by analyzing big data in several ways:

1. **Identifying cultural preferences and trends:** By analyzing large datasets, cultural analytics can identify cultural preferences, trends, and emerging topics in digital media. For example, analyzing social media data can reveal the popularity of cultural movements, the adoption of digital media platforms across different cultural groups, and the dissemination of cultural content.

2. **Understanding cultural influence on content creation:** Big data analysis can provide insights into how cultural factors influence the creation and dissemination of digital content. By analyzing patterns in user-generated content, researchers can understand how cultural identity, values, and norms shape the production and consumption of digital media.

3. **Uncovering cultural biases and stereotypes:** Big data analytics can help uncover cultural biases and stereotypes present in digital media. By analyzing large-scale datasets, researchers can identify patterns of representation or portrayal that may perpetuate cultural stereotypes or

discriminate against certain cultural groups. This understanding can inform discussions and actions to promote cultural diversity, inclusivity, and representation.

4. **Informing cultural policy and decision-making:** Big data analysis can provide valuable insights for policymakers and decision-makers in the cultural sector. By understanding cultural preferences and trends, policymakers can make informed decisions regarding cultural policy, funding, and investment in digital media infrastructure. This can help foster cultural diversity, enhance cultural participation, and support the preservation of cultural heritage.

Applications of Cultural Analytics

Cultural analytics is an interdisciplinary field that combines data science, humanities, and social sciences to analyze and interpret cultural data. It encompasses a range of computational tools and methods to extract meaningful insights from big data. Some of the key applications of cultural analytics include:

1. **Sentiment analysis:** Sentiment analysis is used to analyze the emotional tone and sentiment expressed in digital media data. By analyzing sentiment, cultural analytics can uncover cultural attitudes, perceptions, and reactions towards different topics or events. This can provide valuable insights into cultural perspectives on digital media and aid in understanding the impact of digital media on cultural sentiment.

2. **Topic modeling:** Topic modeling is a technique used to discover latent topics or themes within a collection of documents or data. Cultural analytics can use topic modeling to identify and analyze cultural themes, trends, and discussions in digital media. This can help researchers and practitioners gain a deeper understanding of cultural perspectives and interests in digital communication.

3. **Network analysis:** Network analysis allows for the examination of social and cultural connections within digital media data. By mapping social networks and analyzing network structures, cultural analytics can identify influencers, communities, and the flow of information within cultural groups. This can shed light on cultural dynamics and the diffusion of cultural ideas and practices.

EMERGING TRENDS IN CULTURAL PERSPECTIVES ON DIGITAL MEDIA

4. **Geospatial analysis:** Geospatial analysis involves the exploration and interpretation of data with geographic components. Cultural analytics can use geospatial analysis to understand how cultural factors vary across different geographical regions. This can provide insights into regional cultural differences and their influence on digital media consumption and production.

Ethical Considerations

While the application of big data and cultural analytics offers exciting possibilities, it also raises important ethical considerations. Privacy, consent, and the responsible use of data are crucial aspects to address in the context of cultural perspectives on digital media.

Researchers and practitioners in cultural analytics should ensure the ethical use of data by:

- Obtaining informed consent from participants when collecting and analyzing personal data.

- Anonymizing and de-identifying data to protect individuals' privacy.

- Adhering to relevant data protection and privacy regulations.

- Being transparent about data sources, analysis methods, and potential biases.

- Ensuring data security to protect against unauthorized access or breaches.

Furthermore, cultural analytics should strive for inclusivity and representation by actively considering diverse cultural perspectives and avoiding biases in data collection, analysis, and interpretation.

Conclusion

Big data and cultural analytics have the potential to revolutionize our understanding of cultural perspectives on digital media. By leveraging the vast amounts of data generated through digital platforms, cultural analysts can uncover insights into cultural behaviors, preferences, and trends. However, it is essential to approach the use of big data and cultural analytics with ethical considerations in mind to ensure responsible and inclusive practices. The future of cultural perspectives on digital media lies in harnessing the power of big data and employing sophisticated analytics techniques to gain a comprehensive understanding of the impact of culture on digital communication.

Recommendations for Future Research

Bridging Gaps in Cultural Perspectives on Digital Media

In order to truly understand and appreciate the cultural perspectives on digital media, it is crucial to bridge the gaps that exist between different cultural traditions and contexts. The following sections highlight some strategies and approaches that can help bridge these gaps and foster cross-cultural understanding in the digital age.

Cultural Exchange Programs

Cultural exchange programs provide an opportunity for individuals from different cultural backgrounds to come together and share their experiences, knowledge, and ideas. These programs can be organized at various levels, including educational institutions, government initiatives, and non-profit organizations. By participating in cultural exchange programs, individuals can gain insights into different cultures and develop a deeper appreciation for diversity, which can impact their perspectives on digital media as well.

For example, universities can establish collaborative projects that bring together students and faculty from diverse cultural backgrounds to work on digital media projects. This not only allows for the exchange of ideas and skills but also promotes cross-cultural understanding and appreciation for different perspectives on digital media.

Collaborative Research Projects

Collaborative research projects that involve scholars and researchers from different cultural backgrounds can contribute significantly to bridging gaps in cultural perspectives on digital media. By working together, researchers can bring their unique insights and expertise to the table, leading to a more holistic understanding of the subject matter.

In addition to traditional academic collaborations, online platforms and digital tools can facilitate remote collaboration, making it possible for researchers from different parts of the world to collaborate on projects related to cultural perspectives on digital media. This not only helps bridge gaps in knowledge but also promotes cultural exchange and understanding.

RECOMMENDATIONS FOR FUTURE RESEARCH

Multicultural Digital Content Creation

Promoting multicultural digital content creation can play a vital role in bridging the gaps in cultural perspectives on digital media. This involves encouraging individuals from diverse cultural backgrounds to create and share digital content that reflects their unique cultural experiences, traditions, and values.

Platforms such as social media, blogs, and online forums can be used to showcase and amplify diverse voices, providing a platform for individuals to share their stories and perspectives on digital media. By actively engaging with multicultural digital content, individuals can broaden their understanding of different cultural perspectives and challenge their own biases and assumptions.

Cultural Sensitivity Training

Cultural sensitivity training can help individuals navigate the complexities of cultural perspectives on digital media. This training can focus on developing cultural awareness, empathy, and respect, enabling individuals to effectively engage with people from diverse cultural backgrounds in the digital space.

For instance, businesses and organizations can provide cultural sensitivity training to their employees to ensure a respectful and inclusive approach to digital media communication and marketing. This training can address topics such as cultural norms, communication styles, and potential cultural biases that may arise in digital media interactions.

Engaging with Local Communities

Engaging with local communities allows for a deeper understanding of their cultural perspectives on digital media. This can be achieved through partnerships with community organizations, conducting field research, and actively involving community members in the design and development of digital media platforms.

By working directly with local communities, digital media professionals can gain insights into cultural practices, preferences, and needs, leading to more culturally relevant and sensitive digital media products and services.

Creating Safe Spaces for Dialogue

Creating safe spaces for dialogue is essential for bridging the gaps in cultural perspectives on digital media. These spaces can facilitate open and respectful discussions where individuals from different cultural backgrounds can share their viewpoints, engage in constructive debates, and learn from one another.

CONCLUSION: THE FUTURE OF CULTURAL PERSPECTIVES ON DIGITAL MEDIA

Online forums, community-led initiatives, and moderated social media groups can serve as platforms for meaningful conversations about cultural perspectives on digital media. It is important to establish guidelines that promote respectful communication, encourage active listening, and discourage hate speech or discrimination.

In conclusion, bridging gaps in cultural perspectives on digital media requires concerted efforts from individuals, communities, organizations, and policymakers. By promoting cultural exchange, collaborative research, multicultural content creation, cultural sensitivity training, community engagement, and safe spaces for dialogue, we can foster cross-cultural understanding and create a more inclusive digital media landscape. These strategies can contribute to the development of digital media platforms and practices that embrace cultural diversity and promote cultural empowerment.

Addressing Ethical Challenges in Cultural Research

Ethical considerations play a crucial role in any research endeavor, and cultural research is no exception. When conducting research on digital media from a cultural perspective, it is essential to address the ethical challenges unique to this field. In this section, we will explore some of these challenges and discuss strategies for addressing them.

Informed Consent and Participant Protection

One of the fundamental ethical principles in research is obtaining informed consent from participants. In cultural research on digital media, it is important to ensure that participants fully understand the purpose, procedures, risks, and benefits of the study before agreeing to participate. However, obtaining informed consent can be challenging in the digital space, where anonymity and pseudonymity are common.

To address this challenge, researchers can provide clear and concise explanations of the research and its potential implications. In addition, they should design consent forms that are easily accessible and understandable, taking into account cultural and language differences. Researchers should also consider the potential risks of participation and take steps to protect the privacy and confidentiality of participants, especially in sensitive cultural contexts.

Cultural Sensitivity and Avoiding Harm

Cultural research on digital media involves studying diverse cultures and may touch upon sensitive topics. Researchers must approach their work with cultural

RECOMMENDATIONS FOR FUTURE RESEARCH   215

sensitivity and avoid harming the communities or individuals they are studying. It is crucial to be aware of cultural norms, values, and practices to prevent any unintended harm or offense.

To ensure cultural sensitivity, researchers should engage in self-reflection and cultural self-awareness. They should seek guidance from cultural consultants or community members to understand the potential impact of their research on the cultural group involved. The use of cultural insiders as co-researchers or advisors can help bridge the gap between the researcher and the culture under study.

Additionally, researchers should also be mindful of power dynamics, ensuring that their research does not perpetuate existing inequalities or reinforce stereotypes. They should take steps to include marginalized voices and perspectives in their research and actively work towards empowering the communities they study.

Data Collection and Analysis

Ethical challenges in cultural research extend to the collection and analysis of data. Researchers must handle data responsibly and ensure that it is collected and analyzed in a manner that respects cultural norms, values, and privacy.

When collecting data, researchers should obtain proper permissions and adhere to legal requirements. They should also consider the potential for unintended consequences, such as the re-identification of anonymized data or the misuse of personal information. Researchers must take steps to protect the privacy and confidentiality of participants, both during data collection and in subsequent analysis and publication.

Furthermore, researchers must approach data analysis with caution, recognizing the potential for bias or misinterpretation. They should be transparent about their analytical methods and acknowledge the limitations and potential biases in their research findings. Validating findings through member checking or consulting with participants can help ensure the accuracy and fairness of the analysis.

Interdisciplinary Collaboration and Peer Review

Addressing ethical challenges in cultural research requires interdisciplinary collaboration and rigorous peer review. Researchers should engage with scholars from different disciplines, such as anthropology, sociology, and media studies, to gain diverse perspectives and insights. This collaborative approach can provide a comprehensive understanding of the ethical implications and considerations specific to cultural research on digital media.

Additionally, peer review plays a crucial role in upholding ethical standards in research. By subjecting research papers to rigorous evaluation by experts in the field, peer review helps identify any ethical concerns or methodological shortcomings. Researchers should actively seek out peer feedback and be open to constructive criticism to ensure the integrity and ethical soundness of their work.

Real-World Example: Indigenous Knowledge and Digital Media Research

To illustrate the ethical challenges in cultural research, let us consider a real-world example: research on indigenous knowledge and digital media. Suppose a researcher wishes to study how indigenous communities in Australia use digital media to preserve and transmit their cultural traditions. This research presents several ethical challenges.

First, the researcher must obtain informed consent from the indigenous communities and ensure that they fully understand the purpose and potential implications of the research. This may involve working closely with community leaders and cultural advisors to develop culturally appropriate consent forms and procedures.

Second, the researcher must approach the research with cultural sensitivity, being mindful of the potential harm or offense that may arise from misrepresenting or appropriating indigenous knowledge. They should actively seek input and guidance from the indigenous communities, involving them in the research process as co-researchers or advisors.

Third, the researcher must handle the data ethically, ensuring the privacy and confidentiality of the indigenous participants. This may involve using anonymized data and employing secure data storage and transmission methods.

Finally, the researcher should engage in interdisciplinary collaboration and seek peer review to ensure the ethical soundness and methodological rigor of the research findings. By involving experts from fields such as indigenous studies, digital media, and cultural anthropology, the researcher can navigate the complex ethical landscape inherent in this type of research.

In conclusion, addressing ethical challenges in cultural research on digital media is crucial to ensure the integrity, validity, and fairness of the research findings. By obtaining informed consent, practicing cultural sensitivity, responsibly handling data, engaging in interdisciplinary collaboration, and subjecting research

RECOMMENDATIONS FOR FUTURE RESEARCH

to peer review, researchers can navigate these ethical challenges and contribute to the understanding of cultural perspectives on digital media.

Exercises

1. Choose a research study on digital media that focuses on a specific cultural group. Identify the potential ethical challenges faced by the researchers and propose strategies to address them.

2. Research and discuss a case study where cultural insensitivity or ethical misconduct has occurred in the context of digital media research. Analyze the potential consequences and suggest ways in which such issues could have been prevented.

3. Imagine you are conducting a research project on how digital media has influenced the cultural practices of a specific community. Design a comprehensive ethical framework for your study, addressing informed consent, cultural sensitivity, data collection and analysis, interdisciplinary collaboration, and peer review.

4. Explore the ethical guidelines and codes of conduct established by professional organizations or research institutions for conducting cultural research on digital media. Compare and contrast these guidelines, identifying commonalities and differences.

Additional Resources

- Tufekci, Z. (2014). "Big questions for social media big data: Representativeness, validity, and other methodological pitfalls." In ICWSM (pp. 505-514).
- Ess, C. (2009). "Digital media ethics." In The Handbook of Information and Computer Ethics (pp. 153-178).
- Markham, A. N., & Buchanan, E. A. (2012). "Ethical decision☒making and Internet research: Recommendations from the AoIR ethics working committee." In Decision Support Systems, 54(1), 547-556.
- Mayer, R. E., & Moreno, R. (2003). "Nine ways to reduce cognitive load in multimedia learning." In Educational Psychologist, 38(1), 43-52.

Interdisciplinary Approaches to Cultural Perspectives on Digital Media

In order to fully understand and analyze the cultural perspectives on digital media, it is crucial to employ interdisciplinary approaches that draw from various academic disciplines. By integrating insights from different fields, we can gain a comprehensive

CONCLUSION: THE FUTURE OF CULTURAL PERSPECTIVES ON DIGITAL MEDIA

understanding of the complex interactions between culture and digital media. In this section, we will explore some of the key interdisciplinary approaches that can contribute to the study of cultural perspectives on digital media.

Sociology

Sociology offers valuable theoretical frameworks and research methods to examine the social dimensions of digital media and their cultural impact. Through sociological analysis, we can explore how digital media shape and are shaped by social structures, norms, and institutions. For example, sociologists can investigate how cultural factors influence individuals' online behavior and interactions on social media platforms. By conducting surveys, interviews, and ethnographic research, sociologists can uncover cultural patterns and dynamics within digital communities.

One important aspect of sociological analysis is the study of power and inequality in digital media. This interdisciplinary approach helps us understand how certain cultural groups are marginalized or excluded from accessing and participating in digital spaces. Sociologists can examine the role of digital media in reinforcing or challenging existing power structures, and investigate the ways in which digital media can be used for social and political mobilization.

Psychology

Psychology provides insights into the psychological and cognitive processes underlying individuals' interactions with digital media. By examining cultural perspectives through a psychological lens, we can gain a deeper understanding of how individuals from diverse cultural backgrounds engage with and respond to digital media content. For example, psychologists may study how cultural values and beliefs shape individuals' perceptions and interpretations of online information.

Psychological research can also shed light on the impact of digital media on individuals' well-being and identity formation. For instance, studies can explore how digital media platforms influence individuals' self-presentation and self-esteem, and investigate the psychological effects of online social comparison. By integrating psychological theories and methodologies, interdisciplinary research can provide a more nuanced understanding of the cultural implications of digital media on individuals' mental health and identity.

RECOMMENDATIONS FOR FUTURE RESEARCH

Communication Studies

Communication studies contribute to the interdisciplinary study of cultural perspectives on digital media by examining the process of communication in digital spaces. Communication scholars can investigate how cultural contexts influence the creation, dissemination, and reception of digital media content. They can analyze the role of language, symbols, and visual communication in shaping cultural meanings and representations online.

Furthermore, communication studies draw attention to the power dynamics and ethical considerations in digital media. Interdisciplinary research in this area can explore how cultural biases and stereotypes are perpetuated or challenged through digital communication, and examine the ethical implications of cultural appropriation and misrepresentation in digital media content. By applying communication theories and methodologies, researchers can develop strategies for promoting inclusive and culturally sensitive digital communication practices.

Anthropology

Anthropology brings a holistic and cross-cultural perspective to the study of cultural perspectives on digital media. Anthropologists can conduct ethnographic research to understand how digital media are embedded within specific cultural contexts and how they influence cultural practices and traditions. By immersing themselves in communities, anthropologists can explore the cultural meanings and social functions of digital media within a given cultural group.

Moreover, anthropologists can explore the concept of cultural hybridity in digital spaces. They can examine how different cultural traditions and practices converge and transform in digital environments, leading to the emergence of new cultural forms and identities. Anthropological research on digital media can shed light on how cultural diversity is negotiated and celebrated in online communities.

Design and Human-Computer Interaction

The field of design and human-computer interaction (HCI) plays a crucial role in developing user-centered and culturally sensitive digital media platforms and technologies. Interdisciplinary research in this area incorporates principles from cultural studies, psychology, and anthropology to inform the design process. By considering cultural perspectives in the design of digital media, researchers can create products that are intuitive, inclusive, and relevant to diverse cultural communities.

CONCLUSION: THE FUTURE OF CULTURAL PERSPECTIVES ON DIGITAL MEDIA

Design and HCI also address the ethical considerations and social impacts of digital media. Researchers can explore how the design of digital media interfaces can respect cultural diversity and ensure accessibility for all users. They can also investigate the social implications of emerging technologies, such as artificial intelligence and virtual reality, on cultural practices and identities.

Conclusion

By adopting interdisciplinary approaches, researchers can gain a richer understanding of the cultural perspectives on digital media. Sociology, psychology, communication studies, anthropology, and design and HCI offer valuable insights and methodologies to analyze the complex interactions between culture and digital media. By embracing interdisciplinary collaboration, researchers can develop innovative strategies and solutions to address the challenges and opportunities that arise in the digital age. It is through these interdisciplinary efforts that we can continue to advance our understanding of cultural perspectives on digital media and navigate the complexities of our interconnected world.

Index

-up emoji, 88

ability, 4, 7, 10, 23, 27, 29, 32, 34,
49, 70, 71, 92, 98, 121,
123–125, 127, 129, 130,
135, 136, 164, 165
absence, 90, 132
abundance, 28
academia, 142
acceptability, 185
acceptance, 46
access, 19, 28, 29, 43, 46, 47, 57, 62,
71, 76, 78, 79, 81, 83, 105,
113, 114, 116, 118,
123–126, 133, 135, 136,
141, 142, 145, 149–151,
157, 158, 161, 163–167,
169, 172, 184, 185, 188,
192, 200
accessibility, 38, 46, 75, 84, 105, 114,
131, 136, 139, 146, 148,
149, 172, 182, 185, 186,
192, 220
account, 11, 57, 60, 82, 105, 127,
145, 181–183, 200, 214
accountability, 117, 136
accumulation, 26

accuracy, 28, 76, 80, 82, 84, 132,
134, 188, 198, 199, 215
achievement, 64
acknowledgement, 3
acknowledgment, 192, 194
acquisition, 9, 76
act, 34, 40, 126
action, 7, 41, 70, 71, 116, 118, 128,
136
activism, 20, 70, 71, 73, 117–119,
127–129, 131, 132, 136
activist, 118
activity, 44
actor, 19
adaptability, 11
adaptation, 20, 35–37, 47, 77,
80–84, 87, 94, 98, 134,
141, 187
addition, 129, 143, 172, 212, 214
address, 6, 7, 11–14, 16, 17, 21, 36,
40, 41, 46, 55, 57, 60, 61,
69, 78–81, 84, 86, 88, 89,
97, 99, 106, 115, 119, 122,
129, 134, 136, 144, 154,
156, 157, 169–172, 185,
186, 191, 200, 211, 213,
214, 217, 220
adhering, 41

adoption, 37, 38, 45–47, 62, 111, 129, 133, 143, 166, 167, 171, 185, 192
advance, 2, 44, 134, 220
advancement, 76
advantage, 80, 163
advent, 23, 27, 29, 32, 132, 145, 148, 155, 161
advertising, 82, 86, 87, 128
advocacy, 118
advocate, 70, 112, 119, 127
aesthetic, 84, 87
affordability, 146
age, 3–5, 20, 28, 31, 32, 35, 53, 55, 67, 75, 84, 92, 95, 101, 107, 126, 129, 132, 134, 137, 145, 149, 151, 154, 155, 157, 158, 161, 163–165, 167–169, 173, 183, 188, 199, 212, 220
agency, 18, 19, 106, 126, 168
agreement, 90
alcohol, 89
algorithm, 134
Alistair Duggin, 184
allocation, 136, 176
alternative, 30, 64, 67, 91, 135, 161, 183, 194
ambiguity, 56
amount, 149, 208, 209
amplification, 133
analysis, 15–17, 30–32, 43, 117, 127, 184, 211, 215, 217, 218
animation, 143
anonymity, 135, 214
anthropology, 14, 17, 215, 216, 220
app, 37, 171
appearance, 101

application, 17, 152, 184, 199, 204, 208, 211
appreciation, 38, 66, 94, 114, 115, 122, 154, 169, 176, 194, 204, 208, 212
approach, 4, 11, 13–15, 20, 39, 58, 59, 66, 77, 78, 83, 86, 112, 115, 118, 122, 125, 133, 155, 160, 161, 166–168, 171, 172, 174–176, 182, 183, 185, 195, 208, 211, 213–216, 218
appropriateness, 36
appropriation, 3–5, 20, 21, 25, 33, 38–41, 55, 62–64, 100, 110–113, 115, 141, 143, 146–149, 151, 154, 155, 171, 172, 192–195, 200, 219
approval, 88, 90, 105
archiving, 146
area, 10, 204, 219
array, 79
art, 38, 142, 143, 145, 146, 148, 149
artifact, 148
artist, 148, 207
artwork, 148, 150, 194
aspect, 26, 59, 75, 84, 117, 121, 166, 218
assimilation, 62
assistance, 99
assurance, 82
attempt, 95
attention, 38, 41, 70, 98, 117, 131, 171, 185, 219
attentiveness, 91
attitude, 166
attribution, 25, 193, 194
audience, 6, 28, 33, 35, 36, 47, 52,

Index

64, 66, 70, 82, 87, 91, 100,
101, 105, 114, 132, 140,
142–144, 148, 150, 182,
183, 185, 186, 195
audio, 32, 105, 140, 141, 144, 169,
172, 207
auditory, 32, 173
audits, 7
Australia, 216
authenticity, 3, 36, 103, 104, 106,
110, 111, 113, 132,
149–151, 188
author, 134
authority, 31, 55, 57, 132
automation, 84
autonomy, 41, 66, 181, 199
availability, 31, 46, 146, 155, 209
avenue, 79
avoidance, 181
awareness, 7, 8, 10, 21, 31, 33, 34,
39, 58, 60, 66, 67, 70, 80,
91, 113, 117, 129, 130,
168, 170, 176, 195, 200,
213, 215

background, 4, 6, 8, 53, 55, 172, 184
backlash, 106, 116, 119
balance, 33, 36, 56, 63, 104, 161, 204
barrier, 78
base, 4, 78, 183
basis, 34
battle, 134
beauty, 42, 65, 103, 151
behavior, 6, 18, 30, 45, 49–52, 55,
56, 58, 65, 86, 128, 181,
184, 199, 209, 218
being, 5, 7, 11, 35, 46, 58, 92, 94, 95,
104, 106, 122, 193, 216,
218

belief, 166
belonging, 42, 53, 80, 107, 110, 111,
113, 114, 139, 188
benefit, 76, 80, 81, 123, 173, 194
bias, 6, 7, 20, 133, 141, 215
birth, 103
blending, 61, 67, 68, 122, 142
blogging, 28, 104, 116
board, 170
body, 90–92
bond, 110
book, 19–21, 28
borrowing, 38, 193
bottle, 89
brand, 84, 86, 103, 154
branding, 35
breakdown, 133
bridge, 11, 37, 63, 75, 80, 81, 85, 87,
90, 92, 98, 139, 164, 167,
169, 185, 194, 205, 208,
212, 215
broadcast, 20, 32–35
budgeting, 136
building, 8, 80, 92, 98, 100, 141,
142, 200
burger, 36, 37
business, 154, 161

campaign, 55, 64, 87, 195
capacity, 141, 142
career, 76
case, 4, 10, 18, 55, 57, 63, 64, 111,
128, 154, 157, 161, 183,
184, 187, 194, 207, 217
casting, 129
catalog, 150
Catalonia, 111
categorization, 183
category, 158

cater, 3, 31, 43, 47, 80, 149, 173, 175, 176, 185
caution, 215
celebration, 89, 145
censorship, 60
century, 29, 32
chain, 36
challenge, 3, 16, 18, 31, 33, 34, 62, 70, 71, 73, 79, 91, 111, 113, 114, 117, 119, 127–129, 131, 135, 146, 148, 154, 200, 204, 213, 214
champagne, 89
change, 18, 30, 31, 34, 35, 70, 73, 112, 117–119, 127–132
chapter, 100
character, 79
chat, 169
check, 133
checking, 132–134, 215
China, 37, 42, 51, 52
choose, 59, 105, 207
circle, 200
citizen, 130, 131, 136
citizenship, 170
clarification, 58
clarity, 99
class, 34, 107, 127
classroom, 168
clay, 26
clothing, 38, 111
cloud, 176
co, 215, 216
code, 38
coevolve, 18
coexistence, 3
cohesion, 23, 43, 56, 112, 199

collaboration, 3, 29, 45, 46, 61, 64, 76, 79–81, 83, 97, 100, 115, 118, 128, 140, 144–147, 164, 167, 170, 176, 179, 192, 204, 212, 215–217, 220
collaborative, 16, 77, 142, 157, 173, 176–179, 212, 214, 215
collage, 146
collection, 14, 16, 60, 211, 215, 217
collectivism, 46, 51, 56, 57, 181
collectivist, 41, 46, 56, 59, 181, 184, 199
colonialism, 18
color, 183, 187
combat, 112, 133, 134
combination, 9, 98, 207
comfort, 32, 59, 131
commentary, 30, 31, 34
commerce, 36, 154, 188
commercialization, 146
commodification, 13, 33, 38, 62, 66, 143, 146, 147, 193
communication, 2–4, 7–11, 14, 18, 20, 21, 23–27, 32, 35, 45, 46, 52, 56, 58, 59, 61–66, 75–81, 84–87, 89–100, 110, 124, 131, 164, 172, 173, 175, 176, 179, 184, 187, 188, 204, 205, 211, 213, 214, 219, 220
community, 14, 15, 24, 26, 41, 42, 46, 57, 63, 80, 81, 83, 84, 99, 105, 113, 114, 118, 119, 154, 164, 165, 167, 171, 172, 193, 195, 213–217
company, 36, 78, 86, 87, 89
comparison, 106, 148, 218

Index

compatibility, 183, 186

compensation, 38, 144, 161, 193

competence, 7–11, 20, 94, 172, 176, 179

competition, 123

complexity, 117, 123

compliance, 186

component, 53

comprehension, 166

computer, 79, 134, 164, 165, 206

concentration, 121, 123

concept, 4, 17, 18, 20, 41, 53, 67, 75, 101, 104, 110, 117, 172, 194, 208, 219

concern, 144

conclusion, 19, 29, 67, 87, 134, 172, 214, 216

conduct, 7, 14–16, 164, 193, 217, 219

conferencing, 176

confetti, 89

confidence, 94

confidentiality, 214–216

conflict, 57

conformity, 41

confrontation, 57, 58

confusion, 76, 89, 131

connectedness, 199

connection, 5, 42, 90, 105–107, 110, 117, 163

connectivity, 28, 46, 47, 71, 116, 124, 154, 163, 164, 169

consensus, 56

consent, 13, 16, 25, 60, 61, 106, 141, 193, 201, 211, 214, 216, 217

conservation, 140

conservativeness, 33

consideration, 57, 135, 144, 156, 188

consistency, 86

console, 43

construct, 101, 102, 107, 110, 113

construction, 20, 101, 104–107, 111–113

consultation, 171

consumer, 65, 86, 128

consumption, 3–6, 20, 21, 33, 38, 41–45, 62, 65, 89, 145, 148–151, 158, 161, 196, 209

contact, 90, 91

content, 3–7, 15–19, 21, 27–29, 31–47, 50, 55, 57, 62, 64–66, 77, 79–84, 100, 103–106, 111, 112, 114, 115, 121, 122, 124, 127, 128, 131–135, 143–147, 149–151, 155, 159, 161, 166, 167, 169, 171, 173, 176, 182, 183, 185–189, 193–199, 201, 204, 209, 213, 214, 218, 219

context, 1, 3, 6, 7, 11, 14, 18, 23, 25, 35, 38, 46, 57, 67, 71, 75, 76, 82, 88, 89, 101, 105, 111, 124, 126, 127, 141, 148, 151, 158–160, 163, 166, 168, 171–173, 176, 187, 192, 194, 196, 199, 200, 204, 205, 209, 211, 217

contrast, 42–44, 46, 56, 59, 60, 87, 183, 217

contribute, 8, 17, 28, 33, 37, 38, 47, 55, 57, 58, 63, 65–67, 76, 83, 106, 114, 118, 119, 122, 123, 127, 133, 134, 148, 154, 163, 166, 185,

195, 199, 212, 214, 217–219

control, 13, 57, 59, 60, 66, 105, 121, 134, 144, 193, 201

controversy, 119

convergence, 65

cooking, 63

cooperation, 80

copyright, 141, 147, 148, 150, 154, 155, 158, 161

corruption, 34

counter, 33, 66

country, 35, 42, 148, 157, 187, 207

course, 170

cover, 20, 87

craftsmanship, 154

creation, 21, 28, 34, 43, 61, 67, 114, 115, 128, 132, 140, 145, 146, 149, 158, 161, 194–199, 213, 214, 219

creativity, 3, 5, 21, 30, 70, 104–106, 143–147, 152, 157, 165

credibility, 28, 131, 132, 134

criticism, 17, 106, 194, 216

crowd, 83

crowdfunding, 146

Crowdin, 83

Cues, 100

cuisine, 35, 111

cultivation, 61, 63

culturalization, 185–188

culture, 1, 2, 6, 11, 14–19, 21, 26, 30, 35, 38, 42, 43, 47, 49, 56, 57, 62, 64–66, 68, 82, 90, 91, 99, 103, 106, 113, 122, 125, 126, 135, 143, 145, 149, 171, 181, 185–188, 192–194, 199, 200, 211, 215, 218, 220

cuneiform, 26

curation, 104, 144, 204

curiosity, 98

currency, 82, 186

curriculum, 164, 168

customer, 78

customization, 35, 144

cyberbullying, 106, 131

cybersecurity, 76, 78

damage, 186

data, 15, 16, 19, 21, 43, 60, 91, 136, 137, 140, 141, 151, 186, 200, 201, 205, 208–211, 215–217

date, 82, 164, 186

David Sansone, 89

debate, 135

decision, 49, 122, 127, 133–136, 141, 172

decline, 31

deconstruction, 129

deference, 55

degradation, 140

deliberation, 135

democracy, 21, 134, 136, 137

democratization, 29, 150

depth, 14, 15, 17, 30–32, 43, 89

design, 19, 21, 28, 42, 46, 60, 77, 86–88, 113–115, 127, 136, 166–168, 172, 181–192, 200, 201, 213, 214, 220

destruction, 140

determinism, 18

development, 20, 24, 26, 27, 29, 30, 32, 45, 47, 67, 80, 113, 134, 139, 146, 155, 157,

161, 171, 172, 185, 188, 204, 205, 213, 214
dialogue, 4, 34, 61, 63, 73, 80, 99, 110, 112, 118, 131, 143, 169, 170, 172, 194, 208, 213, 214
diaspora, 42, 113
difficulty, 76
diffusion, 65, 131
digitization, 25, 146
dimension, 29
direction, 183, 186
disadvantage, 164
disagreement, 57
discomfort, 89
discourse, 16, 29, 130, 131, 133–137
discrimination, 76, 117, 124, 214
discussion, 15, 63, 79, 169, 170, 176
disinformation, 112
disparity, 62, 164, 181
disposal, 148
dissemination, 26–28, 30, 33, 61, 80, 111, 112, 132, 133, 135, 140, 142, 145, 150, 151, 155, 157, 193, 219
distance, 8, 181, 208
distortion, 26, 193
distribution, 66, 121, 127, 128, 136, 145, 148, 149, 158, 161, 169, 196
diversity, 2–5, 7, 8, 10–12, 15, 20, 26, 28–30, 32, 34, 35, 41, 44, 45, 47, 55, 61–64, 66, 67, 70, 71, 79–81, 83, 88, 89, 100, 106, 110, 112, 121–123, 128, 131, 139, 145, 150, 151, 157, 161, 168, 170, 172, 176, 183, 189, 192–194, 204, 212,

214, 219, 220
divide, 20, 21, 28, 29, 62, 63, 71, 79, 80, 113, 116, 123–126, 135, 137, 141, 150, 154, 155, 163–166, 169, 172, 185, 200
document, 139, 167, 176
documentation, 80, 142
dominance, 62, 65–67, 122, 123, 171
downloading, 161
dowry, 34
dynamic, 16, 107, 110, 112, 205

e, 10, 27, 36, 136, 154, 184
ease, 38, 106, 116, 132, 144, 146, 149, 159, 183
echo, 6, 19, 131–135
ecology, 18, 19
ecosystem, 80, 123, 134, 143
edge, 185, 188
editing, 82, 105
education, 10, 11, 21, 28, 34, 49, 60, 61, 106, 155, 157, 163–168, 172, 188
educator, 170
effectiveness, 37, 51, 55, 82, 87, 100, 137, 185
efficacy, 80
effort, 83, 94
Egypt, 26
email, 75, 87, 89, 92, 94
emergence, 18, 21, 25, 46, 67, 132, 142, 143, 146, 219
Emma, 94
emoji, 88, 89, 91
empathy, 55, 57, 58, 61, 63, 66, 80, 90, 106, 139, 208, 213
emphasis, 51, 55, 56, 59, 199, 201

empowerment, 18, 20, 29, 33, 70, 71, 73, 80, 114, 126, 131, 167, 214

encoding, 36, 79, 161, 186

endeavor, 214

enforcement, 146, 161

engagement, 5, 10, 16, 35, 37, 43, 51, 70, 78, 117–119, 132, 134–137, 141, 146, 148, 166, 167, 171, 181, 185, 186, 188, 200, 214

enhance, 10, 23, 51, 60, 65, 80–82, 84, 87, 89, 90, 92, 97, 99, 100, 105, 115, 118, 134, 137, 140, 141, 150, 166, 167, 169, 172, 175, 176, 182, 185, 188, 198

entertainment, 32, 111, 188

entrepreneur, 154

entrepreneurship, 21, 151–154

entry, 155

environment, 7, 10, 40, 41, 55, 58, 60, 67, 77, 106, 114, 116, 159, 167, 168, 170, 172, 173, 197, 199, 202, 206

equality, 8, 34

equity, 171, 172

era, 28, 70, 100, 115, 155–157, 208

erasure, 38, 62, 193

erosion, 62, 66, 67, 122, 133

essence, 82, 113

essentialism, 113

establishment, 134, 142

esteem, 106, 218

ethnicity, 42, 53, 107, 125

etiquette, 42, 55–58, 186

Europe, 56

evaluation, 28, 29, 216

event, 6, 16, 58, 64, 148

evidence, 15

evolution, 20, 26, 28, 45–47

examination, 19, 127

example, 6, 14–19, 31, 33–36, 39, 41–43, 46, 51, 55, 56, 59, 60, 63, 65, 68, 82, 86–91, 104, 105, 110, 111, 113, 121, 127, 131, 136, 142, 144, 147, 149, 166, 167, 169, 171, 176, 181, 182, 199, 200, 212, 216, 218

exception, 214

exchange, 3, 7, 38, 40, 41, 47, 61, 62, 64–68, 77–79, 95, 99, 113, 114, 135, 141–143, 145, 172, 176, 194, 212, 214

excitement, 89

exclusion, 76, 78, 113, 123, 127, 204

exercise, 136, 195

existence, 59

exoticization, 33

experience, 10, 25, 31, 32, 42, 44–46, 64, 65, 78, 81, 82, 100, 133, 140, 144, 147, 166, 181–183, 185, 186, 188, 204, 207, 208

experiment, 105, 142, 147

experimentation, 29

expertise, 83, 84, 140, 212

exploitation, 38, 143, 152, 193, 200

exploration, 4, 21, 29, 30, 52, 61, 89, 145, 202, 208

explore, 1, 7, 11, 14–17, 19–21, 23, 25, 26, 29, 32, 37, 41, 45, 50, 52, 55, 58, 59, 63, 64, 67, 75, 76, 81, 84, 87, 91, 95, 104, 105, 107, 110, 113, 115, 121, 126, 132, 139–142, 145, 148, 150,

Index 229

152, 170, 172, 175, 176, 185, 188, 199, 207, 214, 218–220

exposure, 6, 33, 61, 66, 135, 149, 204

expression, 18, 20, 23, 29, 33, 41, 42, 46, 56, 59, 65–67, 76, 80, 91, 101, 104–106, 110, 112, 114, 136, 152, 170

extent, 200

eye, 90

fabric, 26, 133

face, 62, 86, 88, 90, 104, 106, 115, 116, 118, 131, 136, 149, 163, 164, 185, 200

fact, 132–134

factor, 45, 132

faculty, 212

fair, 7, 123, 128, 129, 144, 146, 158, 161, 193, 195, 196, 204

fairness, 136, 198, 199, 205, 215, 216

familiarity, 182

family, 42, 49, 57, 59, 170, 200

fan, 145

fashion, 29, 39, 42, 62, 65, 111, 149, 151, 192, 194

feedback, 7, 37, 64, 87, 100, 105, 114, 146, 164, 188, 216

femininity, 181

festival, 6

field, 11, 17, 21, 112, 210, 213, 214, 216

fight, 134

file, 161

film, 121

filter, 6, 19, 65

finding, 57

flag, 134

flexibility, 11

focus, 15, 17, 20, 36, 42, 80, 87, 99, 141, 213

following, 4, 7, 51, 58, 60, 85, 93, 94, 97, 99, 103, 143, 170, 182, 183, 188, 192, 202, 212

font, 28, 36, 183, 186

food, 36

force, 32

forefront, 129

form, 3, 26, 27, 43, 44, 66, 101, 103, 107, 111, 135, 143

format, 64, 140, 147

formation, 19, 20, 30, 68, 107–115, 218

formulation, 156

forum, 78

foster, 2, 8, 11, 14, 35, 37, 55–57, 60, 63, 66, 67, 69, 77–80, 90, 92, 95, 98, 100, 105, 106, 109, 110, 112, 114, 118, 123, 129, 135, 136, 142, 147, 161, 166, 167, 169, 172, 179, 202, 205, 208, 212, 214

foundation, 27, 32, 192

fragmentation, 133

framework, 17–19, 49, 50, 127, 141, 194, 217

freedom, 41, 112, 136, 199

frequency, 8, 49

friend, 119

frustration, 76, 78

functionality, 46, 127, 185

funding, 140, 141

fusion, 65, 142

future, 21, 25, 27, 47, 52, 73, 100, 112, 123, 129, 132, 139,

141, 145, 146, 161, 211

gain, 6, 14, 15, 19, 36, 38, 47, 49, 61, 105, 116, 143, 176, 182, 185, 188, 193, 206, 208, 209, 211–213, 215, 217, 218, 220
game, 35, 37, 97, 118
gamification, 118
gaming, 41, 43, 44, 96, 97, 127
gap, 90, 123, 163, 164, 169, 194, 200, 215
gatekeeping, 132
gender, 34, 36, 42, 99, 116, 122, 125, 127, 183
generalization, 15, 34
generation, 23
geography, 166
gesture, 88, 90
glitch, 146
globalization, 20, 58, 62, 67, 143
globe, 2, 36
go, 36, 43
goal, 173
gold, 87
governance, 157
government, 60, 112, 136, 212
gratification, 43
gratitude, 88
ground, 57, 58, 132
group, 6, 14, 15, 41, 46, 53, 55–57, 59, 63, 94, 107, 113, 164, 181, 199, 215, 217, 219
growth, 3, 26, 46, 105, 158
guidance, 194, 215, 216
guide, 49, 55, 168, 194, 195
guideline, 194

hand, 25, 33, 35, 41, 56, 59, 62, 66, 90, 91, 113, 122, 127, 134, 152, 163, 166, 185, 188, 199
handling, 201, 205, 216
happiness, 65, 88, 91
harassment, 71, 106, 116, 117, 131, 132, 135, 137
hardware, 124, 163, 164
harm, 16, 112, 215, 216
harmony, 41, 46, 56, 57, 59, 88, 181, 199
hate, 106, 111, 112, 214
health, 133, 218
hegemony, 4, 20
help, 7, 13, 16, 17, 39, 40, 56, 57, 60, 73, 77, 80, 89–91, 94, 98, 114, 122, 123, 133, 134, 140, 164, 167, 184, 194, 209, 212, 213, 215
heritage, 13, 21, 23, 26, 30, 32, 42, 53, 62, 66, 79, 110–113, 139–142, 146, 148, 150–152, 154, 155, 167, 200, 208
hierarchy, 38, 42, 51, 183
history, 1, 23, 29, 31, 32, 60, 111, 113, 139, 144, 167, 170, 193
Hollywood, 66
homogenization, 62, 64–67, 121
humanity, 139
humor, 36, 82
hybridity, 20, 67–70, 122, 123, 219
hybridization, 143

iconography, 194
idea, 17, 18
identification, 53, 152, 215

Index 231

identity, 15, 17, 18, 20, 24, 27, 31, 38, 42, 45, 52, 53, 55, 60, 66, 67, 100, 101, 104–115, 117, 119, 126, 127, 129, 139, 166, 199, 208, 218

ignorance, 193

image, 101, 105, 140

imagery, 87, 171

imagination, 27

imitation, 38

impact, 1–6, 10, 14, 15, 19–21, 26, 29–35, 37, 41–43, 45–47, 49, 55, 57, 58, 61, 64, 66, 67, 71, 73, 75–78, 82, 84, 86, 87, 89, 101, 103, 106, 110, 115, 117, 118, 121, 123, 127, 129, 143, 145, 147–150, 158, 165, 181, 184, 199, 208, 209, 211, 212, 215, 218

imperialism, 18, 66, 122

implement, 13, 80, 84, 97, 123, 164, 205

implementation, 136, 156, 166, 168, 172, 176, 177, 179

importance, 1, 7, 10, 19–21, 45, 49, 57, 59, 66, 88, 92, 94, 110, 127, 148, 157, 167, 168, 185, 187, 199, 208

imposition, 122

impression, 101

improvement, 37, 172, 184, 188

improvisation, 23

inclusion, 81, 144, 168, 172, 189

inclusivity, 3, 7, 8, 10, 11, 26, 34, 35, 71, 73, 79–81, 84, 95, 96, 99, 100, 106, 111, 113–115, 117, 128, 131, 136, 137, 142, 151, 157,

166, 167, 170, 182, 184, 185, 188, 192, 211

income, 124, 163, 164

independence, 31, 111, 112, 189

India, 34, 36, 57

individual, 14, 20, 42, 44, 53, 56, 59, 125, 175, 200, 206

individualism, 46, 56, 181

industry, 4, 66, 161, 186, 194

inequality, 21, 38, 122, 124, 163–165, 218

influence, 1, 2, 4, 6, 18–20, 26, 32, 34, 35, 41–43, 46, 49, 51–53, 55–57, 59, 60, 65, 66, 84, 86–89, 102, 104, 106, 111, 113, 117, 119, 121–123, 126, 127, 151, 166, 167, 184, 199, 209, 218, 219

influencer, 103, 104

information, 6, 7, 19, 23, 26–32, 43, 56–61, 75–78, 81, 84, 90, 91, 95, 101, 106, 112, 116, 118, 129, 131–136, 141, 149, 163–165, 172, 173, 182, 183, 195, 197, 199–202, 204, 205, 215, 218

infrastructure, 28, 46, 47, 62, 124, 163, 166

infringement, 148, 150, 155

initiative, 64

injustice, 117

innovation, 3, 145, 161, 166

input, 186, 216

insensitivity, 35, 217

inspiration, 27, 145

instance, 15, 16, 18, 33, 34, 36, 42, 43, 45–47, 59, 76, 87, 111,

122, 136, 143, 149, 166, 171, 182, 213, 218
integration, 16, 36, 76, 164
integrity, 63, 137, 142, 197–199, 216
intelligence, 21, 61, 63, 81, 84, 141, 204, 220
intent, 132
intention, 89, 127
interaction, 18, 61, 62, 64, 76, 100, 106, 125, 181, 204
interconnectedness, 41
interest, 42, 68, 77
interface, 21, 181–185, 187
internet, 3, 45–47, 62, 71, 76, 105, 116, 124, 135, 154, 159, 163–166, 169
interplay, 17, 18, 20
interpretation, 20, 59, 87–91, 100, 172, 211
intersection, 1, 11, 14, 20, 21, 112, 115, 117, 150, 155, 161, 199, 208
intersectionality, 118, 127, 129
intonation, 23
introduction, 20, 32
invasion, 91
invention, 26, 29, 32
involvement, 77, 82, 84, 119
Isabel H. Twesigomwe, 89
isolation, 181
issue, 38–41, 78, 111, 123, 132–135, 146, 163, 171

Japan, 35, 43, 59, 87, 94, 201
jargon, 99
Johannes Gutenberg, 29
journalism, 131, 133
joy, 89

Juan Antonio Coad-Trainer, 184
justice, 31, 118, 126, 169

Kenya, 110, 207
key, 8, 11, 12, 17, 18, 26, 27, 30, 35, 41, 44, 55, 57, 64, 71, 76, 81, 84, 85, 95, 105, 121, 130, 135, 136, 140, 149, 152, 153, 155, 159, 164, 173, 174, 176, 178, 187, 189, 190, 204, 209, 210, 218
Kimberlé Crenshaw, 117
knowledge, 3, 8–10, 23, 26, 29, 61, 76, 80, 83, 87, 94, 98, 110, 114, 139, 141, 142, 144, 150, 152, 163, 167, 171, 176, 179, 194, 200, 212, 216
Koji, 94

lack, 71, 88, 89, 94, 124, 127, 132, 135, 140, 163, 164, 193, 204
land, 117
landscape, 2, 3, 6, 11, 14, 16, 26, 28, 29, 34, 35, 41, 45, 47, 51, 67, 71, 73, 79, 81, 104, 112, 115, 121, 123, 126, 132–134, 141, 145, 146, 148–151, 153, 155, 161, 192, 195, 199, 214, 216
language, 1, 3, 5, 20, 23, 27, 29, 30, 35, 38, 42, 45, 53, 55–58, 62, 65, 75–84, 90–92, 95, 98–100, 107, 110, 111, 113, 166, 167, 171, 179, 182, 184–187, 204, 205, 214, 219

Index 233

laser, 140
launch, 37
layout, 84, 182–184
learning, 3, 10, 21, 63, 64, 77, 78, 94,
    99, 100, 118, 141, 154,
    163, 164, 166–179, 184
leisure, 44
lens, 1, 17, 127, 199, 218
level, 82, 166
leverage, 26, 152, 154, 168, 204
library, 161
licensing, 161
life, 43, 142, 170, 189
lifestyle, 151
light, 20, 124, 218, 219
likelihood, 134
limitation, 16, 71, 76
listening, 11, 57, 58, 94, 98, 214
literacy, 21, 28, 29, 77, 80, 106, 133,
    134, 136, 150, 154,
    163–167, 183
literature, 27, 29, 30, 145, 147
livelihood, 144
locale, 82
localization, 3, 21, 35–37, 45, 77, 78,
    80, 82, 84, 182, 184–188
location, 125, 135, 149, 163
longevity, 26, 34, 139, 146
look, 51, 57, 63, 73, 145, 147
loss, 26, 62, 65, 66, 140, 141, 150,
    204
Luz Elena Arroyo-López, 184

machine, 77–82, 141
mainstream, 6, 33, 47, 66, 67
maintenance, 141
making, 34, 42, 49, 65, 76, 78, 81,
    98, 122, 127, 133–136,
    140, 141, 149, 150, 155,

    166, 172, 183, 184, 188,
    212
management, 83, 176
manipulation, 112, 136, 137, 145
manner, 40, 100, 105, 149, 165, 215
marginalization, 6, 21, 38, 76, 78,
    113, 123–126
Maria, 154
market, 37, 66, 87, 185, 187, 188
marketing, 35, 36, 43, 82, 86, 213
Masaaki Kurosu, 184
masculinity, 181
material, 150
materialism, 103
matter, 21, 212
McAloo Tikki, 36
meaning, 38, 56, 82, 87, 88, 90, 111,
    124, 171, 193, 194
means, 14, 23, 33, 80, 91, 92, 110,
    116, 144, 167
measurement, 82, 186
mechanism, 65
media, 1–7, 11, 12, 14–21, 23–47,
    49–71, 73, 75, 78, 79,
    81–84, 87, 92, 98, 100,
    101, 103–107, 110–117,
    121–136, 139–155,
    157–161, 163–165, 172,
    173, 175–179, 181, 184,
    185, 187, 188, 190–202,
    208, 209, 211–220
medium, 29, 30, 35, 37, 81, 105
member, 215
memory, 23, 111
menu, 36
Mesopotamia, 26
message, 82, 88, 89
messaging, 34, 75, 87
metadata, 140

mimicry, 100
mind, 51, 58, 104, 114, 184, 211
mindedness, 4, 98
minority, 66
misappropriation, 13, 194
miscommunication, 62, 63, 79
misconduct, 217
misinformation, 116, 117, 131, 133, 135–137
misinterpretation, 6, 35, 62, 79, 89, 91, 215
Misinterpretations, 76
misrepresentation, 6, 7, 17, 38, 111, 122, 143, 193, 200, 204, 219
misunderstanding, 133
misuse, 141, 200, 205, 215
Mixi, 201
mixing, 67
mobile, 27, 37, 47
mobility, 136
mobilization, 21, 111, 112, 129–132, 136, 218
mode, 23
model, 154
moderation, 7, 127, 128
modesty, 33, 36, 59
momentum, 116
mouth, 42
mouthpiece, 29
movement, 16, 31, 111, 112, 117–119
multiculturalism, 33
multilingualism, 20, 77, 79, 80
multimedia, 29, 31, 36, 104, 141, 144, 147, 169, 170, 176, 179
multiplayer, 43, 44
multitude, 172

museum, 170
music, 4, 32, 38, 39, 42, 62, 63, 65, 66, 111, 142, 145, 146, 149–151, 161, 192, 204
musician, 148

narration, 170
narrative, 35, 144, 147, 193
narrowing, 65
nation, 111
nationality, 42, 53, 107
nature, 14, 16, 17, 25, 49, 106, 114, 117, 127, 131, 159, 208
navigation, 182–184
need, 3, 12, 29, 33, 36, 37, 45–47, 52, 60, 62, 63, 66, 79, 80, 88, 91, 117, 118, 129, 137, 142, 146, 149, 150, 153, 154, 168–170, 172, 177, 179, 181, 186, 207, 208
network, 19
networking, 41, 104
news, 15, 21, 29, 31, 32, 43, 111, 112, 131–134
niche, 30, 68, 83, 146
Nishanth Sastry, 89
norm, 199, 200
North Africa, 131
notion, 168
nuance, 88
number, 15, 57, 121

obligation, 123
observation, 14
obsolescence, 141
offense, 62, 215, 216
offering, 20, 115, 140, 145, 149, 151, 165, 179, 205

Index 235

one, 7, 23, 25, 59, 62, 66, 81, 82, 89–91, 101, 122, 143, 149, 168, 169, 176, 208, 213

online, 3, 10, 14–16, 21, 28, 29, 31, 40, 41, 44, 52, 53, 55–61, 63, 65, 67, 68, 70, 71, 75–81, 91, 92, 95–99, 101–107, 110–114, 116, 117, 119, 126–128, 131, 132, 134–137, 141, 142, 145, 146, 149, 151, 152, 154, 163, 164, 169, 170, 173, 176, 183, 200–202, 209, 212, 213, 218, 219

openness, 136

operating, 36, 128

opinion, 29, 30, 34, 117, 134, 136, 137

opportunity, 3, 8, 34, 67, 70, 95, 101, 106, 107, 134, 135, 164, 165, 176, 212

oppression, 117

order, 212, 217

organization, 88, 112, 182, 186

organizing, 31, 117, 118, 131, 136, 140

orientation, 43, 51

other, 14, 18, 24, 26, 29, 32, 33, 35, 41, 46, 56, 59, 61–63, 65–67, 76, 82, 92, 98, 111–113, 122, 124, 127, 134, 145, 146, 152, 154, 163, 166, 185, 188, 199, 204

output, 148

overload, 28, 149

Overreliance, 204

oversharing, 56

ownership, 25, 121, 123, 141, 150, 167

pace, 137, 141, 146

painting, 143

panacea, 136

part, 27, 32, 43, 53, 55, 64, 87, 92, 136

participant, 14, 64, 147

participation, 18, 63, 71, 76, 79, 81, 116, 118, 122, 124, 126, 134, 136, 141, 144, 151, 169, 188, 192, 214

partner, 26, 183

passage, 140

passion, 152

past, 6, 26, 139, 145

patience, 43

patriotism, 110

pay, 89

payment, 183, 187

pedagogy, 21, 166, 168, 169

peer, 161, 215–217

penetration, 185

people, 2, 3, 7, 29, 31, 32, 35, 42, 43, 46, 47, 49, 55, 58, 59, 65, 67, 78, 90, 92, 110, 129, 140, 150, 188, 213

perception, 6, 18, 86, 91, 105, 111, 181

performer, 24

permission, 171, 172, 192, 193, 200

perpetuation, 115, 149

person, 113

persona, 53

personalization, 45, 46, 87, 133

perspective, 18, 19, 64, 98, 185, 214, 219

phenomenon, 65, 103, 104, 132

phishing, 76

photo, 105
photogrammetry, 140
physicality, 31
piracy, 146, 161
place, 7, 59, 65, 132, 199
plagiarism, 146
plan, 64
planning, 71, 73
platform, 4, 5, 20, 28, 30, 31, 33, 35,
　　37, 39–41, 46, 47, 54, 57,
　　60, 62–64, 70, 100–102,
　　106, 107, 112, 117, 119,
　　129–132, 134, 135, 137,
　　183, 184, 187, 188, 194,
　　213
play, 1, 35, 40–43, 46, 49, 52, 55, 59,
　　61, 65, 73, 75, 77, 84, 90,
　　105, 106, 110, 115, 117,
　　121, 123, 125–129, 133,
　　149, 165, 185, 193, 196,
　　199, 204, 205, 213, 214
pluralism, 123
podcast, 169
point, 6, 56
polarization, 112, 133
police, 117
policy, 21, 117, 123, 155–158, 194
pop, 4
popularity, 4, 34, 87, 88, 106, 187,
　　188
population, 16
portion, 38, 121
portrayal, 113, 114
positivity, 88
post, 64, 82, 105
posture, 90
potato, 36
potential, 3, 4, 11, 16, 26, 28, 34, 62,
　　64, 66, 67, 69, 78, 79, 89,

　　100, 111–113, 115,
　　117–119, 121, 123, 127,
　　131–136, 141, 144, 145,
　　147, 148, 150, 151, 157,
　　172, 175, 179, 194, 200,
　　204, 205, 207–209, 211,
　　213–217
pottery, 154
power, 4–6, 11, 17–21, 30, 31,
　　34–36, 38, 53, 55, 66, 71,
　　73, 76, 83, 113–117, 121,
　　124, 126–129, 131, 149,
　　154, 171, 172, 176, 179,
　　181, 193, 208, 211, 215,
　　218, 219
practice, 9, 26, 80, 141, 190
prayer, 88
preference, 43, 187
presence, 34, 55, 118, 185, 188
present, 6, 7, 21, 36, 64, 101, 102,
　　104–108, 116, 139, 185,
　　188, 190
presentation, 53, 101–105, 218
preservation, 26–29, 32, 59, 63, 80,
　　84, 111, 114, 117,
　　139–142, 145, 146, 148,
　　150, 151, 154, 169
press, 29, 32
pressure, 105, 106
prevalence, 16
pride, 110–112, 139, 167
print, 20, 29–32
printing, 29, 32
privacy, 20, 21, 43, 56–61, 91,
　　104–106, 141, 170, 186,
　　187, 197, 199–202, 205,
　　214–216
problem, 132, 134, 176
process, 25, 28, 35, 36, 47, 55, 64,

82, 83, 101, 105, 107, 113, 114, 145–148, 151, 167, 168, 172, 176, 186–188, 205, 216, 219

processing, 77, 80, 81, 140, 182, 209

produce, 27, 29, 82, 105, 143, 146

product, 78, 86, 87, 181, 183, 185, 186, 188

production, 21, 33, 34, 65, 122, 144–149, 151, 209

professional, 36, 76, 77, 105, 172, 217

proficiency, 75, 77, 166

profiling, 182, 184

profit, 38, 66, 146, 193, 212

progress, 116, 163

project, 16, 83, 91, 94, 169, 170, 176, 217

proliferation, 27, 132, 135, 150

prominence, 70

promise, 142

promotion, 42, 56, 63, 67, 110, 111

propaganda, 111

property, 21, 25, 40, 141, 144, 146, 154, 158–161, 170, 193, 194

propose, 37, 55, 169, 184, 194, 217

prosperity, 87

protection, 144, 154, 158, 161

provenance, 142

pseudonymity, 214

psychology, 134, 220

public, 21, 29–31, 34, 57, 106, 117, 131, 133–137, 140, 165, 200

publication, 215

purchase, 86

purpose, 214, 216

pursuit, 106

quality, 79, 82, 105, 135, 146, 149–151, 154, 189, 209

question, 16, 64, 194

quo, 70

race, 116, 125, 127

racism, 31, 117

radio, 32, 33

rainforest, 207

raise, 66, 70, 89, 117, 129

rally, 31

range, 3, 4, 7, 17, 20, 33, 47, 83, 87, 89, 114, 117, 122, 130, 131, 134, 136, 145, 146, 149, 155, 164, 165, 175, 176, 188, 210

rapport, 90

rate, 91

re, 215

reach, 3, 25, 29, 34, 38, 41, 44, 45, 51, 65, 66, 70, 75, 78, 81, 106, 118, 123, 129, 142, 143, 146, 152, 154, 193

read, 182

reader, 147, 183

readership, 31

reading, 27–29, 31, 37, 98, 134, 147, 183

reality, 21, 142, 144, 206–208, 220

realm, 79, 90, 92, 126, 132, 143, 146, 161

reception, 219

recognition, 6, 38, 77, 105, 143

recommendation, 65, 187, 204

record, 26, 142

red, 37, 87

refer, 1, 49, 75, 127, 185

reflection, 9, 11, 43, 94, 101, 168, 208, 215

reform, 131
refugee, 207
regime, 131
region, 35, 66, 111, 131, 154, 187
regulation, 123, 157
reinforcement, 133
reinterpretation, 145, 146, 148
rejection, 133
relatability, 182
relationship, 2, 15, 17–21, 32, 47, 52, 70, 78, 94, 100, 111, 132, 139, 142, 145, 148, 152
relevance, 114, 166, 208
reliability, 28, 209
reliance, 118, 188
relic, 26
religion, 42, 53, 107, 116
remix, 145
replacement, 118
replication, 206
report, 7, 64
representation, 3, 4, 6, 13, 16, 17, 21, 27, 28, 32–35, 47, 52, 54, 62, 66, 67, 79, 88, 110–115, 121–124, 126–129, 141, 144, 145, 149, 151, 172, 193–195, 211
representative, 129, 136, 168
reputation, 104, 186
research, 14–17, 20, 21, 36, 37, 52, 64, 80, 86, 87, 112, 114, 118, 134, 140, 141, 148, 164, 169–171, 176, 182–184, 187, 188, 193, 212–219
researcher, 14–16, 215, 216
resistance, 18, 30, 32, 116

resolution, 57, 58
resource, 136
resourcefulness, 152
respect, 3, 4, 8, 36, 55–58, 62, 63, 70, 91, 94–96, 98–100, 106, 109–113, 123, 141, 143, 144, 146, 154, 161, 170, 192–195, 198, 200–202, 208, 213, 220
response, 91, 94, 117
responsibility, 34, 40, 128, 195
responsiveness, 114
result, 6, 33, 38, 41, 56, 62, 65, 66, 76, 79, 83, 90, 186, 193
retention, 141
review, 215–217
revitalization, 80, 109, 110, 154
revolution, 31
richness, 15, 23, 63, 67, 81, 92, 123, 205
right, 59, 136, 182
rigor, 216
rise, 18, 29, 32, 44, 47, 65, 79, 103, 134, 143, 147, 149, 152, 158
risk, 28, 62, 71, 76, 111, 112, 118, 140, 141, 152, 193
role, 1, 2, 11, 18–21, 23, 25, 27–35, 40–47, 49, 52, 55, 59, 61, 64, 65, 67, 73, 75, 77, 78, 81, 84, 90, 91, 105, 106, 109–115, 121, 123, 125–128, 131, 133, 136, 142, 143, 148, 150, 152, 155, 157, 158, 165, 168, 176, 181, 182, 185, 196, 199, 204, 205, 213, 214, 216, 218, 219

Index 239

safeguarding, 150
sarcasm, 56
satisfaction, 10, 65, 181, 185
scale, 32, 37, 106, 142, 143, 145, 209
scandal, 136
scanning, 140
scenario, 6, 94
scenery, 35
scheme, 183
scholar, 117
science, 134, 210
screen, 183
search, 140
section, 1, 2, 7, 10, 11, 14, 17, 23,
      26, 29, 32, 41, 45, 52, 55,
      58, 59, 61, 64, 67, 70, 75,
      78, 81, 84, 87, 95, 98, 101,
      104, 107, 110, 112, 115,
      121, 124, 126, 129, 132,
      134, 139, 142, 145, 148,
      152, 155, 168, 172, 176,
      185, 188, 195, 199, 208,
      214, 218
sector, 152
security, 21, 43, 59–61, 141, 170,
      199–202, 205
self, 8, 9, 11, 20, 30, 42, 46, 53, 56,
      59, 66, 67, 94, 101–106,
      168, 170, 215, 218
sense, 1, 24, 31, 42, 53, 60, 66, 80,
      90, 105, 107, 110, 111,
      113, 118, 139, 154, 165,
      167, 182, 188
sensitivity, 3, 4, 7, 35, 45, 58, 63, 66,
      70, 77, 87, 92–95,
      98–100, 114, 141, 143,
      167, 169, 184, 193, 195,
      205, 208, 213–217
sensor, 209

sentiment, 31, 112
sequencing, 182
series, 91
service, 165
set, 35, 44, 113, 150, 155, 200
sexuality, 116, 127
shape, 6, 11, 14, 17–21, 25, 26, 30,
      33–35, 41–43, 45, 46,
      49–51, 55–57, 59, 61, 70,
      100, 101, 103, 111, 118,
      123, 126, 127, 134, 144,
      165, 170, 199, 218
share, 3, 28, 31, 33, 41, 47, 50, 52,
      53, 59, 62, 63, 66, 67, 71,
      75, 103–107, 110, 113,
      118, 127, 129, 130, 132,
      135, 141, 143, 145, 146,
      149, 155, 167, 169, 170,
      176, 201, 212, 213
sharing, 3, 15, 23, 41, 46, 56–61, 77,
      80, 100, 104–106, 112,
      116–118, 134, 142, 146,
      149, 154, 161, 167, 176,
      179, 199–201
shift, 20, 32, 47
shopping, 183
show, 42, 55, 57, 65, 94
sign, 91
significance, 23, 25, 26, 38, 59, 62,
      79, 89, 90, 146, 148–150,
      154, 171, 193–195
silencing, 131, 135
simplicity, 99
simplification, 34
Singapore, 157
site, 18
situation, 78
size, 168, 183
skill, 165

240   *Index*

slacktivism, 71
slogan, 82
smiley, 88, 91
soap, 34
socialization, 49
society, 1, 3, 7, 32, 39, 41, 43, 51, 55,
     63, 64, 67, 112, 115, 117,
     119, 123, 126, 166, 189,
     199, 208
socio, 117
sociology, 14, 17, 215
software, 82, 124, 142, 146
solidarity, 113, 118
solution, 89
some Middle Eastern, 88, 90
sound, 29, 147
soundness, 216
source, 29, 82, 88, 139, 193
sovereignty, 117
space, 3, 6, 7, 10, 20, 26, 29, 52, 58,
     59, 61, 64, 65, 70, 71, 78,
     79, 90–92, 95, 106,
     110–113, 115, 116, 131,
     135, 145, 149, 169, 192,
     213, 214
Spain, 111
spark, 70
speaker, 78, 98
specificity, 88, 89
speech, 81, 106, 111, 112, 204, 214
speed, 38, 46, 132, 209
sphere, 67, 133–135, 137
spirit, 82
spread, 21, 29, 38, 65, 66, 116, 117,
     122, 131–137, 143
standardization, 27, 29, 65, 66
status, 70, 117, 125, 163, 166
step, 207
stereotyping, 4

stock, 127
storage, 216
story, 4
storyteller, 24, 144
storytelling, 23, 29, 35, 110, 113,
     114, 129, 141, 144, 147,
     167, 169, 170
strategy, 67, 82, 118
streaming, 44, 121, 149, 150
strength, 117
struggle, 6, 79, 149, 164
student, 94, 168
study, 4, 10, 11, 14, 20, 36, 37, 55,
     57, 63, 64, 111, 112, 128,
     157, 161, 183, 184, 194,
     207, 214–219
style, 58, 94, 100, 194
stylus, 26
subject, 21, 212
success, 4, 37, 42, 45, 64, 65, 118,
     163, 168, 185
summary, 2, 179
support, 31, 36, 47, 70, 71, 77, 78,
     83, 111, 118, 131, 155,
     157, 164, 168, 169, 175,
     179, 186, 191, 193, 198
suppression, 60, 135
surveillance, 60, 106
survey, 15, 16, 91, 151
sustainability, 141, 142, 157, 169
symbiosis, 18
symbol, 88, 89
symbolism, 84, 183, 186
system, 26, 136, 165

table, 212
tagging, 140
tagline, 82
tailor, 3, 46

Index 241

taking, 71, 82, 152, 182, 214
Tanzania, 110
target, 35–37, 43, 64, 82, 86–88,
 105, 114, 182, 183,
 185–188
targeting, 52, 87, 135, 183, 195
task, 88, 176
teaching, 164, 168, 175
team, 86, 87, 89, 183
teamwork, 176
technology, 2, 17, 19, 28, 37, 43, 44,
 46, 47, 71, 77, 80, 84, 86,
 124, 125, 133, 134, 136,
 141, 142, 155, 159,
 163–167, 171, 172, 176,
 185, 188, 204, 206, 208
television, 32, 33, 121
tendency, 6
tension, 106
term, 51, 141
testing, 87, 188
text, 29, 81, 105, 144, 172, 183, 186
the Middle East, 131
the United States, 31, 44, 56, 59, 94
theft, 60
theory, 18, 19
thinking, 29, 71, 73, 165, 168, 170,
 176, 199
Thomas Paine, 31
thought, 21, 29
thumbs, 88, 90
time, 14, 26, 32, 43, 58, 105, 113,
 129, 131, 135, 140, 146,
 176, 204, 208
Tito Rojas-Morales, 184
today, 29, 61, 78, 92, 98, 107, 163
tokenization, 118
tolerance, 8, 61, 139
tone, 58

tool, 7, 30, 34, 61, 71, 114, 127, 136,
 140
topic, 4, 16, 151, 195
touch, 87, 204, 205, 214
tour, 170
tourism, 139
toxicity, 106
trade, 158
tradition, 23–29
training, 7, 10, 99, 154, 163, 164,
 172, 213, 214
transcreation, 82, 84
transformation, 73, 144
transition, 27, 29
translating, 35, 88, 182, 185, 204
translation, 3, 36, 62, 77–84, 99,
 185, 186, 204, 205
transmission, 23, 150, 216
transparency, 60, 61, 134, 136, 201,
 205
trolling, 116, 131
trust, 8, 57, 60, 133, 185
tune, 188
turn, 41, 46, 181
turnout, 136
type, 4, 46, 216
typography, 84

uncertainty, 181
underrepresentation, 6, 17, 122
understanding, 1–8, 10, 14, 16, 17,
 19–21, 33, 36, 38, 41, 44,
 47, 50, 52, 53, 55, 58,
 60–62, 64, 66, 67, 69, 71,
 73, 75, 76, 78, 80–82,
 87–90, 94–100, 109–115,
 117, 118, 122, 123, 129,
 134, 139, 141, 143, 148,
 166, 168–172, 175, 176,

182, 185, 186, 192, 194, 200, 204–206, 208, 211–214, 216–218, 220
Unicode, 89
university, 10
usability, 82, 100, 185
usage, 15, 28, 42, 43, 46, 60
use, 14, 15, 18–20, 39, 49, 50, 53, 55–57, 63, 65, 70, 79, 84, 86–90, 111–113, 118, 123, 134, 137, 143, 146, 154, 158, 165, 167, 170–172, 183, 192–194, 200, 206, 211, 215, 216
user, 4, 15, 18, 21, 37, 45, 46, 61, 65, 78, 80–82, 87, 100, 106, 114, 133, 143, 144, 149, 181–188, 192, 201, 204, 205, 209

validation, 105, 106
validity, 216
value, 25, 41, 43, 56, 57, 59, 66, 67, 149, 152, 154, 171, 199
variation, 88
variety, 118, 169, 209
vegetable, 37
velocity, 209
veracity, 209
version, 101, 103
vice, 17
victim, 76
video, 6, 35, 46, 105, 141, 144, 172, 176
view, 91, 201
vigilance, 70, 134, 141
violence, 34, 117
visibility, 3, 6, 7, 106, 113, 117, 126, 127
visitor, 141

visual, 20, 27, 28, 32, 84–87, 90, 91, 99, 100, 173, 182–184, 219
visualization, 140
vitality, 144
voice, 4, 34, 77, 84, 105, 126, 134, 137
volume, 209
voter, 136
voting, 134, 136
vulnerability, 76

war, 207
wave, 131
way, 6, 8, 27, 29, 31, 32, 41, 45, 47, 55, 57, 58, 65, 67, 73, 84, 104, 110, 116, 129, 132, 139, 142, 147, 150, 152, 155, 161, 172, 181, 188
web, 144
website, 154, 209
wedge, 26
well, 20, 42, 82, 106, 212, 218
whole, 39, 41, 115
willingness, 11, 43, 56, 98, 195
word, 23, 42
work, 6, 40, 41, 112, 123, 128, 129, 134, 142, 143, 146, 148, 155, 161, 165, 172, 176, 194, 212, 214–216
working, 94, 166, 212, 213, 216
world, 1, 8, 10, 11, 19, 44, 45, 47, 49, 55, 61, 65, 68, 77, 78, 81, 86, 89, 92, 95, 98, 100, 104, 109, 115, 124, 127, 136, 142, 149, 150, 169, 184, 206, 207, 212, 216, 220
writing, 26–29

Milton Keynes UK
Ingram Content Group UK Ltd.
UKHW021035111124
451035UK00017B/1298